Hanno Berger
Thinking Revolution Through Film

Cinepoetics

Edited by
Hermann Kappelhoff and Michael Wedel

Volume 10

Hanno Berger

Thinking Revolution Through Film

—

On Audiovisual Stagings of Political Change

Translated by
Alex H. Bush

DE GRUYTER

ISBN 978-3-11-152939-4
e-ISBN (PDF) 978-3-11-075470-4
e-ISBN (EPUB) 978-3-11-075473-5
ISSN 2569-4294

Library of Congress Control Number: 2022936083

Bibliographic information published by the Deutsche Nationalbibliothek
The Deutsche Nationalbibliothek lists this publication in the Deutsche Nationalbibliografie; detailed bibliographic data are available on the internet at http://dnb.dnb.de.

© 2024 Walter de Gruyter GmbH, Berlin/Boston
This volume is text- and page-identical with the hardback published in 2022.
First published in German under the title *Film denkt Revolution. Zu audiovisuellen Inszenierungen politischen Wandels* (Vorwerk 8, 2019).
Cover image: Director Abel Gance and Crew While Filming Scene in NAPOLEON. Bettmann/ Kontributor via Getty Images.
Typesetting: Integra Software Services Pvt.

www.degruyter.com

To June

Acknowledgments

This is the English translation of my book, *Film denkt Revolution*, which was published in German in 2019. For making this book project possible, I want to thank first of all my PhD advisor Hermann Kappelhoff who supervised and supported this project from the very beginning and gave helpful advice and orientation in many crucial aspects. I also want to thank my secondary advisor Michael Wedel, who even though he joined the project in a rather later stage, also gave valuable advice and suggestions.

I wish to express my gratitude to the Collaborative Research Center 626 "Aesthetic Experience and the Dissolution of Artistic Limits" for creating an ideal environment to start a PhD thesis and the Cinepoetics research group, especially the graduate student colloquium, for their support in the conception of this work. Here, a special thanks goes to Danny Gronmaier who, as the first reader and commentator, played an important part in finishing the book. I am also extremely thankful for Cinepoetics' generous financial support that enabled the printing of the English version of the book.

I want to thank Alex Bush for her thoughtful translation. For preparing the typescript for publication, I want to express my appreciation to Eh-Jae Kim, Maximilian Grenz, Charlotte Wettengel and Alexander Wiese. I thank the editors, Myrto Aspioti and Stella Diedrich from De Gruyter, for their support in making the book's English version possible.

Contents

Acknowledgments —— VII

1 Introduction —— 1

2 The Theory of Revolution: Prolegomena —— 19
    2.1   On the Concept of Revolution —— 19
    2.2   Arendt's Conception —— 24

3 The "Machine Which Thinks Temporally" —— 39
    3.1   Film, Time, and Movement: Epstein's and Deleuze's Conception —— 39
            Epstein —— 39
            Deleuze —— 51
    3.2   Film and the Experience of History —— 56

4 NAPOLÉON: The Sublime Conceptualization of Revolution —— 73
    4.1   The Mathematical Sublime and Deleuze —— 73
            The Prewar French School —— 73
            The Snowball Fight —— 84
    4.2   The Thinking of Images and Deleuze —— 94
            How to Think With Images? —— 94
            Revolution as Storm —— 99
    4.3   The Authority of State Foundation —— 105
            The Revolution and the Question of New Beginnings —— 105
            The Question of Authority —— 111
    4.4   After 1945: How Do We Look at Revolution Films With and Against Deleuze? —— 116

5 REDS: The Russian Revolution in Hollywood —— 123
    5.1   Situating the Film Historically —— 123
            "I Was Hoping for a Happy Ending" —— 123
            The Not-So-New-Anymore Hollywood —— 127
    5.2   Revolution —— 129
            The Gaze on Revolution —— 129
            The Asynchronous Rendezvous —— 139
            The Condensed Temporality of Utopia —— 145

		5.3	The Decline of the Revolution —— 157

                    The Confrontational Rendezvous —— 158
                    The Extended Temporality of the Couple —— 162

6 JOHN ADAMS: Before the Birth Comes the Revolution —— 167
    6.1   The Missing Afterlife of the American Revolution —— 167
    6.2   The American Revolution as Mini-Series —— 174
                The Episode INDEPENDENCE —— 174
                Mini-*Series* —— 188
                Mini-Series —— 191

7 Conclusion —— 199

Bibliography —— 205

Filmography —— 217

Name Index —— 219

Film Index —— 223

1 Introduction

This book sets out to examine the potential for a filmic thinking of revolution. This means first and foremost that the book deals with fictional audiovisual stagings of revolutions. In order to avoid treating the formulation 'filmic thinking of revolution' as just a slogan, the first task is to show that films are particularly well suited to thinking about revolution; this is also the book's primary and most fundamental argument. This means that the medium of film is not understood as a mere vessel, as a 'container' [English in original], which holds interpretable content – in this case, representations of revolution. Rather, the medium of film has a special affinity for advancing our understanding of revolution, greater in this capacity than the medium of speech or any other art form. This argument is based on the assumption that both revolutions and cinematic productions can be understood as particular forms of temporality. A very basic, general, and formal definition of the term 'revolution,' from the *Lexikon geschichtlicher Grundbegriffe* [Lexicon of basic historical terms], refers both to a brief *moment* of uprising and to a long-term structural change.[1] An equally fundamental point of reference for this book, to which I will return repeatedly, is that the revolutions of modernity and the modern concept of revolution have enabled a new way of conceptualizing "history." Only since these developments has it become possible to think of history as a contingent evolution of collective human life [*Zusammenleben*], i.e., a way of life that is not trapped in cyclical repetition or eschatological determinacy.

In the next section, I will draw on Hannah Arendt's concept of revolution, developed through her dual portrait of the American and French Revolutions, in order to trace the relationship of these two temporalities (moment of uprising and structural change).[2] My focus will not be on whether history has borne out Arendt's theses on the American or French Revolutions. Rather, I will use her work to establish two central points: 1. Drawing on Immanuel Kant, Arendt ascribes eminently significant meaning to the epistemological spectator position; 2. In theorizing revolution, the decisive parameters for this spectator position are the temporalities of the revolutionary process and the moment of uprising, as well as the corresponding movement formations. More concretely: For Arendt, a

---

[1] Cf. Neithard Bulst/Jörg Fisch/Reinhart Koselleck/Christian Meier: Revolution, Rebellion, Aufruhr, Bürgerkrieg, in: Geschichtliche Grundbegriffe. Historisches Lexikon zur politisch-sozialen Sprache in Deutschland, Vol. 5, ed. by Otto Brunner/Werner Conze/Reinhart Koselleck, Stuttgart 1984, pp. 653–788.
[2] Cf. Hannah Arendt: On Revolution, London 1990.

crucial problem of the French Revolution was that for its agents, but most importantly in the eyes of spectators, the irresistible and unstoppable movement that arose from the Revolution's moment of uprising was transferred onto the second temporality of revolution, the revolutionary process, leading to the death of freedom, and with it, the end of the Revolution. This was not the case in the American Revolution; the problem of the American Revolution, according to Arendt, was that it lacked a spectator position altogether. This section will trace the development of these purely formal aspects of her concept of revolution, which enable a comprehensive understanding of her entire theory of revolution as well as the difference she identifies between the French and American Revolutions. At the same time, I will lay out the content-related questions that Arendt connects to revolution: the questions of freedom, re-foundation, and violence. These aspects – both of form and of content – will guide my observation and analysis of the films.

As a next step, I will draw on Jean Epstein's film theory to show that the medium is particularly well suited to thinking through movement and temporality – and also to reflecting on revolution.[3] Going back to Epstein's writings serves a dual purpose. Admittedly, Epstein is no longer the neglected figure he was once considered to be. However, the productive and fruitful potential of his film theoretical ideas is far from exhausted.[4] This is particularly true when

---

[3] This work is based on German-language editions of Jean Epstein's writings in Jean Epstein: Bonjour Cinéma und andere Schriften zum Kino, ed. by Nicole Brenez/Ralf Eue and trans. by Ralf Eue, Vienna 2008. I consulted other untranslated French-language texts by Epstein, but my book does not claim to present a comprehensive overview of his work. Rather, I aim at a strategic reconstruction of his thought oriented toward the central question of my book. The writings available in German represent about a fifth of his complete works (cf. Alexander Horwath/Brigitte Mayr/Michael Omasta: Vorwort, in: Jean Epstein: Bonjour Cinéma und andere Schriften zum Kino, op. cit., pp. 5–7). There are a few additional excerpts now available in German in Margrit Tröhler/Jörg Schweinitz (eds.): Die Zeit des Bildes ist angebrochen! Französische Intellektuelle, Künstler und Filmkritiker über das Kino. Eine historische Anthologie 1906–1929, Berlin 2016. On this book, see my review in the online publication [rezens.tfm]: Hanno Berger: Rezension – Margrit Tröhler/Jörg Schweinitz (Hg.): Die Zeit des Bildes ist angebrochen! Französische Intellektuelle, Künstler und Filmkritiker über das Kino. Eine historische Anthologie 1906–1929, in: [rezens.tfm], 1, 2017, https://rezenstfm.univie.ac.at/index.php/tfm/article/view/r359 [last accessed 6 May 2022].

[4] On Epstein as a great unknown figure of film theory, cf. Tom Gunning: Preface, in: Jean Epstein. Critical Essays and New Translations, ed. by Sarah Keller/Jason N. Paul, Amsterdam 2012, pp. 13–21, here p. 13; and Sarah Keller: Introduction. Jean Epstein and the Revolt of Cinema, in: Jean Epstein, op. cit., pp. 23–47, here p. 27. Epstein has been centered in English-language scholarship by Stewart E. Liebman: Jean Epstein's early Film Theory, 1920–22, Ann Arbor/New York 1980, as well as by the contributions to Keller/Paul (eds.): Jean Epstein, op.

approaching his work historically. For Epstein, the cinematograph is capable of recording and reproducing the world in motion[5] – the result of this recording differs, however, in his pre-World War Two writings as compared with the essays he wrote after the war. In the prewar texts, there is still a sense of truth that exists beyond human perception, which the cinematograph makes visible. This claim to absoluteness disappears after World War Two – and this is the second reason for my return to Epstein. After the war, he ascribes to cinematographic recordings a variability, relativity, and openness, which – alongside many other possible points of entry – allow us to put Epstein's thought into conversation with the film philosophy of Gilles Deleuze. More specifically, I am interested in connections to Deleuze's first commentary on Bergson. In this piece, Deleuze works with and against Bergson to conceive of film as oriented toward duration and an open whole [*offenes Ganzes*]. Deleuze draws the cinema toward a tendency in the philosophy of history that originated with and achieved validity through the revolutions of the modern era. Film not only has an affinity for understanding revolutions, but also – and this is the second fundamental thesis of my work – is particularly suited to a conceptualization of 'history' whose paradigmatic form is revolutionary transition. Drawing on Deleuze, it is possible to demonstrate film's connection with the intellectual tradition of the history of philosophy that emerged from the revolutions of modernity, regardless of the film's content. Working from this connection, we can ascribe to film an affinity for the conceptualization of revolution itself.

Arendt's theory of revolution and Deleuze's thoughts on film also allow us to establish why the form of movement that is most readily associated with revolution plays no role in this book's approach to the philosophy of history: namely, the movement of dialectics. Writing on dialectics in the postface to the second edition of the first volume of *Capital*, Marx contends that it was Hegel who was "the

---

cit. In francophone scholarship, see Jacques Aumont (ed.): Jean Epstein. Cinéaste, poète, philosophe, Paris 1998. In German, Oliver Fahle's informative study on French cinema in the 1920s provides a helpful background for engaging with Epstein, cf. Oliver Fahle: Jenseits des Bildes. Poetik des französischen Films der zwanziger Jahre, Mainz 2000. For a more recent contribution on Epstein in German, cf. Chris Tedjasukmana: Mechanische Verlebendigung. Ästhetische Erfahrung im Kino, Paderborn 2014, pp. 112 ff.

5 It is thus in response to Epstein's theoretical premises that I refrain from discussing still frames from the films and scenes that I analyze, and instead use precise time codes to refer to the scenes. In the final chapter, when I address the relationship between audiovisual staging and two paintings, I will take up the latter and describe them in the text. As a rule, the time code refers to the indications of the VLC Media Player. Slight differences from the information given by a different viewing method may occur.

first to present its general forms of motion in a comprehensive and conscious manner."[6] He makes it clear that dialectics are a form of movement, a way of conceptualizing movement. Yet shortly after Marx's famous remark that Hegel's dialectics were "standing on its head" and must be inverted,[7] he explains more concretely why this dialectic, once inverted and in its rational form, would be a thorn in the side of the bourgeoisie:

> [...] because it includes in its positive understanding of what exists a simultaneous recognition of its negation, its inevitable destruction; because it regards every historically developed form as being in a fluid state, in motion, and therefore grasps its transient aspects as well; and because it does not let itself be impressed by anything, being in its very essence critical and revolutionary.[8]

Crucially, Marx identifies the "inevitable" downfall of what exists as an inherent part of dialectic movement. Thus in this passage, Marx draws a connection between dialectics and inevitability. It is precisely this connection between movement and inevitability that Arendt contests, and that also contradicts the historico-philosophical tradition that emerges from the revolutions of modernity.

Returning to Epstein and Deleuze, and highlighting the "affinities" between theories of revolution and the filmic medium, also means departing from a film theoretical tradition that sees revolutionary thought realized in the medium per se, i.e., in its technological conditions. In no way do I mean to claim an ontological connection between film and revolution. The filmic medium simply offers a privileged potential for reflecting on revolution. Whether this reflection actually comes to pass is, in my opinion, no longer a question of film theory. To answer this question, it is necessary to move into concrete analysis of cinematic staging. Here I follow Stanley Cavell, who argues convincingly that it is impossible to know in advance what the filmic medium is capable of. What constitutes a film can only be determined by films themselves. What the medium of film is, realizes itself only in concrete films.[9] Thus I absolutely do not intend to argue that every film, simply because it is a film, is or should be a

---

6 Karl Marx: Capital. A Critique of Political Economy, Vol. 1, trans. by Ben Fowkes, London 1976, p. 103.
7 The formulation that made this argument famous comes from Engels, who writes that Hegel's dialectic was placed on its head by Marx, "or rather, turned off its head, on which it was standing, and placed upon its feet" (cf. Friedrich Engels: Ludwig Feuerbach and the End of Classical German Philosophy, in: Karl Marx/id.: MECW 26. Engels 1882–89, London 2010, pp. 353–399, here p. 383).
8 Karl Marx: Capital, Vol. 1, op. cit., p. 103.
9 Cf. Stanley Cavell: The World Viewed. Reflections on the Ontology of Film – Enlarged Edition, Cambridge, MA/London 1979, pp. 29 ff.

reflection on revolution. This refusal distinguishes my book from a broad swath of film theory, particularly early film theory. To quote Béla Balázs:

> By its very nature the technology of film [*Es liegt im Wesen seiner Technik*] has abolished the distance between the spectator and a hermetically sealed work of art. There is an unstoppable revolutionary tendency in this dismantling of the solemn distance of the cult performance that surrounded the theatre. The gaze of the cinema is the intimate gaze of a participant. In film there is no absolute and eternally valid standpoint for the gaze. For film is familiar with the meaning of shifting camera set-ups and hence the relative nature of meaning. And even if this technique can be misused for quite dangerous deceptions its underlying spirit is revolutionary. Despite everything![10]

Of course, Balázs's refusal of an absolute and eternally valid standpoint is consistent with the understanding of film that underlies my work. But there are important differences: First, when it comes to the spectatorial gaze on films about revolution, I am precisely not dealing with the gaze of a participant. Second – and this is the decisive departure from Balázs – he seeks to clarify the relationship between film and revolution through the *essence* of the medium ("its very nature"). Yet the openness of film does not allow for a *definite conclusion* on revolution.[11] Only analyzing concrete staging methods can show whether they actually make use of film's potential for reflecting on revolution. It is not revolution itself, but rather the potential to think revolution, that is inherent to the medium. As a result, my investigation is limited to films that represent revolution – but while I begin with representation, I do not stop there.[12]

Traces of the notion that there might be an intrinsic connection between the filmic medium and (in this case, Communist) revolution also appear in Walter Benjamin's work. Benjamin speaks of the "revolutionary merit" that film possesses, even when it is under the yoke of capital – meaning it has this merit regardless of its circumstances or its use. This merit consists in "the promotion

---

10 Béla Balázs: Béla Balázs. Early Film Theory. Visible Man and the Spirit of Film, ed. by Erica Carter, trans. by Rodney Livingstone. New York/Oxford 2010, p. 229. On this point, see also the entire, quite beautiful closing section of the book with the subtitle "Despite everything!" (Ibid., pp. 228–230).
11 According to Siegfried Kracauer, Balázs's ontologically grounded definition of film as essentially revolutionary is "untenable." Cf. Siegfried Kracauer: Theory of Film. The Redemption of Physical Reality, New York 1960, p. 309.
12 Assuming an overly generalized relationship between film and revolution is also a problem in Lukas Germann: Die Wirklichkeit als Möglichkeit. Das revolutionäre Potential filmischer Ästhetik, Zurich/Berlin 2016. He examines "mainly the canon of *auteur* cinema" as well as "horror and so-called brutal cinema [*Brutalofilme*]" (ibid., p. 44 [Translator's note: my translation]). This includes quite a large number of directors and films.

of a revolutionary criticism of traditional concepts of art."[13] Working with Epstein and Deleuze, who define film by way of movement, also means departing from a theoretical trend that understands film as a trace of the referent, as is the case – roughly speaking – for André Bazin and Siegfried Kracauer. To determine film by movement and not by its indexical power is to relate it to a concept from revolutionary theory, namely that revolution is also a phenomenon of motion and can only be understood as such. The relationship between film and revolution must thus be sought in movement.[14] Furthermore, returning to Epstein and Deleuze enables productive engagement with films about revolution that are digitally shot. This comprehensiveness in turn clearly demonstrates that the answer to the question of the relationship between film and revolution does not reside in film's technological specifications.[15]

In the first chapters and subchapters, I will present and orient the revolutionary theory and the first half of the film theoretical foundations that underlie this book. I complete the film theoretical discussion in the final section of the third chapter. While the first half deals with the conceptualization of the filmic medium that forms the basis of my work, the second half turns to the film spectator, for which I rely on Vivian Sobchack. Just as a revolution is not a revolution

---

13 Walter Benjamin: The Work of Art in the Age of its Technological Reproducibility. Third Version, in: id.: Selected Writings. Vol. IV 1938–1940, ed. by Howard Eiland/Michael W Jennings, trans by Edmund Jephcott et al., Cambridge, MA et al. 2003, pp. 251–283, here p. 261.

14 "Entre le cinéma qui est la représentation du mouvement, et la révolution qui est le mouvement même, il ne pouvait y avoir qu'une longue histoire commune." ["It was inevitable that cinema, which is the representation of movement, and revolution, which is movement itself, would have a long shared history."] – This text appears on the jacket of Raymond Lefèvre: Cinéma et Révolution, Paris 1988. Unfortunately, Lefévre does not support his argument with either film theory or the theory of revolution, and his survey of films about the French Revolution is limited to the level of representational content. Of course, his description of cinema simply as the representation of movement already hints at this limitation.

15 Of course, in principle this interpretation would also be possible for Bazin and Kracauer if one does not read them too reductively. However, it would take a significant hermeneutic effort to rethink the theories of both these writers without reference to analog photography. On the attempt to render Bazin's work productive for digital cinema by way of a time-index for film, see Thomas Elsaesser: Ein halbes Jahrhundert im Zeichen Bazins, in: montage AV, 18 (1), 2009, pp. 11–31. The relationship between digital cinema and realism could also be specified and differentiated, for the "redemption of physical reality" has by no means become impossible with the invention of the digital camera. Simon Rothöhler argues against a hypostatization of media rupture through the digital camera in: id.: Amateur der Weltgeschichte. Historiographische Praktiken im Kino der Gegenwart, Zurich 2011, pp. 11 ff. On the necessary differentiation, see: "Obviously the introduction of digital technology does not pose the same aesthetic and technological questions in the work of Wang Bing and Cong Feng as in relation to CGI practices in contemporary Hollywood cinema" (ibid., p. 13 [Translator's note: my translation]).

without a spectator – to crystallize one of Arendt's arguments – film also cannot be conceived without a perceiving spectator, in whom the film realizes itself. Yet the question is not just about the notion of the spectator, but, following Sobchack, must be simultaneously oriented toward the spectator's capacity to experience historicity through film. More precisely, I seek to represent and interrogate Sobchack's theories about Hollywood's historical epics of the 1950s and 1960s, as well as their return in television mini-series, particularly how these can be grasped and theorized as a form of reflection on history and historicity. They also offer a broader perspective on the audiovisual productions of revolution that I analyze over the course of the book.

Sobchack writes about the *experience* of films through the spectator, and the spectator's experience of historicity. Taking up Deleuze's reflections on NAPOLÉON (Abel Gance, FR 1927)[16] – building on and interweaving with them – I attempt to take the next step, to the thinking of films. Deleuze draws on Kant's concept of the mathematical sublime in order to understand this film primarily as a maximum of movement that overwhelms the spectator and forces the spectator to think. First, I clarify this argument, which Deleuze presents in quite dense prose, with a thorough reconstruction of the Kantian sublime and a detailed scene analysis. I submit the result of this analysis to the question of revolutionary theory as formulated by Arendt. What emerges constitutes my argument on Gance's film: that it conforms to Arendt's theory insofar as the film, like Arendt herself, sees the French Revolution as an uncontrolled and uncontrollable movement, which prevented its protagonists from acting of their own free will. Yet what Arendt can only communicate verbally, the film allows the spectator to experience carnally. Furthermore, the film presents the figure of Napoleon as the only person who is capable of resisting a technically unstoppable revolutionary movement.

This staging then undergoes a second scene analysis, drawing on further writing by Deleuze. The usefulness of emphasizing this staging again, and the surplus value it produces, is that it can demonstrate another capacity of filmic thinking: metaphor. If cinematographic thinking was first enabled by the structure of the sublime, here the production of an audiovisual metaphor is presented as a form of filmic thinking. The importance of metaphor for the theory of revolution should already become clear from my summary of Arendt's position. I pick up this thread in the section on metaphor in NAPOLÉON, as well as in the film analyses that follow. I conclude my observations of Gance's work by reflecting

---

16 The first time I name a film, I indicate its director as well as the year and country of origin. For ease of reading, these are omitted in subsequent mentions. I generally leave the title in the original language, except for Russian titles, which I give in translation in the interest of legibility.

on the question of how this film can be put into conversation with the "problem of authority" that Arendt sees as central for any revolution: How can something established through revolution stabilize itself and achieve lasting legitimacy? This consideration brings into focus another question of the chapter on NAPOLÉON: How can the film be defended against accusations of being a fascist film, dedicated to a Napoleonic cult? This question receives thorough attention in the scene analyses, which argue that this critique focuses too simplistically on the character of Napoleon and overlooks both the staging style as well as the way that this style realizes itself in the spectator. However, this criticism must also be addressed quite directly, by bringing into focus the staging of the character, particularly his relationship to space. My argument will be that the film increasingly detaches the figure of Napoleon from his spatial environment, thereby presenting him as a *mythic* founding father, abstracted from the world around him.

I build a bridge to further film analyses by engaging with the question of how Deleuze's perspective on revolution films (i.e. films that are about a revolution), developed using theories and films from before World War Two, can be put into conversation with films made after the war: a transfer whose possibility Deleuze himself explicitly rejects. My counterargument is dual in nature: First, I refuse to restrict the films in advance, by denying them the capacity to be productive for theorizing revolution before they have even been analyzed. Second, Deleuze's dictum deals primarily with what he calls the "action-thought" of films. However, the selection of the corpus – which results from the revolutionary-theoretical premises that underlie this book, on which I will elaborate in more detail below – does not focus on action-thought. The films in question do not prioritize interventionist agitation, but rather assume an observational and discerning spectatorial stance toward revolution.

This dynamic holds true for the film at the center of the next chapter: REDS (Warren Beatty, US 1981), a Hollywood film about an American who experiences the Russian Revolution as a journalist. My analysis of this film is guided by the basic assumption that the film creates a close interconnection between revolution and the question of love, or more broadly, with the relationship between the private and the political. Based on scene analyses, I attempt to demonstrate that the film thinks through this relationship using multiple temporalities. It stages prerevolutionary conditions as an asynchronous mismatch between the lovers; the revolution, by contrast, is conceived as a utopian coming together of politics, love, sex, work, and free time. Thus, this chapter will address a positive interpretation of the revolutionary moment of uprising, understood by Arendt in negative terms as a loss of control. Here, it is understood as a Kairos moment, a reading that attempts to enrich our theorization of revolution. The second half of the film is examined in two more scene analyses that appear in an excursus, turning to the afterlife and decline of the Revolution after its utopian climax. This excursus seeks not only to do justice to the entire film in its complexity, but also to use the staging of decline to draw conclusions *ex negativo* about how the film thinks revolution and its utopian potential.

The book ends with a chapter on JOHN ADAMS (Tom Hooper, US 2008), a mini-series about the American Revolution. What for Arendt was an extremely important, and chronologically the first, revolution of modernity occupies a prominent position at the end of my book. This chapter is premised on the argument that the mini-series is a much more obvious format than the feature film for thinking the American Revolution. Regarding the way the miniseries uses its staging to think the American Revolution and make it comprehensible, I argue that it presents an antithesis to the way NAPOLÉON and REDS think revolution. There is no excessive or sublime movement formation, no enthusiastic moment of uprising. Rather, the revolution is presented as a confluence of dispassion, consideration, strategy, and hesitation, decisively expanding our concept of what a revolution can be. In this chapter I develop two important arguments: First, drawing on Arendt and the mini-series, I show that a revolution – contrary to common assumptions – can be conceived without a moment of uprising that lends itself to dramatization. And second, this notion allows us once again to rethink the much-discussed relationship between politics and the political: not as two opposing fields, but rather as realms that mutually determine and influence each other. Seen from this perspective, politics loses its negative connotation as mere administration and reveals itself as the actual work of the political.[17]

"Always historicize!"[18] Following this imperative from the American Marxist Fredric Jameson, each film-based chapter of this book contextualizes the film or mini-series historically before delving into analysis. I thereby seek to counter an ahistorical approach to the material that would be diametrically opposed to the search for filmic thinking of history and historicity. However, orienting objects in film historical context can in no way replace concrete film analysis. Since no film is fully identical with or completely explained by its historical context, film historical contextualization serves only as a backdrop against which the valences of staging practices become clear. This approach connects Jameson's credo with an idea from Stanley Cavell. Writing on genre theory, Cavell notes

---

17 On the debate over politics vs. the political, see especially Uwe Hebekus/Jan Völker: Neue Philosophien des Politischen zur Einführung, Hamburg 2012. For more on this topic, see Chapter 6 of this book.
18 Fredric Jameson: The Political Unconscious. Narrative as a Socially Symbolic Act, London 1981, p. 9.

of exemplars of a genre: "They *are what they are* in view of one another."[19] The result of connecting Jameson and Cavell is a concretization of film historical context, as the films I examine enter into conversation with other films of their time. And since my analyses focus on figurations of movement, the surrounding films are also examined in these terms. With regard to NAPOLÉON, this takes place via Deleuze's observations on prewar French cinema, to which he ascribes a search for a *maximum of movement* [Bewegungsmaximum]. I agree with his assertion that among the films that surround it, Gance's film is paradigmatic of this search. In REDS, the movement figurations of New Hollywood Cinema serve as a central point of reference for my analysis. I rely on Hauke Lehmann's work on these films,[20] in which he determines freedom and shock, as well as overwhelming and splitting the spectator, as the essential hallmarks of movement in films of this period. Although REDS appeared shortly after the end of the phase commonly referred to as New Hollywood, the film's connections to this era are strong enough to render its areas of consonance and dissonance with New Hollywood's movement figurations productive for analysis. This chapter extends historical contextualization to include a reconstruction of the concrete conditions of the film's genesis. This film shows in an exemplary way how reducing a film to the conditions of its origin can cause it to be misunderstood. I seek to demonstrate that the analysis of a film can make it more productive than its production history might indicate. With that, this chapter also serves as a proof of concept and substantiation of my methodology for examining films – knowledge acquisition through film analysis – and continues the discussion over the relationship between films and the conditions of their production. In the final chapter, film historical contextualization means engaging with the broad lack of other fictional audiovisual material on the American Revolution.[21] I explain this lack through the process of the American Revolution, which cannot be condensed in a dramatic moment of uprising. This in turn leads us back to the argument laid out above, that the mini-series format is especially well suited to thinking the American Revolution in the context of audiovisual media.

---

19 Stanley Cavell: Pursuits of Happiness. The Hollywood Comedy of Remarriage, Cambridge, MA/London 1981, p. 29.
20 Hauke Lehmann: Affect Poetics of the New Hollywood. Suspense, Paranoia, and Melancholy, trans. by James Lattimer, Berlin/ Boston 2020.
21 This chapter includes a shift in perspective: While the chapters up to this point address the relationship of the films in question to other films of their era, in the final chapter I turn to the relationship to (the lack of) films of a similar thematic context. A temporal contextualization of the mini-series with regard to other mini-series, e.g. to their production methods and figurations of movement, appears in the third chapter. There, I take up Sobchack's argument that the TV mini-series can be regarded as a successor to Hollywood epics of the 1950s and 1960s.

In my observations of the films as I have framed them thus far, I attempt to use detailed scene analyses to find answers to theoretical questions of revolution. In most cases, the basis for this work will be working through "expressive movements" in the respective scenes.[22] The concept of expressive movements and the method of a film analytical understanding of expressive movements are at the center of Hermann Kappelhoff's work on film theory. In the background of this work is Gilles Deleuze's work on the theory of art. Together with Félix Guattari, Deleuze identifies the work of art as a bloc of sensations, which must be understood as a combination of percepts and affects. They write:

> Percepts are no longer perceptions; they are independent of a state of those who experience them. Affects are no longer feelings or affections; they go beyond the strength of those who undergo them. Sensations, percepts, and affects are *beings* whose validity lies in themselves and exceeds any lived.[23]

The foundational concept of affect that underlies the theory of expressive movement (and this book) is not individual psychological emotion, but rather something impersonal that exceeds the individual and precedes every emotion. Affect refers to the interplay of bodies and their capacity to affect and to be affected.[24] And affects are only realized in the body as effects. The film analytical model of expressive movement conceptualizes this body of the spectator with reference to Sobchack's neophenomenological film theory.[25] Another notable feature of expressive movement is that it is organized according to form [*gestalthaft organisiert*]. Expressive movement refers to an audiovisual *form*,

---

[22] In sections "The Question of Authority" and "The Episode INDEPENDENCE" respectively, I present two analyses that are not conceived on the basis of expressive movement of the scenes. I do so because in these cases, I am interested only in a particular aspect of the scenes and not their entire form. In section "The Question of Authority" I am interested in the staging of characters and their relationship to space, and in section "The Episode INDEPENDENCE" I focus on performance.

[23] Gilles Deleuze/Félix Guattari: What is Philosophy?, trans. by Hugh Tomlinson/Graham Burchell, New York 1994, p. 164.

[24] On this distinction between affect and emotion, cf. Hermann Kappelhoff: Front Lines of Community. Hollywood Between War and Democracy, trans. by Daniel Hendrickson, Berlin/Boston 2018, pp. 108 ff. Deleuze discusses affect as an image type in Gilles Deleuze: Cinema 1. The Movement-Image, trans. by Hugh Tomlinson/Barbara Habberjam, Minneapolis 1986. On the affection-image, see also pp. 90 f. of my book.

[25] Later in the book, I introduce Deleuze's understanding of film, Sobchack's notion of the spectator, and Eisenstein's description of the fourth dimension in film. This explication is intended as an extended introduction to the theoretical background of expressive movement as a concept in film analysis.

into which all formal parameters of film analysis flow. Kappelhoff summarizes this phenomenon as follows:

> The model was based on the idea that audiovisual images, in their compositional movement – that is, the construction and arrangement of moving images – structure the temporal matrix of affective and perceptive processes of viewing films. The dynamic course of shaping cinematic images, that is, moving images, model the temporal structure of the spectator's bodily sensations which is performed by film perception. The audiovisual moving image structures this affective sensation in its temporal shape.[26]

As previously mentioned, one vanishing point of the concept of expressive movement is a method of film analysis. In an analysis that examines films through the question of expressive movement, one aim is to describe the audiovisual form of a film – which is realized in the spectator's body – in its temporal process. This temporal structure usually unfolds following the pattern "preparation, hold, and retraction." The analysis attends to all parameters of filmic form: the camera (meaning focal length, camera movement, and camera angle), as well as editing and rhythm, sound design, gesture and facial expressions, the constellation of characters (understood as *mise-en-scène*, i.e. the choreography and constellation of characters and objects), and image composition (the distribution of contrast and color, values [*Valeurs*], visual patterns and segmentations as well as the dynamics within the image). The scene analyses that appear in this book follow a systematic process for describing expressive movement.[27] In order to make the scene analyses more manageable, I focus on the dominant level of description, as well as two subdominant levels. Analyses begin with a description of the entire scene's dynamic pattern, which consists of one or more expressive movement units (EMU). A detailed description follows of the given expressive movement unit. Both the descriptions of scenic composition and the EMUs begin with a standardized phrase, which identifies the dominant levels of description. In

---

26 Kappelhoff: Front Lines of Community, op. cit., p. 116. On the concept of expressive movement, see also id./Jan-Hendrik Bakels: Das Zuschauergefühl. Möglichkeiten qualitativer Medienanalyse, in: zfm – Zeitschrift für Medienwissenschaft, 5 (2), 2011, pp. 78–95, here p. 84. Further central points of reference for Kappelhoff's conceptualization of expressive movement are Wilhelm Wundt, Karl Bühler, and Helmuth Plessner, as well as Georg Simmel and Konrad Fiedler (cf. ibid., p. 84).
27 On the systematic process, see the survey "eMAEX – eine systematisierte Methode zur Untersuchung filmischer Ausdrucksqualitäten" https://www.empirische-medienaesthetik.fu-berlin.de/emaex-system/emaex_kurzversion/index.html [last accessed 13 May 2022], especially "Ebene 3: Analyse der Pathosszenen [Level 3: Analysis of Pathos Scenes]" in "Kapitel B: Analyse" https://www.empirische-medienaesthetik.fu-berlin.de/emaex-system/emaex_kurzversion/entwicklung_emaex/05_analyse/index.html [last accessed 13 May 2022], as well as the unpublished manuscript "Entwurf für ein Manual zur Szenen-Beschreibung in ELAN".

addition, I address the staged affective domain and identify what principle of composition[28] is used to achieve it. This standardized process has the advantage of creating a basis for comparison between the analyzed scenes. It also ensures that the analyses do not remain mere analyses, but rather that the analyzed object is re-synthesized in the description such that temporal process, form, and the staged affective domain become legible. In this way, depictions of scenes and EMUs extend far beyond mere logs or charts of sequences (although these provide the foundation), as the analysis provided by a sequence log stops at mere dissection. Kappelhoff understands expressive movement as a form of filmic thinking: a thinking in images, without recourse to concepts or linguistic structures.[29] Alongside this thinking in images, this book takes up two other forms of filmic thinking. First, with reference to Deleuze, I examine how films use the sublime (in the Kantian sense) to take the spectator out of sensory elements and into thought. Second, with the audiovisual metaphor I present another Deleuzian form of filmic thinking. This form, which Deleuze outlines only briefly, is further specified and differentiated through Kappelhoff's research.

Thus, this book draws on a variety of theoretical positions from quite different areas. While Arendt is my primary point of reference for the theory of revolution, Deleuze's research takes precedence in the chapters that deal with film. This is not to say, however, that these two positions can be effortlessly unified.[30] There is obvious friction, for instance, between the ways in which each theorist attempts to account for the creation of the new. While Arendt sees novelty as ensured by the existential conditions of any individual's birth, Deleuze

---

[28] On the significance of composition, see also: "Composition, composition is the sole definition of art. Composition is aesthetic, and what is not composed is not a work of art." Deleuze/Guattari: What Is Philosophy?, op. cit., p. 191. Neither in this text nor in the discussion of expressive movement, however, should composition be mistaken for intention.

[29] Cf. a similar argument in Hermann Kappelhoff: The Politics and Poetics of Cinematic Realism, trans. by Daniel Hendrickson, New York 2015, pp. 36 ff. Deleuze and Guattari also understand art – alongside philosophy and science – as a form of thinking: thinking through sensation. For example, they write of painting: "In any case [...] painting is thought: vision is through thought, and the eye thinks, even more than it listens." Deleuze/Guattari: What is Philosophy?, op. cit., p. 195.

[30] Reconciling them would require an extensive discussion of the commonalities and differences between the positions – something that is not a central focus of this book. If one were concerned with bringing the two authors together, American pragmatism or its close counterpart in American literature might offer opportunities. On Deleuze's engagement with American literature, cf. Gilles Deleuze: Bartleby; or, The Formula, in: id.: Essays Critical and Clinical, trans. by Daniel W. Smith/Michael A. Greco, Minneapolis 1997, pp. 68–90; a few of his remarks on American pragmatism can be found in the same text, pp. 86 ff. Arendt's book on revolution includes a recourse to Melville, cf. Arendt: On Revolution, op. cit., pp. 82–88.

locates the creation of the new in affect.[31] As discussed above, however, Deleuze conceives of affect as a phenomenon that transcends the individual, as "nonhuman becoming."[32] This contradiction should not present a significant obstacle for my argument: a unification of the two positions is not absolutely necessary, as they deal with quite different areas. While Arendt's theories refer to the agents of a revolution, Deleuze is concerned with the relationship between films and spectators.

Spectators bring us to another fundamental point, one which acts as a crucial hinge between the various positions, as well as the glue that holds them all together. Upon first glance, the variation in the spectator concept comes to the fore. Arendt's book on revolution presents a spectator that can be traced back to the one conceived by Kant; Sobchack invokes a spectator derived from Merleau-Ponty and his phenomenology of the body; in his writings on NAPOLÉON, Deleuze assumes a spectator and in turn borrows from Kant's subject theory; and the film spectator in whom the expressive movements realize themselves is once again understood with recourse to Sobchack. What then unites these positions in all their obvious differences? What is the common foundation of all the spectators that appear in this book? First, it is important to stipulate that this spectator is a *theoretical construct*. None of the positions I have mentioned deal on any level with an empirically researched spectator or the empirical conditions of reception. This theoretical construct, however, can be historicized and historically located. It is – in Deleuzian terms – a spectator that thinks, or is able to think, the Whole (understood as historical development or as duration) as the Open. That is, all theoretical positions address a spectator that only became conceivable through the revolutions of modernity, the American and French Revolutions. Yet in building on this concept, a difference emerges: The spectator presumed in film analysis is an embodied spectator. This is the case only to a very limited extent for Arendt or Kant.

Even if the spectator position assumed by the various theorists is not the same – and I will not attempt to force the different backgrounds closer to each other – the basic commonalities should prove broad enough to keep the assumed

---

31 "The affect is independent of all determinate space-time; but it is none the less created in a history which produces it as the expressed and the expression of a space or a time, of an epoch or a milieu (this is why the affect is the 'new' and new affects are ceaselessly created, notably by the work of art)." Deleuze: Cinema 1, op. cit., p. 99.
32 "The affect is [...] man's nonhuman becoming." Deleuze/Guattari: What is Philosophy?, op. cit., p. 173. Similar differences characterize the question of what causes thought: for Deleuze it is a shock that comes from outside, while for Arendt it is human mortality that makes a person think.

spectator position from collapsing under the weight of eclecticism. For instance, both the Kantian spectator of revolution and the film spectator are affectively connected with what they observe. Yet in film, the affective realm is certainly more directly comprehensible. Thus, the relationship of spectator concepts in my work can be described as follows: The experiential spectator of film takes over the function of the spectator found in Arendt and Kant. This is certainly the most significant shift in this book. But the films-as-spectators and the spectator-in-the-film can also be understood to take over the spectatorial role that Arendt and Kant regard as central for a revolution.

Each of the chapters that follow is tailored to the central intellectual question of the book – how can films think revolution? That is, the book is not conceived, and certainly not primarily intended, as a contribution to research on Epstein or even the extensive work on Deleuze and Arendt.[33] Similarly, my return to the Kantian sublime does not attempt a comprehensive discussion of this topic as it relates to cinema, but simply seeks to help clarify Deleuze's arguments on Gance's film.[34] Furthermore, in each chapter I examine the films according to the book's central inquiry, and not as comprehensively as would be necessary and appropriate in a monograph dedicated to a single film.[35] Neither am I attempting to use the films to draw conclusions about the time in which they were produced.[36] To pose this question, it would be necessary first and foremost to look at films that address revolutions from the perspective of genre. The complex relationship between film and society, which can never be reduced to a simple relationship of causality or reflection, is best clarified with genre theory. The goal of my work, however, is neither to proclaim the genre of revolution film, nor to trace the theme "revolution" through film history. Such

---

[33] For a recent examination of Arendt's book on revolution, cf. Judith Mohrmann: Affekt und Revolution. Politisches Handeln nach Arendt und Kant, Frankfurt/Main / New York 2015. The author does not, however, closely attend to the significance Arendt ascribes to spectators of a revolution, and instead deals exclusively with Kant on this point.

[34] The relationship between film and the sublime is discussed more extensively in Jihae Chung: Das Erhabene im Kinofilm. Ästhetik eines gemischten Gefühls, Marburg 2016. Although Chung, also working with Deleuze, writes about Gance's NAPOLÉON, she does not draw a connection between the sublime and revolution, and in this way her approach differs from mine.

[35] For a monograph on NAPOLÉON, cf. Paul Cuff: A Revolution for the Screen. Abel Gance's Napoleon, Amsterdam 2015. Cuff's book is particularly notable for its extensive contextualization of the film.

[36] This is Wolfgang Koller's interest in relation to NAPOLÉON in: id.: Historienkino im Zeitalter der Weltkriege. Die Revolutions- und Napoleonischen Kriege in der europäischen Erinnerung, Paderborn 2013, pp. 100 ff.

a reconstruction could begin with films produced by the Lumière Brothers like LA MORT DE ROBESPIERRE (Georges Hatot, FR 1897), and could extend into a contemporary interweaving of revolution film, zombie film and gay porno at OTTO; OR, UP WITH DEAD PEOPLE (Bruce LaBruce, DE/CA 2008). What connects the three works that I address in this book, however – beyond thematic concerns – is that all three find answers to the questions posed by the theory of revolution. The framework, the question posed to the films, comes from this theory: the question of how to think revolution, and in particular the processes of movement and time that go with it. That is, in all three case studies, the central question is about the relations of movement and time in a revolution, and the forms of filmic thinking. These concerns represent the common thread of the argument. It would have been entirely possible to draw on different films or series that deal with revolution. Thus, especially in its relationship to the films analyzed here, the perspective I develop can be extended to other audiovisual stagings of revolution as well.

What stands out in this overview of the questions, the process, and the limitations of this book, however, is likely its greatest provocation: the attempt to clarify the relationship between film and revolution without recourse to Russian revolutionary cinema and in particular without referencing the films of Sergei Eisenstein.[37] As a theorist, Eisenstein does function as an important point of reference, but when it comes to thinking in images, his *films* play no role in my book. It is thus important not to equate Eisenstein the theorist with Eisenstein the filmmaker. For omitting Eisenstein the filmmaker is not intended merely as a provocation, but rather results from the theoretical premises that undergird the book. For Kant and Arendt, it is the spectators and commentators, the observers and theorists of a revolution who lend it relevance or cause it to be forgotten, presumed unimportant. It is thus a question of shifting the locus of meaning from the agents of a revolution to its spectators. And this shift is reflected in the selected corpus of films, since I am not interested in researching the possibilities for artistic engagement in revolutions.[38] Deleuze is right, however, to connect Eisenstein's films with action-thought. Both in their stated intention and empirical

---

37 Although Eisenstein is named here as a representative of the Soviet revolutionary cinema, these films are by no means monolithic. Vertov's "camera eye" is certainly closer to my approach than Eisenstein's films. However, on the difference between Vertov and JOHN ADAMS, cf. pp. 187 f. of my book. On the "camera eye," cf. Dziga Vertov: Kinoks: A Revolution, in: id.: Kino-Eye. The Writings of Dziga Vertov, ed. and with an introd. by Annette Michelson, trans. by Kevin O'Brien, Berkeley/Los Angeles 1984, pp. 11–21.
38 On this question, cf. Gerald Raunig: Kunst und Revolution. Künstlerischer Aktivismus im langen 20. Jahrhundert, Vienna 2005.

reactions, and – most importantly for my work – in the staging methods of the films themselves, they are invested in moving the spectator to action. This goal is exemplified by Eisenstein's BATTLESHIP POTEMKIN (SU 1925).[39] Hans-Joachim Schlegel ascribes an activating effect to the film's production – that is to say, an effect that is transmitted to the spectator. He sees the film as embedded in an avant-garde context in which art was expected to have a functional relationship to reality.[40] Consequently, it is hard to imagine something that departs further from an approach grounded in the theory of Arendt and Kant than the films of Eisenstein.[41] This point is underscored by the preceding discussion – and rejection – of the inevitable motion of dialectics, a central point of orientation for the Russian revolutionary cinema. In order to avoid simply reproducing the films' own self-image, it would be necessary to show whether and to what extent the films have liberated themselves from the "inevitability" of dialectics. Furthermore, in my examination of the films, I am interested in revolution as a way to access the openness of politics. Revolution is thus – following Arendt's conception of politics – not a manufactured product, not a product of *homo faber*. Russian revolutionary

---

39 On the intention behind the film: Eisenstein was particularly invested in the film's "emotional power of persuasion;" Eisenstein qtd. in Hans-Joachim Schlegel: Die Verfilmung der Revolution und die Revolutionierung des Films: Panzerkreuzer Potemkin (1925), in: Fischer Filmgeschichte, Vol. 2. Der Film als gesellschaftliche Kraft. 1925–1944, ed. by Helmut Korte/Werner Faulstich, Frankfurt/Main 1991, pp. 42–57, here p. 44. On the empirical consequences: "In 1933, his vision even sparked an insurrection by Indonesian sailors against their Dutch naval officers: Eistenstein's film 'left the screen and came to life,' as the director declared with satisfaction in an essay" (ibid., p. 46 [Translator's note: my translation]).
40 Cf. ibid., p. 45 and p. 47. Benjamin also saw the strength of Eisenstein's film precisely in its potential to mobilize people (cf. ibid, p. 46).
41 I do not seek to establish an emphatic notion of art in this book. This would be a misguided approach to films, for they have always undermined a strict distinction between art and non-art in conflictual but productive fashion. "Film is *simultaneously* art and mass medium, including all the implications that belong to each realm [...]. In each filmic image, an aesthetic, incommensurable, intransigent mode of perception, of visibility and contemplation is basically interwoven with a transparent, communicative approach to perception, visibility, and contemplation that is suited to the medium's character of addressing the masses" (Thomas Morsch: Filmische Erfahrung im Spannungsfeld zwischen Körper, Sinnlichkeit und Ästhetik, in: montage AV, 19 (1), 2010, pp. 55–77, here p. 66 [Translator's note: my translation]). Yet from my references to the theory of revolution, it should already be apparent that I do not orient myself toward the artistic aspect of the films in a functional and interventionist way, but rather take an approach informed by Kant's understanding of art. This tack is characterized primarily by disinterested pleasure. Cf. Immanuel Kant: Critique of Judgement, trans. by J.H. Bernard, New York 1951, pp. 38 f. (B 5 ff.). Yet this is precisely how art obtains its political value, as Jacques Rancière insists (cf. Jacques Rancière: Aesthetics as Politics, in: id.: Aesthetics and Its Discontents, trans. by Steve Corcoran, Cambridge/Malden 2009, pp. 19–44).

cinema, however, aims at precisely this kind of construction, mounting, and production of revolution.

Thus, rather than turning to the classics of revolutionary cinema, this book examines films that have sometimes been denied any relationship to revolution, in the Arendtian sense of revolution as a new formation of freedom. Existing interpretations disqualify NAPOLÉON as fascist and REDS as apolitical.[42] And JOHN ADAMS deals with a revolution that has itself been classified as conservative.[43] This book aims to show, however, that precisely these films can be productive for theorizing revolution. And even if this does not mean reconciling these films with historical reality – an approach that is problematic for a number of reasons[44] – it is crucial to remember that the events depicted cost an enormous number of human lives. While this book is not centered on examining the failure of revolutions, which can be seen as another consequence of Arendt's understanding of revolution since for Arendt, a revolution is always about the (re-)foundation of freedom. In other words, a political uprising that does not lead to an establishment of freedom is not a revolution. Yet at the same time it cannot be ignored that liberatory movements have often come to embody their opposite. This transition is particularly true for the aftermath of the Russian Revolution.[45] And filmic aestheticizations should never take precedence over the experiences and stories of historical victims.[46] Rather, this book attempts to keep the capacities and conceptual possibilities of political emancipation open.

---

[42] For my engagement with criticism of the films, see the respective chapters.

[43] Cf. Cotten Seiler: The American Revolution, in: The Columbia Companion to American History on Film. How the Movies Have Portrayed the American Past, ed. by Peter C. Rollins, New York 2004, pp. 49–57, here p. 49.

[44] For a discussion of this position on a theoretical level, cf. the beginning of section 3.2, "Film and the Experience of History;" on the reification of critiques of this position, see Chapter 5.

[45] For an interrogation what the catastrophes of the twentieth century mean for thinking film, cf. section 4.4, "After 1945: How Do We Look at Revolution Films With and Against Deleuze?".

[46] An oft-cited sentence from Adorno gets to the heart of this problem: "All post-Auschwitz culture, including its urgent critique, is garbage." Theodor W. Adorno: Negative Dialectics, trans. by E. B. Ashton, London 1996, p. 367. Here, 'Auschwitz' can stand in for the catastrophes of the twentieth century. The context of Adorno's statement, however, is more complex than the sentence itself might indicate. He revises here his earlier judgment that after Auschwitz, no more poetry could be written (cf. Theodor W. Adorno: Cultural Criticism and Society, in: id.: Prisms, trans. by Samuel and Shierry Weber, Cambridge, MA 1986, pp. 17–34, here p. 34).

2 The Theory of Revolution: Prolegomena

2.1 On the Concept of Revolution

"'Revolution,' at least in its ubiquitous use as a buzzword, is perhaps a more well-worn term than its users could possibly realize. Academically, it certainly requires more precise and verifiable definitions to remain useful, even if only to find consensus in dissent."[1] Even if one disagrees with the tendentious value judgment in Reinhart Koselleck's concluding sentences to the entry 'Revolution' in the *Lexikon geschichtlicher Grundbegriffe* from 1984, the demand it makes for a precise definition of the term is welcome. The introductory sentence of this entry also makes a first and fundamental contribution to this refinement: "The concept of revolution is modern."[2] Of course, this claim does not mean that the idea appears out of the blue in modernity; its genealogy has been extensively studied.[3] Yet the word first appeared in a political context in the late Middle Ages and has only been used broadly since the French Revolution. According to Koselleck, this modern concept of revolution covers at least two "realms of experience." First, it refers to "the violent unrest of an uprising," whose goal is to change the constitution. As a second realm of experience, Koselleck describes "a long-term structural change, which extends from the past into the future. In this case the term, through formulations like 'permanent revolution,' comes to resemble 'process' or 'development.'"[4] Already from this general definition, it is clear that the term implies duration, or to be more precise: It contains, or can contain, two distinct forms of duration. These are on the one hand the short-term uprising – which this book will further emphasize as a revolutionary *moment* – and on the other, the long-term

---

[1] Neithard Bulst/Jörg Fisch/Reinhart Koselleck/Christian Meier: Revolution, Rebellion, Aufruhr, Bürgerkrieg, in: Geschichtliche Grundbegriffe. Historisches Lexikon zur politisch-sozialen Sprache in Deutschland, Vol. 5, ed. by Otto Brunner/Werner Conze/Reinhart Koselleck, Stuttgart 1984, pp. 653–788, here pp. 787 f. [Translator's note: my translation].
[2] Ibid., p. 653 [Translator's note: my translation].
[3] An extensive reconstructing of the history of the term, or of the reasons for its development is not my goal here. I will only lay out the groundwork for Hannah Arendt's concept of revolution. For a comprehensive reconstruction of the history of the term, cf. ibid. as well as Reinhart Koselleck: Historical Criteria of the Modern Concept of Revolution, in: id.: Futures Past: On the Semantics of Historical Time, trans. by Keith Tribe, New York 2004, pp. 43–57; or the even more extensive and elaborate work by Karl Griewank: Der neuzeitliche Revolutionsbegriff. Entstehung und Geschichte, Frankfurt/Main 1973. Griewank also argues in this standard reference that the political use of 'revolution' first appears in modernity.
[4] Bulst/Fisch/Koselleck/Meier: Revolution, op. cit., p. 653 [Translator's note: my translation]; the formulations are Koselleck's.

development of structural change. And even if both of these realms of experience, with their respective temporal forms, do not necessarily belong together, and the term 'revolution' can refer to only one or the other, since the French Revolution it has been common for these two temporal forms (each of which implies a distinct form of movement, as I will demonstrate with Arendt) "to mutually define each other in one and the same concept of revolution."[5] According to Koselleck, the long-term development unfolds and clarifies the political goals of the uprising (which Koselleck also calls a "short-term violent change"[6]). Conversely, the uprising's political goal opens up long-term development (Koselleck writes of the "historical dimension"[7]). For Koselleck, this dynamic gives the term a dual function: It is both a conceptual guide [*erkenntnisleitend*] and a director of the action [*handlungsweisend*]. This duality is also the basis of the term's modernity. Thus, when I speak of 'revolution' in this book, I always intend to invoke this dual aspect of the term. In so doing, I do not wish to ignore the fact that there can be quite different types of revolutions, e.g. the Industrial Revolution. And one could certainly examine the relationship between a political revolution and a phenomenon like the Industrial Revolution.[8] Here, however, the focus is primarily on the relations of time and movement through which a revolution is to be understood, and less on examining these kinds of interdependencies. Furthermore, answers to questions about

---

5 Ibid., p. 654 [Translator's note: my translation].
6 Ibid. [Translator's note: my translation].
7 Ibid. [Translator's note: my translation].
8 Griewank emphasizes the close connection between industrial and political revolution in Karl Marx's theory of revolution (cf. Griewank: Der neuzeitliche Revolutionsbegriff, op. cit., p. 219). As a consequence of this emphasis, he also describes the preface to *A Contribution to the Critique of Political Economy* as "a consummate expression of Marxist revolutionary theory" (ibid., p. 220 [Translator's note: my translation]). More recent work on Marx, however, warns against overemphasizing this introduction's significance for the entirety of Marxist theory, particularly the sentence "It is not the consciousness of men that determines their existence, but their social existence that determines their consciousness," for fear that it gives rise to an overly simple and causal base-superstructure determinism (cf. Michael Heinrich: An Introduction to the Three Volumes of Karl Marx's Capital, trans. by Alexander Locascio, New York 2012, p. 200; the comment by Marx is in Karl Marx: A Contribution to the Critique of Political Economy. Part One, in: id./Friedrich Engels: MECW 29. Marx 1857–61, London 2010, pp. 257–417, here p. 263). On Marx's own complications of this relation, see the third thesis on Feuerbach: "The materialist doctrine that men are products of circumstances and upbringing, and that, therefore, changed men are products of changed circumstances and changed upbringing, forgets that it is men who change circumstances and that the educator must himself be educated" (Karl Marx: Theses on Feuerbach, in: id./Friedrich Engels: MECW 5. Marx and Engels 1845–47, London 2010, pp. 6–8, here p. 7). According to Marx, the *coincidence* [*Zusammenfallen*] of change to each side is the revolutionary praxis.

2.1 On the Concept of Revolution

the causes, linkages, and interrelationships of a political revolution should not be predetermined on a theoretical or historical level, but instead sought in the films themselves.

Following Hannah Arendt, "each new appearance among men" – especially in the political realm – "stands in need of a new word, whether a new word is coined to cover the new experience or an old word is used and given entirely new meaning."[9] If one digs deeper into the historical etymology of the term 'revolution,' and examines pre-political usages, interesting similarities to and differences from its modern usage emerge. Similarities include the different temporalities and movement in particular, as demonstrated by the following remarks on the word's usage in late antiquity:

> The word 'revolutio' first appears in Christian literature of late antiquity; its use is not political. It means 'rolling back,' 'rolling over,' 'rotation.' We find it only in a few examples: for the rolling of a stone away from Christ's grave; for the orderly cycle of the year and the heavenly bodies, for return (e.g. *revolutio temporis, lunaris cursus revolutio; incarnationis divinae mysterium [...] a nobis annua revolutione celebratur*). Further uses refer to the transmigration of souls, *opinio translationis vel revolutionis animarium*, which anticipates eternal repetition of the same; Augustine contrasts this term with *resurrectio*, according to which everything in the world has a beginning; and finally the term appears in the context of cholera (as *ventris sive stomachi nimia tortio et subita revolutio*).[10]

Four points stand out in the term's ancient usage. First, it is important to stipulate that the term referred to various *movements*, and various *forms of movement*. In addition – and this is of course the fundamental difference from the modern usage – the term was used to refer to a return, a turning back (re-volution), a repetition. Third, the connection to cholera reveals a usage of the word that is directly associated with human corporeality. Seemingly trivial upon first glance, this aspect becomes important for exploring a filmic approach to the topic of revolution and can furthermore be traced through the term's historical development. Goethe described his first reaction to the French Revolution as follows, in a letter to Jacobi: "You can understand that the French Revolution was also a revolution for me," by

---

[9] Hannah Arendt: On Revolution, London 1990, p. 35. The relationship between politics and speech in Arendt's work can be roughly summarized in the idea that for her, speech is what makes humans political beings. Cf. Hannah Arendt: The Human Condition, Chicago 1998, p. 3. Another decisive element of her theory of politics is of course action. See also Seyla Benhabib: The Reluctant Modernism of Hannah Arendt, Thousand Oaks 1996, p. xxix. Yet another basic condition of politics for Arendt is that *the human* does not exist, but rather people must always be conceived in their plurality. Cf. Hannah Arendt: Introduction into Politics, in: id.: The Promise of Politics, ed. by Jerome Kohn, New York 2005, pp. 93–200, here p. 93.

[10] Bulst/Fisch/Koselleck/Meier: Revolution, op. cit., p. 669 [Translator's note: my translation]; the passage is by Christian Meier.

which he meant that the news made him feel nauseated.[11] Particularly significant is, fourthly, the indication that the term was used to indicate the cycle of heavenly bodies. This usage became central in the medieval period, while the others fell away. Although it is not yet a political usage of the word, according to the *Lexikon geschichtlicher Grundbegriffe*, this astronomical-astrological use of the term contains two elements that became significant in the later, political idea of revolution. The movement of stars served to measure time. Thus, the term's temporal dimension also becomes central. It designated a temporal unit, served to measure time, and therefore necessarily possessed its own temporality. Furthermore, in the Middle Ages there was already talk of a *revolutio mundi* (for example in Thomas Aquinas). By the medieval period, the term already referred to the entire world.[12]

The term was likely first used in a political sense in the Middle Ages in mid-fourteenth-century Italy, to mean 'overthrow.'[13] And only once it was used politically did the term become a fundamental historical concept. Quite soon after the French Revolution and regardless of a given commentator's political orientation, people realized that the events of the Revolution impacted all of humanity and thus the past and future of the entire world. While before the French Revolution, unrest and civil war were always conceived and carried out according to an existing system (whether theological, legal, or political), now

---

11 On this point, see Griewank: Der neuzeitliche Revolutionsbegriff, op. cit., p. 130 (Griewank cites Johann Wolfgang von Goethe: Goethe's letter to Jacobi from March 3, 1730, in: id.: Goethes Werke, Weimarer Ausgabe, Briefe, Vol. 9, Sec. 4, ed. by Eduard von der Hellen, Weimar 1891, p. 184). For another example of this use of 'revolution' in the sense of mental or physical "disturbances, turbidity, and convulsions," Griewank notes that Camille Desmoulins referred to a seizure [*Schlaganfall*] as a 'revolution' as late as 1789 (cf. Griewank: Der neuzeitliche Revolutionsbegriff, op. cit., p. 130).

12 Cf. the section on the term's medieval usage by Neithard Bulst: Bulst/Fisch/Koselleck/Meier: Revolution, op. cit., pp. 670 ff. Bulst cites Thomas Aquinas: In libros physicorum 2, 7, 6, in: id.: Opera omnia, Vol. 4, ed. by Roberto Busa, Stuttgart 1980, p. 72: "revolutio mundi, et motus stellarum." Arendt will refer to yet a third point of reference for the modern notion of revolution: the *irresistibility* of astronomical movement. On this topic, cf. the following subchapter of this book.

13 Cf. ibid., pp. 671 f. Italy would remain significant for the term's political development. Particularly important are the thoughts and theories of Niccolò Machiavelli during the Renaissance, even if he did not use the term itself nor have any sense for the pathos of new beginnings that is so important for modern revolutions. On Machiavelli and his relationship to the modern concept of revolution, cf. Griewank: Der neuzeitliche Revolutionsbegriff, op. cit., pp. 110 ff. and Arendt: On Revolution, op. cit., pp. 35 ff. Arendt situates the rise of the term's political sense in the seventeenth century and particularly in connection with events in England in 1660 and 1668, where it was still used to indicate return and restoration (cf. ibid., pp. 43 f.).

these systems themselves were being questioned: The French Revolution made a static final justification impossible. This in turn enabled for the first time the concept of 'history': "The modern concept of revolution cannot be understood without its interdependence with the term 'history,' which emerged simultaneously [...]."[14]

In antiquity, political change was conceived in the framework of a circular return of conditions[15] and was part of what Koselleck calls a *transhistorical* concept. This transhistorical notion of political change did not allow for any development or profound change of the existing order; instead, it suspended all political positions. By contrast, Koselleck characterizes the modern idea of revolution as *metahistorical* and describes it as follows:

> As with the German concept of *Geschichte*, which in the form of "history pure and simple" contained within itself the possibilities of all individual histories, Revolution congealed into a collective singular which appeared to unite within itself the course of all individual revolutions. Hence, revolution became a *metahistorical concept*, completely separated, however, from its naturalistic origin and henceforth charged with ordering historically recurrent convulsive experiences. In other words, Revolution assumes a transcendental significance; it becomes a regulative principle of knowledge, as well as of the actions of all those drawn into revolution.[16]

In contrast to a transhistorical concept, in which fundamental changes and developments of human life are unthinkable, and instead disappear into monotonous repetition, but also in contrast to a singular event with no consequences, the metahistorical concept that crystallized in modernity into the collective singular 'revolution' is a "historicophilosophical concept, based on a perspective which displayed a constant and steady direction."[17] The modern concept of revolution was what made it possible to reflect on the development of humanity and human life from a perspective that extends beyond cyclical repetition. Only

---

14 Cf. Bulst/Fisch/Koselleck/Meier: Revolution, op. cit., p. 739. With reference to Friedrich Schlegel's commentary on the French Revolution, they make this point as follows: "The singularity of the French Revolution did not determine that it – like everything else in the course of time – has a particular place, but rather the French Revolution challenges the entire past and future to reorganize themselves with regard to one another. 'French Revolution' became, quite simply, a basic provision of the history of philosophy" (ibid., p. 738 [Translator's note: my translation]). The passages from p. 738 and p. 739 are by Koselleck.
15 Cf. Koselleck: Historical Criteria of the Modern Concept of Revolution, op. cit, pp. 45 ff. Roughly speaking, the medieval period differed in that theories of human life were eschatologically oriented. In Luther's time, according to Griewank, one "always saw Judgment Day looming" (Griewank: Der neuzeitliche Revolutionsbegriff, op. cit., p. 79 [Translator's note: my translation]).
16 Koselleck: Historical Criteria of the Modern Concept of Revolution, op. cit., p. 50.
17 Ibid., p. 51.

through the concept of revolution is something new in the realm of politics conceivable. A precise discussion of what this thesis means in terms of the American and French Revolutions can be found in Hannah Arendt's work.

2.2 Arendt's Conception

For Arendt too, the decisive difference between the revolutions of modernity and earlier notions of political change and transition was that in the former, something fundamentally new was beginning and could be conceived. In two central passages from her book on revolution, a dual portrait of the American and the French Revolutions, she writes:

> Antiquity was well acquainted with political change and the violence that went with change, but neither of them appeared to it to bring about something altogether new. Changes did not interrupt the course of what the modern age has called history [...].

Furthermore, she argues:

> The modern concept of revolution, inextricably bound up with the notion that the course of history suddenly begins anew, that an entirely new story, a story never known or told before, is about to unfold, was unknown prior to the two great revolutions at the end of the eighteenth century. Before they were engaged in what then turned out to be a revolution, none of the actors had the slightest premonition of what the plot of the new drama was going to be. However, once the revolutions had begun to run their course, and long before those who were involved in them could know whether their enterprise would end in victory or disaster, the novelty of the story and the innermost meaning of its plot became manifest to actors and spectators alike. As to the plot, it was unmistakably the emergence of freedom.[18]

I want to draw attention to four points in these passages. Not only does a revolution give rise to an entirely new political order – this was precisely what was alien to the political upheavals of antiquity and the Middle Ages, and even *at first* to American and French revolutionaries – one can also sense that this new beginning is loaded with extreme pathos. Arendt connects this intense feeling with the introduction of the revolutionary calendar after the French Revolution, for instance.[19]

A second point that shines through in the above-cited passages is the question of violence. Arendt understands revolutions as profoundly violent

---

[18] Arendt: On Revolution, op. cit., p. 21 and pp. 28 f.
[19] Cf. ibid., p. 261.

phenomena. For her, however, they are always more than simple eruptions of violence, since they are political phenomena (Arendt strictly distinguishes between politics and violence.) They thus initially have more to do with power than with violence – two concepts that Arendt considers to be opposites: she defines 'power' as the human capacity to join together with others. Only a group can have power, and their power emerges from their cohesion. If one claims that an individual has power, it means that this person is backed by a certain number of people who have empowered this person to act in their name. When this group of people stops supporting the individual, he also loses his power, and must instead use violence to keep others on his side. In this sense, for Arendt, solidarity is power.[20] Consequently, a revolution only occurs when there has first been a shift in power, which is why she argues that revolutions generally begin without bloodshed.[21] On the other hand, however, she does not exclude violence and does not work with a necessarily pacifist concept of revolution. Rather, she sees a profound connection between origin, new beginning, and violence. She reminds us that there are no origin stories free from violence, and refers to Marx's remark that violence is the midwife of history. Though with Arendt, this metaphor should be understood precisely. Violence is neither the siring nor the birthing parent; it is only the *midwife*,

---

20 Cf. Hannah Arendt: On Violence, San Diego/New York/London 1970, pp. 50 f. In the fifth chapter of her book on revolution, Arendt makes a point-by-point comparison between the American and French Revolutions based on the concepts 'violence,' 'power,' and 'authority;' cf. Arendt: On Revolution, op. cit., pp. 179–214.
21 Cf. Hannah Arendt: Über die Revolution, Munich/Zurich 2014, p. 148 and Hannah Arendt: Macht und Gewalt, Munich/Zurich 2013, p. 50 [Translator's note: In some cases, the author refers to passages in the German version of Arendt's work that do not correspond completely to the earlier English version. Arendt translated her own work and in some cases revised in translation. In general, I use the English versions, unless there is an important element in the German version that is missing from the English, as in this case]. The value of Arendt's distinction between 'power' and 'violence' becomes clear when one considers the problems faced by Herbert Marcuse, for instance, when he reduces the question of a revolution's legitimacy to the question of violence. He weighs the victims to be expected under an existing society against the victims to be expected from a revolution and comes to the conclusion that ten thousand victims are better than twenty thousand. A utilitarian ethic, which Marcuse himself describes as brutal and inhumane, which he nonetheless sees no way around. Yet in the process he misses the significant question of 'power' in a revolution. Cf. Herbert Marcuse: Ethics and Revolution, in: Richard T. de George (ed.): Ethics and Society. Original Essays on Contemporary Moral Problems, Garden City, NY 1966, pp. 133–147.

and can never suffice alone or in its own right to complete a revolution and to found a new political order.[22]

Third, the passages cited above suggest that Arendt sees a quite close connection between revolution and freedom. For her, the aim of every revolution is freedom.[23] The new entity that emerges with revolutions is freedom. The rights to life, freedom and property were first expressed as inalienable human rights during the revolutions of the eighteenth century. When it comes to freedom, Arendt distinguishes between negative and positive freedom. As she understands them, negative freedoms are experienced as liberation *from* something. More concretely, she means freedom from servitude, protection from unlawful force, and freedom from hunger and fear.

These liberatory aspects, however, are not the most important part of Arendt's concept of revolution, and particularly not for the American case, which is more central to Arendt's work than the French Revolution, especially with regard to freedom. For these aspects could theoretically also be achieved through the establishment of a constitutional monarchy. And it is particularly important to Arendt that the American Revolution was not concerned with freedom from hunger and poverty. Wealth in America was what first broke down the notion of an unchangeable distribution of riches and poverty, she argues. Only through wealth did it become possible to think of political relations beyond the form of cyclical motion. Thus, for Arendt, the American Revolution has nothing to do with the social question, or the fact of poverty, which she furthermore excludes from the realm of politics. The reason for the American Revolution was not great poverty among the population. To the contrary, wealth showed that the world and the way it is structured are not immutable, which encouraged the revolutionaries in Europe.[24]

---

22 Cf. Arendt: Über die Revolution, op. cit., p. 21 and p. 268. Arendt gives no citation for Marx's comment, but she is probably referring to the first volume of *Capital*, where Marx writes: "Force is the midwife of every old society which is pregnant with a new one" (Karl Marx: Capital. A Critique of Political Economy, Vol. 1, trans. by Ben Fowkes, London 1976, p. 916). In Engels' *Anti-Dühring*, this becomes: "That force, however, plays yet another role in history, a revolutionary role; that, in the words of Marx, it is the midwife of every old society pregnant with a new one [...]" (Friedrich Engels: Herr Eugen Dühring's Revolution in Science, in: Karl Marx/id.: MECW 25. Engels, London 2010, pp. 5–309, here p. 171).
23 For the following paragraphs, cf. the first chapter from Arendt's book on revolution; on the connection between revolution and freedom, see also the introduction of that book.
24 At this point I could begin a critical discussion of Arendt's theory of revolution, but that would exceed the scope of this book. I will at least remark, however, that first and fundamentally, the complete exclusion of the social question from the political realm merits discussion (a discussion that would end with the question of Arendt's relationship to Marx's theory of *political* economy). Secondly, the nearly complete absence of slavery and the Indian Wars in

The reason why the American Revolution in particular is so important for Arendt is that it focused on the foundation of freedom in a positive sense; this freedom could only exist in a republic, and could not be realized in a constitutional monarchy. By "freedom in a positive sense," Arendt means political and public affairs: reflecting, talking, discussing, persuading, and acting, as well as general activities in public. Thus, for Arendt, true political freedom, i.e. positive freedom, is the freedom to think and speak as well as to gather and organize. These positive freedoms make up "public happiness" for Arendt. She connects them with joy, with a form of happiness: "It turned out that acting is fun."[25] All of this existed already in antiquity yet disappeared by the Middle Ages and only resurfaced again with the American Revolution. For this reason, in the revolutions of modernity, this freedom was associated with the pathos of new beginnings.

Fourth, in the passages cited above, Arendt speaks of both the actors and the spectators of revolution. This distinction is significant for her concept of revolution. Referring to the spectators of revolution invokes a critically important perspective for Arendt. As is apparent from her notion of positive freedoms, the level of acting is eminently important for her concept of politics. It quickly becomes clear that the same is true in her concept of revolution – and particularly for her understanding of the American Revolution. The latter emerged through praxis and action rather than in theory: "[...] the [American] Revolution, in particular, was the result not of 'bookish' learning [...] but of the 'practical' experiences of the colonial period."[26] Upon closer examination, however, she clearly does not

---

Arendt's observation of the American Revolution begs attention. A few thoughts on these topics can be found in Benhabib: The Reluctant Modernism of Hannah Arendt, op. cit., pp. 130 ff., 138 ff. and especially 155 ff.

25 Hannah Arendt: Thoughts on Politics and Revolution. A Commentary, in: id.: Crises of the Republic, San Diego/New York/London 1972, pp. 199–233, here p. 203; for the German original, see Hannah Arendt/Adelbert Reif: Interview mit Hannah Arendt. Von Adelbert Reif, in: Arendt: Macht und Gewalt, op. cit., pp. 105–133, here p. 109. With the term "fun," Arendt refers to American students in the late 1960, yet she also relates it to the "public happiness" of American revolutionaries. I take the reference to this quotation from the presentation title "'*It Turned Out: Acting is Fun!*': Medienaffekte in den neuen Politik-Serien" by Chris Tedjasukmana, held on February 10, 2016 as part of the lecture series "Abseits des Kinos [Beyond the Cinema]" in the Seminar für Filmwissenschaft at the FU Berlin.

26 Arendt: On Revolution, op. cit., p. 219. Arendt's emphasis on action and praxis leads to her polemic against the concept of the professional revolutionist, propagated by Lenin especially. According to Arendt, the professional revolutionist may have studied revolution in coffeehouses and libraries but had never brought about the outbreak of revolution. He could, however, pick up power if it lay in the street (for Arendt, a necessary condition of revolution is that a regime loses power). On this polemic, cf. ibid., p. 329. On Lenin's theory of the professional revolutionist, cf. Vladimir Ilyich Lenin: What Is To Be Done? Burning Questions of Our

dismiss the perspective of the thinking spectator as unimportant. Quite the contrary, she writes: "Wherever knowing and doing have parted company, the space for freedom is lost."[27] That is, for Arendt the goal of the revolution can only be achieved through the interplay of knowledge and action, theory and praxis, reason and experience, observing and participating.[28] So according to Arendt, besides the experiences that the men of the American Revolution had both in and before the revolution, they also possessed "book-learning and thinking in concepts" – here too, the epistemological position has a role to play.

What does she say about this spectator position with regard to the revolutions she examines? Here it is worth first addressing her observations on the French Revolution, as Arendt sees its great influence on world history as coming from the fact that people have so often attempted to understand its events and dress them up with theory.[29] Arendt too tells the story of the night of July 14, 1789, according to which the Duc de la Rochefoucauld-Liancourt, probably one of the first spectators of the French Revolution, told the King of the people's uprising and the storming of the Bastille, whereupon Louis XVI responded, "It's a revolt!" Liancourt, however, corrected him: "No, Sire, it is a revolution."[30] For Arendt, what is most important about Liancourt's correction is the following:

> Here we hear the word still, and politically for the last time, in the sense of the old metaphor which carries its meaning from the skies down to the earth; but here, for the first time perhaps, the emphasis has entirely shifted from the lawfulness of a rotating, cyclical movement to its irresistibility. The motion is still seen in the image of the movements of the stars, but what is stressed now is that it is beyond human power to arrest it, and hence it is a law unto itself.[31]

In the preceding section of this book, one side of the concept of revolution is defined as the uprising that has a short, momentary duration and whose paradigmatic example might be the storming of the Bastille. In Arendt's description,

---

Movement, in: id.: Lenin Collected Works. Volume 5, May 1901–February 1902, Moscow 1977, pp. 347–529, there especially "Chapter 4C. Organisation of Workers and Organisation of Revolutionaries," pp. 451–467.
27 Arendt: On Revolution, op. cit., p. 264.
28 With this remark, I certainly do not seek to flatten the difference between knowledge, theory, reason, and observation. Yet all these terms refer to an epistemological position. Arendt traces 'theory' etymologically to the Greek 'theōrein,' 'to look at.' Cf. Hannah Arendt: Lectures on Kant's Political Philosophy, ed. by Ronald Beiner, Chicago 1992, p. 55.
29 Cf. Arendt: On Revolution, op. cit., p. 220.
30 Ibid., p. 47 [Translator's note: In French in Arendt's original]. I am not interested here in the accuracy of this historical anecdote.
31 Ibid., pp. 47 f.

we find the form of movement that corresponds to this temporality: an "irresistible" movement that cannot be controlled by human power, like the movement of the stars. With regard to the French Revolution, she writes – and this is perhaps the most important sentence for Arendt's theorization of the French Revolution, as it concisely expresses the kernel of her critique:

> The notion of an irresistible movement, which the nineteenth century soon was to conceptualize into the idea of historical necessity, echoes from beginning to end through the pages of the French Revolution.[32]

Regarding the forms of movement and temporality in the concept of revolution, the sentence can be reformulated as follows: The irresistible movement of the fourteenth of July is transferred onto structural change. Or in other words, the movement of the moment comes to characterize the temporality of structural change; the movement of one side of the revolutionary idea becomes imbricated with the temporality of the other side.

Arendt reinforces this argument when she lists the metaphors that have been used to try to make the events of the French Revolution comprehensible: as streaming lava, as a mighty current, tempest or as rushing waves.[33] When Arendt places such emphasis on the metaphors used in attempts to understand the French Revolution, she anticipates a basic idea of the metaphor scholars George Lakoff and Mark Johnson: the notion that for the ways in which a given phenomenon can be understood and conceived, the metaphors used to explain it are not simply accidental rhetoric. Rather, these metaphors set the framework of comprehension and to a large extent determine how the phenomenon will or

---

[32] Ibid., p. 48.
[33] Ibid., pp. 48 f. Other authors also use kinetic metaphors to capture revolution. Marx writes: "*Revolutions are the locomotives of history*" (Karl Marx: The Class Struggles in France, 1848 to 1850, in: id./Friedrich Engels: MECW 10. Marx and Engels 1849–51, London 2010, pp. 45–145, here p. 122). And Benjamin responds: "Marx says that revolutions are the locomotive of world history. But perhaps it is quite otherwise. Perhaps revolutions are an attempt by the passengers on this train – namely, the human race – to activate the emergency brake" (Walter Benjamin: Paralipomena to "On the Concept of History", in: id.: Selected Writings. Vol. IV 1938–1940, ed. by Howard Eiland/Michael W. Jennings, trans. by Edmund Jephcott et al., Cambridge, MA et al. 2003, p. 402). Koselleck postulates a close connection between metaphors and historical knowledge in general: "Unlike other sciences, the science of history lives through metaphor" (Reinhart Koselleck: Über die Theoriebedürftigkeit der Geschichtswissenschaft, in: Werner Conze [ed.]: Theorie der Geschichtswissenschaft und Praxis des Geschichtsunterrichts, Stuttgart 1972, pp. 10–28, here p. 16 [Translator's note: my translation]). An overview of metaphors used in historical writing can be found in Alexander Demandt: Metaphern für Geschichte. Sprachbilder und Gleichnisse im historisch-politischen Denken, Munich 1978.

can be conceptualized.³⁴ While the above-named examples come from the actors of the French Revolution themselves, the impression of an 'irresistible movement' was even stronger among the revolution's spectators. Arendt writes:

> If the new metaphorical content of the word 'revolution' sprang directly from the experiences of those who first made and then enacted the Revolution in France, it obviously carried an even greater plausibility for those who watched its course, as if it were a spectacle, from the outside. What appeared to be most manifest in this spectacle was that none of its actors could control the course of events, that this course took a direction which had little if anything to do with the willful aims and purposes of the anonymous force of the revolution if they wanted to survive at all.³⁵

Especially from the spectator position unleashed by the action, the impression is of unstoppable and necessary movement.³⁶ According to Arendt, the most consequential observer of the French Revolution was Hegel, who developed his philosophy of history and theory of historical necessity with an eye to the French Revolution³⁷ – as the passage cited above already hinted at. The reference to necessity, however, means the death of revolution for Arendt: After all, a revolution is always about the foundation of freedom, which is extinguished when it is replaced by necessity. And while Arendt correctly states that talk of historical necessity can be used to justify violence and terror, her assessment that this talk

---

34 Cf. George Lakoff/Mark Johnson: Metaphors We Live By, Chicago/London 1980. For Lakoff and Johnson, metaphors are not only a question of language, i.e. of words, but as metaphorical concepts they structure human thought processes (cf. ibid., p. 3). On the significant role that Arendt herself assigns to metaphors in thought, cf. Hannah Arendt: Denktagebuch 1950 bis 1973. Vol. 2, Munich/Zurich 2002, p. 728 ("Metaphor is what connects thinking and writing. What is called a concept in philosophy is called a metaphor in poetry. Thinking creates 'concepts' from what is visible in order to describe the invisible. [...] Everything that thought 'transmits' [is] metaphorical." [Translator's note: my translation]) and p. 729 ("The role of metaphor: the connection (as – though) of the visible with the invisible, the conscious with the unknowable." [Translator's note: my translation]), as well as and especially Hannah Arendt: The Life of the Mind, San Diego 1971, pp. 98 ff. (cf. the conclusion that "language, by lending itself to metaphorical usage, enables us to think, that is, to have traffic with non-sensory matters, because it permits a carrying-over, *metapherein*, of our sense experiences" (ibid., p. 110)).
35 Arendt: On Revolution, op. cit., p. 51.
36 Cf. ibid., p. 52.
37 Cf. Georg Wilhelm Friedrich Hegel: Werke in zwanzig Bänden. Vol. 12. Vorlesungen über die Philosophie der Geschichte, Frankfurt/Main 1970, especially pp. 520 ff. Formulations that refer to history as a process of necessity can also be found in Marx. For example, see Karl Marx/Friedrich Engels: Manifesto of the Communist Party, in: id.: MECW 6. Marx and Engels 1845–48, London 2010, pp. 477–519, here especially pp. 495 f.; or in Marx: Capital, Vol. 1, op. cit., pp. 927 ff. Fredric Jameson, however, argues that for Marx, the goal of this development is never the end of history, but simply the end of prehistory. Cf. Fredric Jameson: 'End of Art' or 'End of History'?, in: id.: The Cultural Turn. Selected Writings on the Postmodern, 1983–1998, London/New York 1998, pp. 73–92, here p. 88.

means the end of freedom and the death of revolution should not be accepted uncritically. Florian Grosser argues that it was precisely the Hegelian concept of history and the reference thereto that led to an increase in political and revolutionary activity.[38] Yet regardless of how one evaluates Arendt's assessment, the important takeaway for this book is that metaphors of movement and forms of temporality used to grasp and understand the French Revolution are far from being mere rhetorical accessories. Rather, they are situated at the core of what Arendt considers to be the quandary of the French Revolution. Arendt creates a connection between the necessity of the course of the French Revolution and the needs of the body (among which the necessity of nourishment reigns supreme). It is therefore associated with the social question that was at the heart of the French – unlike the American – Revolution, and that in her eyes led to the death of the former.[39]

For if one looks with Arendt at the American Revolution and how it is perceived, one sees a quite different picture. First, no one had the feeling of being compelled to follow an irresistible movement, and of losing control of their own ability to act.[40] Second, in the American Revolution there is no moment that serves as a crystallization of the entire phenomenon. There was the Boston Tea Party in 1773, which might have had the potential to function as a paradigmatic moment; yet it took place three years before the Declaration of Independence. And the Declaration of Independence certainly lacks the drama of the storming of the Bastille. Furthermore, according to Arendt it would be a mistake to limit the American Revolution to the war for independence and the rebellion against British colonialism. The war for independence could "be completed much more quickly [...] than the American Revolution." For the latter continued after the rebellion: "the actual course of the revolution" only came later.[41] According to Arendt, the American Revolution had a much longer duration than has frequently been argued, particularly by historians. Nonetheless, the American Revolution can be understood in the matrix of movement forms and temporalities. It is only missing the singular moment of uprising that would condense the dramatic events, as well as the associated irresistible and uncontrollable movement. Rather, the process of this revolution had a much longer duration than is often assumed, and included the Constitutional Conventions. Thus, the movement of the American Revolution can also be described positively as a free and open movement that was not devoured by the moment of uprising and its form of movement.

---

[38] Cf. Florian Grosser: Theorien der Revolution zur Einführung, Hamburg 2013, p. 99.
[39] Cf. footnote 24 in this chapter.
[40] Cf. Arendt, On Revolution, op. cit., p. 51.
[41] Both formulations are in Arendt: Über die Revolution, op. cit., p. 184 [Translator's note: my translation].

Yet – and this leads me to the last point that I want to draw out of Arendt's book on revolution – the American Revolution lacks a spectator position. Precisely this lack, the absence of an appropriate theorization of the Revolution, according to Arendt, led to the gradual death [*Absterben*] of the revolutionary spirit in America.[42] It was the French Revolution, because it was so intently observed and theorized, that attained world historical significance. Every revolution that came after it, and particularly the actors of the Russian Revolution, took their cues from the process of the French Revolution, according to Arendt. But significantly – herein lies the deadly tragedy – because the Russian revolutionaries succumbed to the idea of obeying historical necessity, they followed the *course* of the French Revolution, which had deadly results, sometimes for the revolutionaries themselves. Here too, it is worth attending to the metaphors used by Arendt to describe these observations:

> For the true tragedy of the Russian Revolution can only be appreciated when one realizes the absurd degree to which the men of this revolution consciously modeled their actions on the experiences of the French Revolution, as though it were a question of *simply performing the old play on the world stage once again* under radically changed circumstances.

Later in the same section, she goes on:

> What the men of the Russian Revolution had learned from the French Revolution – and this learning constituted almost their entire preparation – was history and not action. They had acquired the skill *to play whatever part the great drama of history was going to assign them*, and if no other role was available but that of the villain, *they were more than willing to accept their part* rather than remain outside the play.[43]

Here as elsewhere,[44] Arendt relies on theatrical metaphors. And her rhetoric is only consistent in this case. After all, she wants to express the idea that participants in the Russian Revolution were no longer independent actors, but instead

---

42 Cf. ibid., p. 283.

43 Translator's note: Both of these quotes are taken from Arendt's German version in the original. Here, because the English version offers no similar passage, the first passage is my own translation from Arendt: Über die Revolution, op. cit., p. 70. The second is from Arendt's English work, On Revolution, op. cit., p. 58. In both passages, the emphases are mine.

44 Cf. the explanations cited below. On this point, see also Hermann Kappelhoff: Front Lines of Community. Hollywood Between War and Democracy, trans. by Daniel Hendrickson, Berlin/Boston 2018, p. 375 and Benjamin Wihstutz: Urteilende Zuschauer. Über Geschmack und Öffentlichkeit um 1800, in: Geschmack und Öffentlichkeit, ed. by Matthias Grotkopp/Hermann Kappelhoff/Benjamin Wihstutz, Zurich 2019, pp. 103–120. Both authors indicate that the theatrical metaphor becomes inappropriate when Arendt uses it to grasp the political significance of aesthetic judgment and the *sensus communis* – the goal of Arendt's argumentation in her lectures on Kant's political philosophy. Kappelhoff recommends that films and film vision be

played a predetermined role, just as an actor or actress is bound to the script of an old drama. Nor is Arendt alone in deploying theatrical metaphors, for interestingly, these can already be found among the actors of the Revolution; by contrast, according to Arendt, historians and theorists of the revolution tended to use the metaphor of birth pangs.[45] Beyond Arendt's negative view of theatrical metaphors – which for her articulate victory for the idea of historical necessity – she draws on the realm of performing arts to characterize the epistemological perspective whose eminent significance she repeatedly highlights.

The use of theatrical metaphors can also be found in Arendt's lectures on Kant's political philosophy.[46] Like the book on revolution, this work begins with the significance of spectators for a revolution. Here, the origin of Arendt's emphasis on the importance of the spectator position becomes clear: Immanuel Kant's remarks on the French Revolution.[47] The fundamental argument of these remarks is that the uninvolved spectators in particular, with their enthusiastic

---

substituted as paradigmatic metaphors, a suggestion that I take up in this work to theorize revolution.

45 Cf. Arendt: On Revolution, op. cit., p. 106. With regard to the birth metaphor, she again refers to Marx, yet without giving a concrete citation (cf. footnote 22 in this chapter). At least in "The Eighteenth Brumaire of Louis Bonaparte," however, the circumstances seem different. From the beginning of this essay, it is clear that Marx uses theatrical metaphors when speaking about revolutions of the past. For example when he comments on Hegel's thesis that all great historic facts and personages recur twice: "He forgot to add: the first time as tragedy, the second as farce" (Karl Marx: The Eighteenth Brumaire of Louis Bonaparte, in: id./Friedrich Engels: MECW 11. Marx and Engels 1851–53, London 2010, pp. 99–197, here p. 103). He further writes with regard to past revolutionary crises of "disguise," "costumes," and a "new scene of world history" that is being "present[ed]" (ibid., p. 104). And when it comes to the revolution in which Marx was more or less directly involved, the social revolution of the nineteenth century, which "cannot draw its poetry from the past," but "only from the future" (ibid., p. 106), he uses a metaphor that once again emphasizes the New which is the element that the birth metaphor also brings into focus. Marx then characterizes revolution as a leap and writes: "Hic rhodus, hic salta!" (Ibid., p. 107). For a more detailed discussion of the dramaturgical representation in the "Eighteenth Brumaire," and in other texts by Marx, see Hauke Brunkhorst: Kommentar, in: Karl Marx: Der achtzehnte Brumaire des Louis Bonaparte. Kommentar von Hauke Brunkhorst, Frankfurt/Main 2007, pp. 133–328, here p. 191.

46 Cf. Arendt: Lectures on Kant's Political Philosophy, op. cit. The theatrical metaphor is especially clear on pp. 61 f. In the following, I am interested solely in elaborating the meaning of the public for Arendt with regard to revolutions, which she then develops for aesthetic judgment in a second step, drawing on the *sensus communis*. I am not attempting to use the *sensus communis* to draw a connection from the films to the concept of community. On this point, cf. Kappelhoff: Front Lines of Community, op. cit., pp. 344 ff.

47 Cf. Immanuel Kant: The Conflict of the Faculties, trans. by Mary J. Gregor, Lincoln, NE 1992, here pp. 139 ff. and especially pp. 153 ff.

commentary, were the primary figures through whom this revolution achieved its historical significance.⁴⁸ What is important for Arendt is that this approach produces a separation of acting from observing, of actors from adjudicators. This separation can certainly lead to a contradiction: While Kant criticizes the actions of the French Revolution and does not see it as worthy of imitation, he enthusiastically welcomes its results.⁴⁹ It is precisely as initially disinterested, i.e. non-partisan non-actors, that the spectators become meaningful, for they have an epistemologically privileged position and could understand the significance of the Revolution.⁵⁰ At the same time, they hardly seemed inclined to carry out a revolution themselves. Their contribution lies solely in their commentary, their applause, their judgment. Yet this judgment must have a way of being expressed. For the spectator to be important, there must be a public: Kant "spelled out man's basic 'sociability' and enumerated as elements of it communicability, the need of men to communicate, and publicity, the public freedom not just to think but to publish – the 'freedom of the pen' [...]."⁵¹ According to Arendt, Kant understands this public not merely as a supplement to thinking or judging. Rather, it is a *precondition* for thinking, judging, and forming opinions. A completely isolated person who cannot verify his views or relate them to other opinions would ultimately not be capable of passing his own judgment. All intellectual capacities presume the existence of other people and at least the potential for exchange with these others. Sociability is the very basis of humanity, not its end.⁵²

---

48 For Kant, the historical significance of the French Revolution – regardless of its result, i.e. its success or failure – lies in its contribution to human progress, which always occurred behind the backs of its primary actors. On this topic, see Arendt: Lectures on Kant's Political Philosophy, op. cit., p. 45. Arendt draws attention to the problems caused by the talk of progress for the immanent coherence of Kant's philosophy in ibid., p. 77. On the critique of the concept of progress with regard to humanity, see also footnote 28 in Chapter 6 of this book.
49 Cf. ibid., p. 48.
50 See: "The spectator, because he is not involved, can perceive this design of providence or nature, which is hidden from the actor. So we have the spectacle and the spectator on one side, the actors and all the single events and contingent, haphazard happenings on the other. In the context of the French Revolution, it seemed to Kant that the spectator's view carried the ultimate meaning of the event, although this view yielded no maxim for acting" (ibid., p. 52).
51 Ibid., p. 19. Yet it is not only with regard to revolutions that the public plays a significant role. Drawing on Kant and Arendt, one could argue that it is precisely the public and its commentary that decides whether a democracy deteriorates into an ochlocracy, or mob rule. This decision is determined not only by the quality of the commentary, but also by what is deemed worthy of comment.
52 Cf. ibid., p. 26 and pp. 73 f. Arendt characterizes sociability as "the very essence of men" (ibid., p. 74).

2.2 Arendt's Conception

Thus, Arendt argues that a spectator ultimately never exists as a singular entity, but instead must always be conceived in the plural form as an audience, along with fellow spectators.[53] And the capacity that unites all onlookers, which they all have in common, is the power of judgment. Therein lies, for Arendt, the decisive connection between aesthetics and the political significance possessed by spectators in a revolution. After all, Kant's *Critique of Judgement* is primarily a theory of taste.[54] Arendt first lays out that here, Kant also assumes a split between actors and spectators: on the one side the public that needs taste in order to judge works of art, and on the other side the artist and his genius, which also requires taste in order to be communicable. Here too, the spectator position is privileged, since taste is ultimately more important than genius. Genius without taste can create only inaccessible, uncommunicable, and therefore worthless art. Art achieves value only through the critical public:

> The condition sine qua non for the existence of beautiful objects is communicability; the judgment of the spectator creates the space without which no such objects could appear at all. The public realm is constituted by the critics and the spectators, not by the actors or the makers.[55]

Like other forms of discernment, aesthetic judgment is never made in isolation, but always with regard to other people.[56] Thus the 'maxim of enlarged thought' applies with regard to both political and aesthetic judgment. This maxim is fulfilled when a person verifies and evaluates his judgment by considering other possible standpoints, i.e. a potential public.[57] Enlarged thought is one of the maxims of the human *sensus communis*. Although aesthetic judgment is subjective, it still makes a claim to generality.[58] Summarizing very briefly, the contradiction is resolved through the existence of a "subjective principle which

---

53 Cf. ibid., p. 63. With regard to Kant, Arendt specifies that he is thinking of the reading and writing public of the late eighteenth century (cf. ibid., p. 60).
54 Cf. Immanuel Kant: Critique of Judgement, trans. by J.H. Bernard, New York 1951. At this point I am not interested in the question of how Arendt's reconstruction of taste relates to Kant's conception, but rather solely in laying out the significance of spectators for taste and for a revolution.
55 Arendt: Lectures on Kant's Political Philosophy, op. cit., p. 63.
56 Additionally, according to Arendt, Kant conceives of both judgment in general and aesthetic judgment as disinterested, i.e. impartial, which stands in contrast to the partisanship of actors (see ibid., p. 73).
57 Cf. ibid., p. 43 and p. 73. On the maxim of enlarged thought in Kant, see Kant: Critique of Judgement, op. cit., pp. 352 ff. (B 158 ff.).
58 "The judgement of taste requires the agreement of every one; and he who describes anything as beautiful claims that every one ought to give his approval to the object in question and also describe it as beautiful" (ibid., p. 227 (B 63)).

determines what pleases or displeases only by feeling and not by concepts, but yet with universal validity."[59] This is the community sense, the *sensus communis*. According to Kant, it is a precondition for the judgment of taste. For Arendt – who reveals its political relevance – it is an "extra sense […] that fits us into a community."[60] Man's true humanity is manifest in this sense, since it requires communication and speech in particular – in this way also it is a political sense. Thus, I can never force another person to agree with my aesthetic judgments: "[…] one can only 'woo' or 'court' the agreement of everyone else. And in this persuasive activity one actually appeals to the 'community sense.' In other words, when one judges, one judges as a member of a community."[61]

To summarize: In both political judgment and the judgment of taste, the spectator holds a privileged position. In both cases, the question is not of an isolated spectator; instead, the spectator's judgment is inflected by the idea of a public. This public is a necessary condition for the spectator position to be privileged. Even aesthetic judgment, which is subjective in the first instance, does not remain purely subjective, but is always – via the *sensus communis* – related to a community. In this way, the *sensus communis* of aesthetic judgment proves to be a deeply political sense. It is ultimately the power of judgment, developed by Kant in the context of aesthetics and reflection on art, that Arendt elaborates to explain how the spectator position achieves so much political significance. And in a certain way, the spectatorial entities that are important for this book also turn up in Arendt's lectures on Kant's political philosophy: not only the observer who can make an aesthetic judgment, here understood as a film spectator, but also the spectators of revolution, who appear in Arendt's book on revolution and whose role in my work will be assumed by the films I examine. After all, when it comes to their topic, the films primarily adopt an observational stance and do not understand themselves, as is the case for Eisenstein, to be leading the action.

For Arendt, revolution (and the spectacle it represents) can only be adequately understood and appropriately described with metaphors from theater and an emphasis on the importance of the spectator position. From this perspective, it is possible to revisit and reconceptualize her aforementioned polemic against professional revolutionaries.[62] With their time "spent not in revolutionary agitation […] but in study and thought, in theory and debate, whose sole object was revolution," and their history belonging to "the as yet unwritten history of

---

59 Ibid., p. 228 (B 64).
60 Arendt: Lectures on Kant's Political Philosophy, op. cit., p. 70.
61 Ibid., p. 72.
62 See footnote 26 in this chapter.

productive idleness," Arendt conceives of professional revolutionaries primarily as spectators of a revolution communicated by media.[63] In the position they occupied, however, they studied the wrong revolution, and most importantly they drew the wrong conclusions from it. The question would then be whether stagings of revolution might exist that do not attempt to write the course of history in stone, but instead create an opportunity to rethink revolution altogether. This notion may not depart so drastically from Arendt's thought: At the very end of her book on revolution, she argues that "the storehouse of memory is kept and watched over by the poets, whose business it is to find and make the words we live by."[64] Given that the preceding pages demonstrate that temporality and forms of movement are decisive parameters in the observation and theoretical analysis of revolution, perhaps the art form best suited to revolution is neither theater nor poetry, but film, which can be characterized in Jean Epstein's words as "a machine which thinks temporally."[65]

---

63 Arendt: On Revolution, op. cit., p. 259; Arendt: Über die Revolution, op. cit., p. 332. On this subject, see also the prominent role played by newspapers, i.e. media, in Lenin's revolutionary theory: Vladimir Ilyich Lenin: Where to Begin?, in: id.: Lenin Collected Works. Volume 5, op. cit., pp. 13–24, here pp. 20 ff.
64 Arendt: On Revolution, op. cit., p. 280. From this reference to art, we can read an implicit assumption that historicity is mediated. Detailed explorations of the role of the arts in Arendt's thought can be found in Wolfgang Heuer/Irmela von der Lühe (eds.): Dichterisch denken. Hannah Arendt und die Künste, Göttingen 2007 and the catalogue Barbara Hahn/Marie L. Knott (eds.): Von den Dichtern erwarten wir Wahrheit. Hannah Arendts Literatur (Texte aus dem Literaturhaus Berlin), Berlin 2007.
65 Jean Epstein: Timeless Time, in: Magnification and Other Writings, in: October, 3, 1977, pp. 9–25, here p. 16.

3 The "Machine Which Thinks Temporally"

3.1 Film, Time, and Movement: Epstein's and Deleuze's Conception

Epstein

Like so many early film theorists, Jean Epstein sought to explain the immense impression that the new medium had made on its first viewers.[1] His answer seems quite simple upon first glance: movement. For Epstein – unlike Bazin or Kracauer – the basis of cinema is not the indexical relationship to extrafilmic reality, as it is for analog photography.[2] Epstein, by contrast, vehemently distinguishes film from photography.[3] For the specificity of the cinematograph inheres in the fact that it sees movement even when the human eye sees only stillness. Epstein understands this movement first and foremost as an acceleration. For Epstein, the cinema is an expression and intensifier of a general accelerating tendency in artistic expression, artistic modes and thought in general. It is constantly speeding up its metamorphic rate, changing faster and faster.[4] For

---

[1] For an autobiographical yet still mythically exaggerated report of Epstein's first experience in the cinema, see Jean Epstein: Mémoires inachevées, in: id.: Écrits sur le cinéma. 1921–1953. Edition chronologiques en deux volumes. Vol. I: 1921–1947, Paris 1974, pp. 27–57, here pp. 27–29.

[2] Cf. André Bazin: The Ontology of the Photographic Image, in: id.: What Is Cinema? Vol. 1, trans. by Hugh Gray, Berkeley/Los Angeles/London 2004, pp. 9–16; Siegfried Kracauer: Theory of Film. The Redemption of Physical Reality, New York 1960. I do not mean to claim, however, that either Bazin or Kracauer reduces film to this characteristic. On the concept of the index, cf. Charles Sanders Peirce: New Elements, in: id.: The Essential Peirce. Selected Philosophical Writings. Vol. 2, 1893–1913, ed. by Nathan Houser et al., Bloomington 1998, pp. 300–324. He defines the index as a sign that is "in a real reaction with its object" (ibid., p. 306), and thereby guarantees that object's reality.

[3] On Epstein's distinction between cinema and photography, see Jean Epstein: Bilan de fin de muet, in: Écrits sur le cinéma I, op. cit., pp. 229–237, here p. 229 and pp. 230 f. An essay in which Epstein goes into more detail on photography and does not simply see it in contrast to film is Jean Epstein: Le cinématographe dans l'archipel, in: Écrits sur le cinéma I, op. cit., pp. 196–200. On this essay and its arguments, see pp. 137 f. of my book.

[4] On the relationship between film and acceleration, see especially Jean Epstein: Cinema and Modern Literature, trans. by Audrey Brunetaux/Sarah Keller, in: Jean Epstein. Critical Essays and New Translations, ed. by Sarah Keller/Jason N. Paul, Amsterdam 2012, pp. 271–276. Epstein seems to be aware that in this essay, he comes perilously close to the Futurists. While he does not engage with them in any detail, he offers multiple polemics against Marinetti and the Futurists; see ibid., p. 274 and Jean Epstein: The Cinema Seen from Etna, trans. by Stuart

Epstein this quality also means that the cinema at first creates problems for comprehension: "We had to understand. It was a different affair. For a long time, we understood nothing, nothing, nothing, yet again nothing."[5] What Epstein means is that people have tried for too long to understand cinema on the wrong level. In limiting the cinematograph to filmic narrative, one misunderstands its potential. Instead of plots and stories, which could be told through theater or literature, the effect of cinema according to Epstein manifests "in suspense," in the "situations" and "seconds with their own particular flavor" which, regardless of their narrative import, are full of drama, tension and harmony.[6] As examples of such situations, Epstein names the drift of cigarette smoke or the actor Sessue Hayakawa's graceful strides through a room, which hold a power that inheres in the figuration of movement alone, remote from any symbolism.

Yet the significance and complexity of Epstein's reference to cinema's potential to record and play back movement can hardly be overestimated. On one hand, Epstein sees this potential as a criterion that establishes cinema as an art and also constitutes its essence, i.e. distinguishes itself from the other arts. For him, "absolute films" – for example RHYTHMUS 21 by Hans Richter (DE 1923), which is made up entirely of constantly changing abstract geometric shapes – demonstrate the essence of cinematographic pleasure.[7] Yet on the other hand, he also writes of these films: "Like all abstractions, they quickly lose interest."[8] Through their abstraction and for the same reasons Epstein also frequently speaks out against films shot in the studio, preferring natural settings[9] – they

---

E. Liebman, in: Jean Epstein, op. cit., pp. 287–292, here p. 289. The problems of futurism are clear in Filippo Tommaso Marinetti: The Manifesto of Futurism, in: Paths to the Present. Aspects of European Thought from Romanticism to Existentialism, ed. by Eugene Weber, New York 1960, pp. 242–246. On the critique of futurism, see Walter Benjamin: The Work of Art in the Age of its Technological Reproducibility. Third Version, in: id.: Selected Writings. Vol. IV 1938–1940, ed. by Howard Eiland/Michael W. Jennings, trans. by Edmund Jephcott et al., Cambridge, MA et al. 2003, pp. 251–283, here pp. 269 f.

5 Jean Epstein: Bonjour Cinéma. Collection des tracts, Paris 1921, p. 28 [Translator's note: my translation].

6 The phrases in Epstein's original are "en suspens," "des situations," and "des secondes d'un goût particulier" (ibid., pp. 86 f.). My book recommends understanding these situations as expressive movements.

7 See Epstein: Bilan de fin de muet, op. cit., p. 236.

8 Ibid.

9 For instance in Epstein: Mémoires inachevées, op. cit., pp. 29 f.; Epstein: Bilan de fin de muet, op. cit., p. 232; Epstein: Le grand œuvre de l'avant-garde, in: Jean Epstein: Écrits sur le cinéma. 1921–1953. Edition chronologiques en deux volumes. Vol. II: 1946–1953, Paris 1975, pp. 72 f., here p. 72.

miss the second great potential of cinema. In the cinema and its capacity to show movement, Epstein sees an entirely new perspective opening onto the world: film offers an opportunity to see and think the world differently than through human perception. This is the meaning of the term *photogénie*, which is likely and for good reason the best known element from Epstein's writings on film.[10] Yet photogénie, which Epstein characterizes as "rhythmic movement"[11] is not easy to grasp or to explain. Epstein himself warns in "Bonjour Cinéma," his early manifest on the significance of cinema: "Your chops get beaten up trying to define it."[12] If we refuse to be distracted by the somewhat crude, almost vulgar writing style, we can deduce two points from this sentence. First, problems arise when one attempts to *define* photogénie. Apparently one of the essential qualities of photogénie is to demonstrate constant change, thereby escaping determination, petrification. The second point that I wish to draw from this sentence is related to this malleability: "Your chops get beaten up" refers to the linguistic mode of expression that creates problems in attempted definitions. Epstein indicates that photogénie demands a mode of access to the world that refuses and exceeds language.[13] Working from the above-quoted sentence, photogénie is a movement that cannot be fixed. Oliver Fahle correctly

---

10 Here I seek only to clarify Epstein's terms, and not to reconstruct their history completely. However, it bears mentioning that before Epstein, Louis Delluc had already done significant work to elaborate this term. Cf. especially the excerpts "La Photogénie" and "Photographie n'est pas photogénie" in: Louis Delluc: Écrits cinématographiques I. Le Cinéma et les cinéastes, Paris 1985, pp. 31–77, here pp. 34 f. and p. 36. For the history of the term see also Frank Kessler: Photogénie und Physiognomie, in: Geschichten der Physiognomik. Text, Bild, Wissen, ed. by Rüdiger Campe/Manfred Schneider, Freiburg 1996, pp. 515–534, here pp. 516 ff.
11 Epstein: Bonjour Cinéma, op. cit., p. 33.
12 Ibid., p. 35.
13 Epstein is certainly not alone among early film theorists in arguing that in the cinema, an alternative expressive form to language comes into its own. See e.g. Béla Balázs's remark that the cinema has the same significance for the development of visual culture that print had for the culture of the word. Cf. Béla Balázs: Béla Balázs. Early Film Theory. Visible Man and the Spirit of Film, ed. by Erica Carter, trans. by Rodney Livingstone, New York/Oxford 2010, pp. 9 f. In the course of his work, Epstein repeatedly discusses the cultural significance of the non-linguistic, visual mode of expression made possible by the cinema. Cf. Jean Epstein: La Langue de la grande révolte, in: Écrits sur le cinéma I, op. cit., pp. 359–361, here p. 359; Jean Epstein: Alcool et cinéma, in: Écrits sur le cinéma II, op. cit., pp. 240–246, here p. 240; Jean Epstein: Cinéma, hysterie, culture, in: Écrits sur le cinéma II, pp. 253–259, here p. 253. My book does not offer a detailed discussion of these texts, as the question of the relationship between film and society is not a focal point. In addition, Epstein's explanations are problematic insofar as he insists on a static dichotomy between language and reason on one hand, and film and emotions on the other. The notion of folding the two together remains foreign to him.

identifies the "paradoxical task" of photogénie as "to describe movement, and thereby to pin it down conceptually."[14]

Yet Epstein of course does not stop with his warning but attempts to explain the term more clearly in his writings. He offers a first clue when he characterizes photogénie as "something that wasn't existing before [i.e. before the recording of the camera]"[15] Photogénie makes something visible that previously was invisible. For Epstein, the camera lens is a perceptual apparatus that is upstream of our own sensory apparatus during the screening in the cinema. That is, in the cinema we see what the camera has seen – and this is not equivalent to human perception. To Epstein, or more precisely: to the young Epstein, the camera is the

> [...] unexpected discovery of a subject that is an object – without consciousness, i.e. free from hesitation or scruples, with neither venality, nor complacency, nor possible errors. An entirely honest artist, an artist and nothing else, the prototype of an artist.[16]

Epstein does not mean that in a film no human actors can influence the recording – yet the gaze of the director or the cameraman is always located behind the gaze of the camera, and is not the decisive factor in the emergence of *photogénie*. Rather, it can only accentuate or emphasize it to a certain degree. Epstein goes into more detail on the specific quality that becomes newly visible through the camera's perception of movement: "What is '*photogénie*'? I would describe as photogenic any aspect of things, beings, or souls whose moral character is enhanced by filmic reproduction."[17] Yet this explanation seems to obscure more than it clarifies. One page later, Epstein attempts to specify:

---

14 Oliver Fahle: Jenseits des Bildes. Poetik des französischen Films der zwanziger Jahre, Mainz 2000, p. 29. Fahle also writes of the "*necessarily* lacking linguistic precision of the concept" photogénie (ibid., p. 34 [emphasis mine]).
15 Epstein: Bonjour Cinéma, op. cit., p. 37.
16 Ibid., p. 39. Epstein repeats this characterization of the camera in quite similar terms in Epstein: Le Cinématographe vu de l'Étna, in: Écrits sur le cinéma I, op. cit. pp. 131–152, here p. 132. Jacques Rancière uses this definition of the camera as a cornerstone of his discussion on the relationship of film to the aesthetic regime of art. Cf. Jacques Rancière: L'historicité du cinéma, in: De l'histoire au cinéma, ed. by Antoine de Baecque/Christian Delage, Brussels 1998, pp. 45–60, here pp. 50 ff. The passage cited above could spark a discussion of Epstein's relationship to surrealism. For a discussion of this relationship that also includes other central figures of French cinema in the 1920s, cf. Fahle: Jenseits des Bildes, op. cit., pp. 64 ff.
17 Jean Epstein: On Certain Characteristics of *Photogénie*, trans. by Tom Milne, in: Jean Epstein, op. cit., pp. 292–296, here p. 293.

> A moment ago I described as photogenic any aspect whose moral character is enhanced by filmic reproduction. I now specify: only mobile aspects of the world, of things and souls, may see their moral value increased by filmic reproduction.[18]

The maneuver that enables Epstein to see practically every element of the world as photogenic is his interpretation of movement in the broadest possible sense: meaning that he also applies it to movements *in time*. Epstein situates the photogenic aspect of an object in the dependents of its variations in the space-time system. Cinema offers not only a spatial, but also a temporal perspective on what it records. For Epstein, the cinematograph is thus not only the medium *par excellence* for the recording and playback of movement, but also for the playback and staging of temporal relations – whereby slow motion, time-lapse and montage are only the most apparent of the possibilities that are available to film.

Yet what follows from these very basic observations on the capacities of the cinematograph? What is made visible by *photogénie*? How does the filmic image differ from the image that humans perceive? At this point it is important to distinguish between the older and the younger Epstein. In his early text, the answer is frequently metaphysical: "It [the cinema] inscribes a bit of the divine in everything."[19] Cinema transforms reality, *photogénie* elicits a dimension that appears supernatural to us. What he means is that the cinema gives rise to a general animism. In the cinema, everything seems to be moving and thereby animate, possessed of a soul. In time-lapse one can see the germination of a wheat kernel, and with it the animation of nature. Yet movement is not the only element of film that causes a general vitalization of the world. Closeups also made a deep impression on Epstein, like on many early film theorists, and he argues that the closeup, too, changes our perception of things in the world:

> On screen, nature is never inanimate. Objects take on airs. Trees gesticulate. Mountains, just like Etna, convey meanings. Every prop becomes a character. The sets are cut to pieces and each fragment assumes a distinctive expression. An astonishing pantheism is reborn in the world and fills it until it bursts. The grass in the meadow is a smiling, feminine genie. Anemones full of rhythm and personality evolve with the majesty of planets. A hand is separated from a man, lives on its own, suffers and rejoices alone. And the finger is separated from the hand.[20]

---

18 Ibid., p. 294.
19 Epstein: The Cinema Seen from Etna, op. cit., p. 289. See also: "Le cinema est surnaturel par essence [the cinema is essentially supernatural]," in Epstein: Bonjour Cinéma, op. cit, p. 43.
20 Epstein: The Cinema Seen from Etna, op. cit., pp. 289 f. See also: id.: Magnification and Other Writings, in: October, 3, 1977, pp. 9–25, in which the closeup is characterized as the "soul of the cinema" (ibid., p. 9).

In this passage, the decisive observation for Epstein's theoretical project is that through movement and closeups, things and objects in film can be assigned a *personality*. Later in the essay, Epstein defines the concept of personality as a *spirit visible in things and people* that goes beyond intelligence. Personality reveals their origin, makes their past present; in their personality, one can recognize that their future is already present. Personality is thus evidently a crystallization of temporal forms, a condensation of past, present, and future, that only becomes visible with the cinematograph. For Epstein, this concept of personality also reveals cinema's ability to exceed our everyday understanding of time.[21] He illustrates the definition of personality, which is quite alien upon first glance, through one of his own experiences with film. Invited to a screening of family films – a grandfather had spent 20 years capturing every important family event on camera – Epstein made a discovery: Through the cinema, in this case understood as the capacity to line up multiple family members of different generations and visualize them alongside each other within a brief time frame, that which unites a family across multiple generations becomes visible. All the similarities, but also all the differences of individual family members meld into a single person. The family becomes a totally unified being that differentiates itself through various family members, yet only comes into being through this process of differentiation. Every individual contains both forefathers and descendants. This quality only becomes visible and recognizable through the arrangement of filmic recordings, i.e. through the condensation of a long period into a short one – and although Epstein rarely mentions montage, this passage makes clear that this technique is integral to his understanding of the cinema. He makes a similar observation about the visibility of disease: Through the juxtaposition of sick people, the face of disease, which exceeds individual sufferers, becomes visible. Thus, the cinema can introduce extra-individual beings. This is the synthetic capacity of cinema.[22] In this way, especially in its manifestation as personality, *photogénie* is not an exclusively metaphysical notion, but can also be based in biological processes that exceed individual temporality.[23]

---

21 On the concept of personality, see Epstein: On Certain Characteristics of *Photogénie*, op. cit., pp. 295 f. With regard to the everyday understanding of time, I am thinking of Augustine, who at first saw time as quite simple before he thought about it, but with upon closer consideration of the question experienced great difficulty and did not know how to answer it. See Augustine: Confessions of St. Augustine. Book XI, trans. by F.J. Sheed, New York 1943, pp. 271–286.
22 For these examples, see Jean Epstein: Photogénie de l'impondérable, in: Écrits sur le cinéma I, op. cit., pp. 249–253, here pp. 251 f.
23 To compare Epstein with Balázs on this point: both authors saw great potential in the cinematograph to rediscover the world and experience it anew. While Balázs saw the cinema as making man and his soul visible, for Epstein the new visuality also extends to objects and to a

3.1 Film, Time, and Movement: Epstein's and Deleuze's Conception

Yet according to Epstein, the cinema has not only a synthetic, but also an analytical capacity. This analytical capacity emerges with the spatial emphasis on individual objects as closeups, yet it is once again in the capacity for temporal manipulation that this potential finds its full expression. Epstein thinks of police investigations that seek to convict someone who denies guilt. If he is a good enough actor, he may be able to trick people; but he will not fool the implacable camera and especially the temporally extended playback of filmic recordings:

> That which the mind does not have time to retain, that which the eye has neither the time nor the field of vision to perceive: the precursors, the beginning, the development, and the struggle between conflicting feelings that ultimately produce a result; slow motion can reduce its speed at will. And the enlargement for the screen allows us to examine it as though under a magnifying glass. There, the most beautiful lies remain powerless, while truth erupts into view, strikes the spectator with the suddenness of evidence, triggers an aesthetic emotion in him, a sort of admiration and infallible pleasure.[24]

Toward the end of this passage, Epstein mentions twice that cinema makes *the truth* visible. Where human perception is partial and deceptive, the perception of the cinematograph is not.[25] It brings to light that which escapes human vision. So, Epstein touches on three possible effects of photogénie: What can become visible through the filmic image and through photogénie, which is the essence of film, are the metaphysical plane, biology, and truth. All three evade and exceed 'mere' human perception. They refer to a plane behind or above human perception and generate a new form of reality that differs from everyday reality: "The cinema is poetry's most powerful medium, the medium most capable of realizing the unreal, the 'surreal,' as Apollinaire would have said."[26]

It is thus unsurprising that Epstein repeatedly writes about how a person who sees himself on the screen will be frightened, because the person on the screen seems so alien.[27] A person's own image in film demonstrates irrefutably

---

level that exceeds the individual (regardless of whether this level is metaphysical or not). On this point in Balázs, see Balázs: Early Film Theory, op. cit., p. 10.

24 Epstein: Photogénie de l'impondérable, op. cit., p. 253 [Translator's note: my translation].
25 Epstein mentions that this cinematographic perception is then perceived in turn by the spectator, yet does not go into further detail on the relationship between these two modes (see Epstein: Bonjour Cinéma, op. cit., pp. 37 ff.). Vivian Sobchack discusses this point in more depth. Cf. the end of my subchapter "Film and the Experience of History".
26 Epstein: On Certain Characteristics of *Photogénie*, op. cit., p. 296.
27 Considering only the essays translated into German, Epstein describes this phenomenon four times (cf. Epstein: Le Cinématographe vu de l'Étna, op. cit., p. 136; Epstein: Le cinématographe dans l'archipel, op. cit., p. 199; Epstein: Photogénie de l'impondérable, op. cit. p. 249; Jean Epstein: Le doute sur la personne, in: Écrits sur le cinéma I, op. cit., pp. 392–397, here p. 392).

that the camera's perception does not correspond to one's own perception. In his early essays, Epstein is very clear on this point: In the film image we see who we really and truly are. The film image brings our true essence to light. Yet Epstein interprets this phenomenon differently in the essay "Le doute sur la personne [Doubting the self]," which he wrote after World War Two. There, he argues that film absolutely does not reveal the true, supratemporal essence of a person, but only a *variation* thereof. And different film recordings show different aspects of the person. Film recording has lost its claim to universality. In this essay as well, Epstein reiterates his characterization of the camera as a recording device free from any subjectivity, which can be assumed to have privileged access to reality. Yet immediately after that, his argument takes a decisive turn:

> But this photochemical truth proves incoherent. It has its angles and caprices; it manifests inexplicable preferences; it expresses successive and discordant sincerities; it is influenceable and partial; in the end, it too allows for a certain subjectivity. The subject who hoped to find a reliable gauge, a touchstone that could serve to separate the real from the false in all its other images, encounters nothing but a renewed sense of instability and confusion.[28]

The difference here from the characterization of the camera in his early essays could hardly be greater. One could see this passage as merely revealing Epstein's discovery of film's capacity for staging. Yet the difference expressed here goes further. In essays written after World War Two, Epstein disputes the camera's ability to capture the true essence not only of people, but also everything else in the world. The reason for this change, however, is not that Epstein abandoned his assumption that the camera could capture a reality that differs from or exceeds that of human perception. Rather, he lost his belief in a supratemporal, absolute plane – or at least the recognizability of this plane. Whereas in his early texts, he often endowed film recordings with an absolute, religious, metaphysical quality, and made liberal use of the concept of truth, these elements are absent from his later writings after the Second World War. On the contrary, here he declares war on the absolute.[29]

This declaration of war is at first based on problematizing the recognition of reality. While his early essays clearly argue that the film camera has unobstructed access to reality, Epstein questions this assertion in his postwar writing. In the 1946 essay "The Law of Laws,"[30] he also disputes the idea that any philosophical

---

28 Epstein: Le doute sur la personne, op. cit., p. 393 [Translator's note: my translation].
29 The title of one of his postwar essays is: Guerre à l'absolu [War on the absolute], in: Écrits sur le cinéma I, op. cit., pp. 361–363.
30 On the following, see Jean Epstein: The Law of Laws, in: id.: The Intelligence of a Machine, trans. by Christophe Wall-Romana, Minneapolis 2014, pp. 87–92.

school or system could have access to reality or truth (Epstein does not distinguish between the two terms). Although logical in their own right, according to Epstein they can contain only immanent truths. If one thinks like Plato, Platonic thought is true; if one thinks like Rousseau, Rousseauism is true; and even pragmatism is only true for those who think like William James. Which of these (or any other) philosophies is the 'truest' or 'most correct' cannot be determined, since such a determination would require a common measure, a criterion external to the systems. Yet no such thing exists; reality constantly escapes and remains opaque. And the cinema in particular – in this passage Epstein uses the elegant phrase "cinematographic robot-philosopher"[31] – is no exception. The cinema, too, can only see the world as its premises and its mode of construction allow, and can only transmit one of many possible perspectives on reality. In answering the question of how this cinematographic perspective on the world is obtained, however, Epstein remains true to himself:

> In its very innate and inescapable construction, the cinematograph represents the universe as an always and everywhere mobile continuity, much more continuous, fluid, and agile than our directly sensible continuity. Heraclitus had not imagined such an instability in all things […]."[32]

Here once again, the cinema's ability to manipulate time enables it to represent the universe in motion. The cinema can allow for variations in temporal perception, and time itself becomes a variable in the cinema. The cinema frees people from the steady tempo of linear time, and thus opens up another perspective on the world. Through the cinema, our understanding and conceptualization of time are no longer set in stone. This openness allows a new experience of reality: Things are reclothed to suit to the respective dimension of time on display. An "unspeakable reality," i.e. a reality that is not yet linguistically accessible, opens up, "that we assume to be subjacent to all these qualities created by a temporal perspective."[33] Through changed forms of temporality, according to Epstein, things and reality also change. Finally, this general malleability of the cinematographic universe leads Epstein to a philosophical monism whose derivation or plausibility do not require discussion here. Significantly, however, in Epstein's later work the cinema is unable to unlock what stands behind this general changeability: "Indeed, whether we call it God or the Quintessence of

---

[31] Ibid., p. 87.
[32] Ibid., p. 88.
[33] Ibid., p. 89.

Energy, the unique essence of all things divided into appearances remains unapproachable."[34]

In this same vein, Epstein writes of a "return to Pythagorean and Platonic poetry."[35] This is the title of an essay that also begins by problematizing the possibility of recognizing reality. Reality is not a simply given fact, but rather emerges through each different perception of the world: "Reality, the only knowable reality, does not exist: it is manufactured, or more precisely, it must be manufactured."[36] And the relativity of our grasp on reality, according to Epstein, is not limited to human perception. He also disputes the ability of scientific experiments to obtain direct access to reality. Their design and method already prescribe a particular direction. A totally impartial observation of reality cannot exist, since observation changes reality.[37] Cinematic recordings do not have a privileged access to reality: "The cinematograph is also an experimental apparatus that constructs, that is to say, thinks an image of the universe whose reality is predetermined by the structure of its plasmatic mechanism."[38] With these words, Epstein turns decisively away from a logic of representation with regard to film. The cinematograph does not depict a pre-existing reality or truth; prior to any fictionalization, i.e. before it starts to tell stories, it presents its own perception of the world. Every film recording is always already a construct and thus can only communicate a relative, not a universal, perspective on the world. The decisive parameters for constructing reality in the cinema – here too Epstein remains consistent with his earlier work – are space and time, or more precisely: the combination and variation thereof. Epstein sees the relationship to Pythagoras and Plato in the fact that for both of them, reality was nothing more than the harmony of ideas and numbers. That is, in their theories too, reality as we perceive it is preceded by ideas and numbers that determine how we perceive reality. Epstein recognizes this phenomenon in the way in which cinema perceives the world. The cinema is preceded by other mathematical and

---

[34] Ibid., p. 90.
[35] See Jean Epstein: Return to Pythagorean and Platonic Poetry, in: The Intelligence of a Machine, op. cit., pp. 103–105.
[36] Ibid., pp. 103 f.
[37] The Heisenberg uncertainty principle lurks in the background of these remarks; at another point, Epstein references it explicitly (see Epstein: Le doute sur la personne, in: Écrits sur le cinéma I, op. cit., p. 394). In this passage, however, Epstein also echoes a fundamental concept from Saussure's theory of linguistics: "Far from it being the object that antedates the viewpoint, it would seem that it is the viewpoint that creates the object [...]." Ferdinand de Saussure: Course in General Linguistics, ed. by Perry Meisel/Haun Saussy, trans. by Wade Baskin, New York 2011, p. 8.
[38] Epstein: Return to Pythagorean and Platonic Poetry, op. cit., p. 104.

mechanical laws. What the cinema shows us with its alternative modes of perception is that there can be no such thing as absolute perception. Every person and every machine has a particular perspective on the world.

Thus, in Epstein's later work, the cinematograph is one of the most important weapons in the war on the absolute.[39] As a symbol of this absolute, he draws on the concept of an eternal and unmoving god, around which all stable values are organized. When Epstein speaks of the absolute, he means a "fixist representation of the universe,"[40] which is derived from a Christian conception of God. According to Epstein, this standpoint, i.e. the idea of a God who is perpetually congruent with Himself, leads to a static image of the world. For him, the most precise expression of this image is a chronology that is as solidly measurable as marble. By that Epstein means the idea that time is uniform and enduring. Yet it is precisely this durability and uniformity of time against which the cinematograph rebels. The cinematograph challenges the idea of time's durability as well as the universal applicability of this idea, and shows it to be just one among several possibilities:

> Space, time, and causality have been understood as revealed by God, and as immutable as He, the preconceived and cardinal categories of universal being. Yet the cinematograph presents them as concepts that are sensory in origin and experimental in nature, like relative and variable data systems.[41]

Through its ability to stage the variability of time, the cinema leads to a realignment of how we think about the universe. In this essay, even more explicitly than in his other post-World War Two work, Epstein links the relativity of the filmic image, i.e. the relativity that is expressed through the filmic image, and the cinematograph's capacity to stage different forms and relations of time.

For someone as conscious as Epstein was of cinema's fundamental significance for theorizing the world, it is not surprising that this cinematographic capacity also performs an important function when it comes to imitating the world. The reference to Aristotle that reverberates in the term *imitation* is no coincidence. Epstein draws on ancient philosophy when he takes up Aristotle's definition of man in his essay "Timeless Time," characterizing man as "the imitative animal *par excellence.*"[42] Aristotle gave two reasons for man's imitation of the world: First, humans are born imitators. And second, humans are also born enjoying imitation (in this way, the joy of imitation is a variation on the joy of

---

39 Cf. for the following Epstein: Guerre à l'absolu, op. cit.
40 Ibid., p. 361 [Translator's note: my translation].
41 Ibid., p. 363 [Translator's note: my translation].
42 Epstein: Timeless Time, in: Magnification and Other Writings, op. cit., p. 16.

learning). Furthermore, it is not even necessary to be familiar with what is being imitated in order to enjoy the imitation. If one is unfamiliar, the performance alone brings joy.[43] In the following, Epstein contemplates the historical development of temporal stagings of imitations. At first, he argues that merely by occurring, every imitation of a series of events has its own temporal course, which can be understood as a modification or deformation of objective historical time. Epstein begins his historical development with "primitive theatrical manifestations,"[44] in which efforts were made to minimize the deviations of staging time from 'objective' time – as well as space. Over the course of time, however, people took more liberties: Man became "accustomed to providing himself with fictive spaces and times which [...] progressively distanced themselves from their original models."[45] Epstein sees a teleology at work in this development of art away from simple realism: The better man developed his capacities as an imitative animal, the more freedom he took in staging time, and the more fictive these stagings became. At the end of this development, at the time he was writing, came the time-condensation-machine of cinema, which he describes as a "machine which thinks temporally."[46] The cinema, to which Epstein attributes "a kind of psyche"[47] in this essay, can stage multiple temporal perspectives and thereby enables people to see something that they would not otherwise have seen; it enables people to think thoughts that could not be thought without the cinema.

In Epstein's later work, the relationship between film, time, and movement is no longer conceptualized as merely a relationship of acceleration. Although he writes in his 1946 essay "Naissance d'une académie [The Birth of an Academy]" that the cinema evolves with "spontaneous rapidity,"[48] and that a possible film academy can and should not be content to preserve what has already been achieved, he also challenges the view that the continuous molting of cinematic language is necessarily positive, and writes a sentence that would have been unthinkable for the young Epstein: "The excess of speed calls for brakes."[49]

---

43 Cf. Aristotle: The Poetics of Aristotle, trans. by S.H. Butcher, Hazleton 2000, pp. 7 ff. (1448b5–1448b20). Theo Girshausen discusses how these two joys complement each other and are not mutually exclusive. Cf. Theo Girshausen: Ursprungszeiten des Theaters. Das Theater der Antike, Berlin 1999, p. 140.
44 Epstein: Timeless Time, op. cit., p. 16.
45 Ibid.
46 Ibid.
47 Ibid.
48 Jean Epstein: Naissance d'une académie, in: Écrits sur le cinéma II, op. cit., pp. 73–75, here p. 75 [Translator's note: my translation].
49 Ibid. [Translator's note: my translation].

Deleuze

If one looks for positions in film theory that were influenced by Epstein's work on cinema, one quickly finds the film philosophy of Gilles Deleuze.[50] Even if Deleuze did not deal with Epstein in a systematic way, he refers to Epstein's writings or films at significant points in his books on cinema.[51] This affinity is not terribly surprising, given both Epstein's and Deleuze's close proximity to the philosophy of Henri Bergson. For Epstein, this proximity remains unspoken.[52] He does not engage systematically with Bergon's philosophy, yet Oliver Fahle is correct to emphasize Bergson's importance not only to Epstein, but to all French film theory in the 1920s.[53] Deleuze, by contrast, openly acknowledges Bergson's influence by opening the first of his two books on cinema, *The Movement-Image*, with a commentary on Bergson's theses on movement.[54] This commentary allows a more precise assessment of Epstein's work as well – and leads back to the question of the conceivability of revolution and history.

Deleuze begins his first commentary on Bergson by asserting that the latter put forward three theses on movement. According to Bergson's first thesis, "movement is distinct from the space covered."[55] Movement cannot be reconstituted from positions or motionless sections, i.e. individual points of movement; it has a quality that cannot be reduced to these elements. Movement always occurs in the interval *between* individual points of movement. It cannot be obtained by way of static incisions. Using Bergson, Deleuze separates movement

---

50 See Lorenz Engell/Oliver Fahle: Film-Philosophie, in: Moderne Film Theorie, ed. by Jürgen Felix, Mainz 2003, pp. 222–245, here p. 226.
51 For example, Deleuze writes that Epstein was the first to focus theoretically on the observation that the movement-image appears as a fundamentally aberrant and abnormal movement, and thus already implies the possibility of time-images (cf. Gilles Deleuze: Cinema 2. The Time-Image, trans. by Hugh Tomlinson/Robert Galeta, London/New York 1989, p. 36). He also calls Epstein's La chute de la maison Usher (FR 1928) one of the first great works to show the movement of the world and to follow the laws of an 'implied dream' (cf. ibid., p. 59).
52 In Epstein's collected works, according to the index in the French edition of his writing, Bergson is named only once: in a list of philosophers who see movement and change as an essential aspect of being, yet unlike cinema have no influence on the masses. See Epstein: Alcool et cinéma, op. cit., p. 210. The fact that Epstein read Bergson can be seen not only in the conceptual proximity of his film theoretical work to Bergson, but for instance in the fact that he characterizes Chaplin's comedy as Bergsonian (see Epstein: Le Cinématographe vu de l'Étna, op. cit., p. 150).
53 See Fahle: Jenseits des Bildes, op. cit., p. 56 and p. 185.
54 See Gilles Deleuze: Cinema 1. The Movement-Image, trans. by Hugh Tomlinson/Barbara Habberjam, Minneapolis 1986, pp. 1–11.
55 Ibid., p. 1.

from the space covered, which he characterizes as a divisible, homogeneous space, and which he connects with the aforementioned motionless sections and their abstract time. Instead, movement exists, indivisible, in a heterogenous space, and unfolds in a concrete duration. Given that, Deleuze concludes that "each movement will have its own qualitative duration."[56] These quite condensed and abstract remarks on movement and its relationship to duration become clearer when they are illustrated using the movement of a melody, as demonstrated by Balázs, who also draws on Bergson in his film theory. A melody cannot be divided into individual notes and broken down temporally. It exists only as a whole (a whole shape [*Gestalt*]) and lies not in the individual notes, but in the relationship between notes; every new note changes the shape of the entire melody.[57] This relationship between movement and duration, which is expressed through melody, also emerges from the first of Bergson's theses on movement reconstructed by Deleuze.

Yet Bergson himself does not see the filmic image as realizing this phenomenon. For Bergson, cinematographic movement remains a pure illusion. He characterizes cinema as a false friend and a textbook example of false movement: Film works with still images that are set into motion. In this way, film resembles natural human perception, which also sees only in snapshots and thus fails to recognize actual movement. Much in line with Epstein's thoughts, however, Deleuze contradicts Bergson on this point. Not only does Deleuze assume a fundamental difference between human and cinematographic perception, like Epstein he considers the filmic image unthinkable without movement. Film does not show us a photogramme (or a number of photogrammes) to which movement is subsequently added, but rather "the intermediate image," to which movement belongs "as an immediate given."[58] Film thus "immediately gives us a movement-image" that cannot be reduced to individual still frames.[59]

---

56 Ibid.
57 Balázs: Early Film Theory, op. cit., p. 101. Balázs relates Bergson's ideas to closeups of human faces which – this is his plausible thesis – are being perceived as a visual melody, a visual Gestalt.
58 Deleuze: The Movement-Image, op. cit., p. 2.
59 Ibid. Deleuze's explanation for Bergson's misinterpretation of film, however, is not very convincing. "We know that things and people are always forced to conceal themselves [...] when they begin," he writes. His argument becomes problematic when he asserts that therefore cinema was "forced to imitate natural perception" at its outset (ibid., pp. 2 f.). With this characterization of early cinema as 'primitive' cinema, Deleuze fails to comprehend early cinema. On this point, see Chris Tedjasukmana: Mechanische Verlebendigung. Ästhetische Erfahrung im Kino, Paderborn 2014, p. 44; on the qualities of early cinema, see Thomas Elsaesser: Filmgeschichte und frühes Kino. Archäologie eines Medienwandels, Munich 2002, pp. 20–46.

3.1 Film, Time, and Movement: Epstein's and Deleuze's Conception — 53

Bergson's second thesis first addresses the illusionary conceptualization of movement as something that can be reconstructed out of individual images. According to Bergson, there are two entirely different versions of this illusion: one ancient and one modern. In antiquity, movement was understood as a "regulated transition from one form to another, that is, an order of *poses* or privileged instants" that embody the endpoint or climax of a movement.[60] In this understanding, movement refers to eternal and changeless forms and ideas. Even developments based on the scientific revolutions of modernity (the first example named by Deleuze is Kepler's modern astronomy, which relates the path of orbit to the time needed to traverse it) misunderstand movement as consisting of individual moments. In contrast to ancient ways of thinking, however, these developments relate movement to "any-instant-whatever."[61] Movement was no longer reconstructed from transcendental forms (poses), but rather from immanent, arbitrary points – and upon first glance, the cinematograph corresponds precisely to this model. This understanding of the cinematograph, however, cannot stand, since both versions share the same problem:

> In fact, to recompose movement with *eternal poses* or with *immobile sections* comes to the same thing: in both cases, one misses the movement because one constructs a Whole, one assumes that 'all is given' whilst movement only occurs if the whole is neither given nor giveable. As soon as a whole is given to one in the eternal order of forms or poses, or in the set of any-instant-whatevers, then either time is no more than the image of eternity, or it is the consequence of the set; there is no longer room for real movement.[62]

At the end of this section, I will take a closer look at the affinity that emerges in this passage with revolutionary theory and the attempt to theorize history. First, it is important to ascertain what, according to Deleuze, Bergson draws from this predicament: Modern science demands a new philosophy that corresponds to it and is capable of thinking movement differently. Movement must not remain stuck in the wholeness of arbitrary instants; rather, it must become possible to conceive of creating something new. This argument amounts to a new concept of the whole. And film – this is Deleuze's addition – is capable of making a significant contribution to this new philosophy. This argument leads Deleuze to Bergson's third thesis on movement:

---

60 Deleuze: The Movement-Image, op. cit., p. 4.
61 Ibid., p. 5.
62 Ibid., p. 7.

> Not only is the instant an immobile section of movement, but movement is a mobile section of duration, that is, of the Whole, or of a whole. Which implies that movement expresses something more profound, which is the change in duration or in the whole.[63]

Drawing on Bergson, Deleuze defines duration as ceaseless change, constant becoming, and in this way directly related to movement. Movement too always refers to change, migration, shifting, and as in a melody, always means a change to the whole as well. Deleuze illustrates this connection between movement, duration, and the whole with Bergson's famous example of sugar water. If one wants to create sugar water, one must put some sugar into a glass of water and wait for the sugar to melt. The decisive factor is that over the course of the process, there is a change to the whole, to the content of the glass: "a qualitative transition from water which contains a sugar lump to sugared water."[64] And just as the natural sciences are incapable of fully grasping this emergence of something qualitatively new, the subdivision of motion into individual snapshots cannot encompass movement itself. Chemistry is limited to examining the shifts and displacements of masses and molecules; the actual transformation into sugared water cannot be explained in this way. For this process occurs only in time, in duration. Deleuze calls this duration "mental, spiritual reality," immediately adding that it "bear[s] witness, not only for me who wait, but for a whole which changes."[65] Duration does not refer to a purely subjective sense of temporality, but rather relates to the glass of sugared water. Neither is it possible to think the constantly changing whole without attending to duration. This is the fundamental redefinition of the whole, of which Deleuze suggests, drawing on Bergson: "[...] the whole is neither given nor giveable (and the error of modern science, like that of ancient science, lay in taking the whole as given, in two different ways)." Clarifying further, Deleuze expresses this point as follows: "[...] if the whole is not giveable, it is because it is the Open, and because its nature is to change constantly, or to give rise to something new, in short, to endure."[66] Only through the *relations* of objects contained in a whole can this phenomenon be defined, not through the objects themselves. As a counter term to the whole, Deleuze introduces *sets*. Deleuze defines a *set* as a collection of particular substances in an (artificially closed) container, as represented by water and sugar in a glass, for instance. In contrast to the whole, which resides in duration, sets exist in space. Sets are kept open by the whole, which drives the set from one qualitative state to

---

63 Ibid., p. 8.
64 Ibid., p. 9.
65 Ibid.
66 Both these passages are in ibid. Cf. also ibid., p. 11: "the whole, the wholes are in duration, are duration itself, in so far as it does not stop changing".

another. The connection between set and whole, in turn, is movement. More precisely, there are two sides of movement that determine the relationship between whole and set. Movement is on one hand that which occurs between substances, and on the other, it reproduces duration and the whole. Through these two sides, movement connects substances and duration; through movement, substances and duration also relate to each other. In this way, movement is a mobile section of duration. Against this background, Epstein's characterization of the cinema through *photogénie* also seems like an attempt to create a productive connection between Bergson's theses on movement and the new medium. Not only does Epstein treat movement as more than a mere supplement that is implemented in the filmic image, he (like Deleuze) conceives the filmic image as a movement-image, which cannot be grasped through arresting motion (whether this occurs through the various points in time, the photogrammes from which movement is composed, or a linguistic specification).

For the purposes of this book, however, the following point is more central: Epstein's later refusal of absolute truths and his turn to relativity, variability, diversification, and the openness that emerges through cinema, seem in this light to anticipate Deleuze's definition of the whole. If one further considers that another of Deleuze's examples of the whole is an organism, because the organism too is an Open, capable of creating something new, then it is plausible to relate the whole not only to an individual organism, but also to the collective life of organisms, and to conceive it in a political-historical sense. Film, understood in Deleuze and Epstein's sense as a movement-image, reveals an astonishing affinity to the attempts that have existed since the revolutions of modernity to understand history theoretically. As already mentioned, the revolutions of modernity made it possible to break free of eschatological and cyclical models of history, and thus paved the way for the modern concept of history. Only through the revolutions of modernity did it become possible to see something qualitatively new in human political life. The revolutions of modernity enable human history to be thought as a whole in the Bergsonian and Deleuzian sense. From this perspective, film seems like the ideal medium to communicate the historical-philosophical thought that emerged through the revolutions of modernity.

This kind of political interpretation of Bergson's thought is not idiosyncratic, but can be found in Ernst Bloch's work, for instance.[67] Although this

---

[67] Bloch, however, offers a critical reading. For him, Bergson ultimately does not truly think the new, since the latter neglects to consider possibility and finality (cf. Ernst Bloch: The Principle of Hope. Vol. 1, trans. by Neville Plaice/Stephen Plaice/Paul Knight, Cambridge, MA 1986, pp. 200 ff.). It is not possible here to engage in depth with Bloch and his critique of

political interpretation produces important connections between film (or Bergson and Deleuze's theories of film) and the theory of revolution, on its own this assessment does not show how films think revolution. It cannot be said that all films in and of themselves, or as a medium, think revolution. Rather, films are particularly suitable for thinking revolution and the concepts of temporality and historicity that are fundamental thereto. Now I want to show which genre offers a productive perspective on films about revolution: the historical epics of Hollywood. In a further effort at concrete analysis, the following chapters will then be anchored by direct engagement with individual films, showing how these films think revolution.

3.2 Film and the Experience of History

Working from the banal but fundamental observation that revolutions are historical events and that films about revolution – at least those that are examined in this book – are *historical films*[68] raises the question of these films' relationship to the historical events they depict. A famous passage from Aristotle's *Poetics* can help begin to answer this question. He compares the work of the poet, which can be understood as the entire realm of fictional narratives – a realm that includes not only films generally, but also historical films in particular – with the work of the historian:

> It is, moreover, evident from what has been said, that it is not the function of the poet to relate what has happened, but what may happen, – what is possible according to the law

---

Bergson. However, regarding the reproach that at first seems counterintuitive, that Bergson fails to consider possibility, it can be said that Bergson derives the possible from the real – and this indeed contradicts Bloch's approach (cf. Henri Bergson: The Possible and the Real, in: Henri Bergson. Key Writings, ed. by Keith Ansell Pearson/John Mullarkey, New York/London 2002, pp. 223–232, here p. 232). The criticism that Bergson's thinking omits finality highlights a problem in Bloch's own philosophy. While Bloch defines his anticipated finality as a homeland [*Heimat*] in which "no one has yet been" (Ernst Bloch: The Principle of Hope. Vol. 3, trans. by Neville Plaice/Stephen Plaice/Paul Knight, Cambridge, MA 1995, p. 1376), this "homeland" is the homeland of the unalienated man (cf. ibid., p. 1359), whom he sees as sketched out by Marx. Thus, in Bloch's work, finality ultimately requires an unalienated state of humanity – a highly problematic thought. A productive reading of Marx would have to separate Marx from the idea of alienation.

68 I do not mean to argue that science fiction films – such as V FOR VENDETTA (James McTeigue, US/GB/DE 2005) or ELYSIUM (Neill Blomkamp, US 2013) – cannot be productive for a filmic thinking of revolution; the question of which films achieve this goal is not decided by the characters' costumes.

of probability or necessity. The poet and the historian differ not by writing in verse or in prose. The work of Herodotus might be put into verse, and it would still be a species of history, with metre no less than without it. The true difference is that one relates what has happened, the other what may happen. Poetry, therefore, is a more philosophical and a higher thing than history: for poetry tends to express the universal, history the particular. By the universal, I mean how a person of a certain type will on occasion speak or act, according to the law of probability or necessity; and it is this universality at which poetry aims in the names she attaches to the personages. The particular is – for example – what Alcibiades did or suffered.[69]

Aristotle privileges the poet and his work (which he characterizes as a higher thing and more philosophical), for this work is less specialized, its themes more general. The decisive distinction, the factor that brings Aristotle to this conclusion – to push his argument a bit further – is fiction.[70] Rather than 'merely' reproducing what has happened, the poet is capable of creating possible worlds, and should thus be judged by different standards than the historian. While the latter is concerned with the facticity of past events, poetry addresses the question of what could happen, without any imperative to realize it. This is not to say that poems have no relationship to the world from which they emerge. But they cannot be reduced to it.[71]

---

69 Aristotle: The Poetics of Aristotle, op. cit., p. 14 (1451a–1451b). For a discussion of this passage in the structure and context of the Poetics, see Girshausen: Ursprungszeiten des Theaters, op. cit., p. 144.
70 For a basic definition of fiction, see: all forms of fiction "have their own 'as-if-character': 'imagine X behaved as if such and such were true ...' Counterfactual sentences like this one are paradigmatic of the fundamental character of possibility, as well as the negative character of fictional content. We imagine something precisely in the way it is not, about which we also know that it is not as we imagine it. The fact that we do not fool ourselves about the fictional status of our thoughts is a condition of fictional operations" (Gertrud Koch/Christiane Voss: Einleitung, in: "Es ist, als ob". Fiktionalität in Philosophie, Film- und Medienwissenschaft, ed. by Gertrud Koch/Christiane Voss, Paderborn 2009, pp. 7–11, here p. 8 [Translator's note: my translation]).
71 See Gertrud Koch: "In aesethetics, communicating a world happens through worldbuilding. It is centered not on depiction and description, but the construction of worlds that can hold implicit positions on the world. What the autonomy of art enables is, briefly, the construction of worlds: the construction of a world that is fallibilistically related to all other worlds; a world that remains virtual, i.e. takes effect without becoming real, not a potential world that aims to become possible" (Gertrud Koch: Filmische Welten – Zur Welthaltigkeit filmischer Projektionen, in: Dimensionen ästhetischer Erfahrung, ed. by Joachim Küpper/Christoph Menke, Frankfurt/Main 2003, pp. 162–175, here p. 162 [Translator's note: my translation]).

The passage from Aristotle is productive for looking at films about revolution.[72] It would be misguided to evaluate historical films on the basis of their 'accuracy' and reduce them to this question. Aristotle's insistence that works of poetry and fiction cannot be measured against reality in the same way as a book of history also undergirds the tradition of film theory introduced in the preceding chapter.[73] Étienne Souriau, one of the founders of the filmology school,[74] asserts that the filmic universe and the diegetic world surrounding a film function according to different principles than reality does. And this goes for every narrative film; the only difference is the way in which, and to what degree, reality is adopted or ignored as a point of reference.[75] For Deleuze, even Italian neorealism is not characterized by an accurate reproduction of reality. He has this idea in mind when he summarizes Bazin's position on neorealism as follows: "The real was no longer represented or reproduced, but aimed at. Instead of representing an already deciphered real, neo-realism aimed at an always ambiguous, to be deciphered, real [...]."[76]

Yet if films, including historical films, cannot be productively compared with 'reality,' the question remains of how to positively determine the relationship between films and the themes they address. If these two phenomena are not simply to run on in parallel, one must ask how films can think not only revolution, but *revolution as a historical event*. Vivian Sobchack answers this question with regard to the historical epics of Hollywood.[77]

---

[72] The title of a *New York Times* article on historical films from 21 May 1995 describes the liberation of historical films from historical accuracy somewhat more informally, but quite poignantly: "They're Movies, Not Schoolbooks." See Caryn James: They're Movies, Not Schoolbooks, in: The New York Times, May 21, 1995. For a more concrete discussion of this concept, see my chapter on REDS.

[73] This is not to say that other lines of thought that place more emphasis on the medium's relationship to reality, for instance Siegfried Kracauer's work, necessarily develop a limited perspective on historical films.

[74] On filmology, see Frank Kessler: Etienne Souriau und das Vokabular der filmologischen Schule, in: montage AV, 6 (2), 1997, pp. 132–139; and of course Epstein's essay Naissance d'une académie, op. cit.

[75] Cf. Étienne Souriau: Die Struktur des filmischen Universums und das Vokabular der Filmologie, in: montage AV, 6 (2), 1997, pp. 140–157, here pp. 141 ff.

[76] Deleuze: The Time-Image, op. cit., p. 1. Deleuze himself goes further and sees the particularity of Italian neorealism not in its relationship to the real, but in its break with the sensory-motor system (ibid., pp. 1–13).

[77] Cf. Vivian Sobchack: "Surge and Splendor": A Phenomenology of the Hollywood Historical Epic, in: Representations 29, 1990, pp. 24–49.

Although she refuses to give a clear definition of the historical epic, Sobchack does list a few formal features, family resemblances that help delimit the set of films designated by this generic label.[78] After an early heyday in Italian silent cinema, and via the work of D.W. Griffith and Cecil B. DeMille historical epics reached their apex in Hollywood cinema of the 1950s and 1960s.[79] Measured against other Hollywood films of this period, these films are characterized by their extravagance and excess.[80] The first generic exemplars named by Sobchack are GONE WITH THE WIND (Victor Fleming, US 1939) and LAWRENCE OF ARABIA (David Lean, GB/US 1962). Excess and extravagance can be found on many levels in this genre: from film format and mode of presentation (Cinerama, Cinemascope, 70mm) through the number of extras that are used in crowd scenes and the 'greatness' of Hollywood stars who play the protagonists of world history (accompanied by a historiography reduced to the deeds of individual heroes), to a plot introduced by panels of text or an offscreen narrator (who is thereby endowed with godlike qualities[81]) that clearly mark it as being in the past; from extravagant costumes, spectacular furnishings, and grand sets and structures, through grandiose landscapes, to sentimental music that is also 'too much'; and not least the reliance on extraordinary, 'historically significant' plots, battles and events.

---

[78] Were Sobchack to give a definition of historical films, she would immediately be mired in the antinomies of genre taxonomy. For an overview of the problems of taxonomic approaches to genre, see Hermann Kappelhoff: Front Lines of Community. Hollywood Between War and Democracy, trans. by Daniel Hendrickson, Berlin/Boston 2018, pp. 82 ff. On the idea of seeking generic coherence in Wittgensteinian family resemblance, see Jörg Schweinitz: "Genre" und lebendiges Genrebewußtsein. Geschichte eines Begriffs und Probleme seiner Konzeptualisierung in der Filmwissenschaft, in: montage AV, 3 (2), 1994, pp. 99–118, here p. 114. Stanley Cavell too sees a connection between Wittgenstein's family resemblances and the question of genre theory, yet cautions against applying the idea too simply. He specifies the connection between exemplars of a genre: "they *are what they are* in view of one another" (Stanley Cavell: Pursuits of Happiness. The Hollywood Comedy of Remarriage, Cambridge, MA/London 1981, p. 29). On the model of family resemblance, see especially paragraphs 66 and 67 in: Ludwig Wittgenstein: Philosophical Investigations. The German text, with an English trans. by G.E.M. Anscombe, P.M.S. Hacker/Joachim Schulte, Chichester/Malden 2009, pp. 36 f.
[79] Sobchack maintains that for her, 'Hollywood' is a conceptual rather than a geographic designation (cf. Sobchack: "Surge and splendor", op. cit., p. 45, n2).
[80] As is clear throughout Sobchack's essay, she is aware that excess always implicitly requires a norm to confirm its existence.
[81] On this topic, see Michel Chion: The Voice in Cinema, ed. and trans. by Claudia Gorbman, New York 1999, pp. 17 ff.

Given the circumstances, it is no wonder that such films are hardly considered relevant to a 'serious' transmission of historical images,[82] and on the contrary are not taken seriously. But Sobchack contradicts this notion:

> Indeed, I would suggest that the Hollywood historical epic is as central to our understanding of what we mean by the 'historical' and 'History' as any work of academic scholarship. Obviously, its modality is different from the latter. [...] However, in that both the work of academic scholarship and the Hollywood historical epic construct interpretive narratives formulated around and foregrounding past human events as coherent and significant, both are temporally reflexive and both respond – if in different ways and through different experiences – to the same central philosophical question: *how to comprehend ourselves in time.*[83]

Thus, according to Sobchack, Hollywood epics have an understanding of history that is just as legitimate as that of academic historiography.[84] This argument, provocative on first glance, seems more reasonable when one considers the shared task of academic history and Hollywood epics, all differences aside (she does not claim the two are identical – this would be absurd). In a decisive break from the approach that sees historical films as a *representation* of history and historical events, Sobchack is interested in how the films answer the question of how we can understand ourselves in time and in history. In other words, she asks how we can understand ourselves as historical beings, as people with history and historicity. Yet this question has only become meaningful since the emergence of the modern concept of revolution. Epic historical films that are about not just great events of history, but about revolutions, are thus even better suited to answer this question.

As the title of Sobchack's essay indicates, she attempts to answer this question for Hollywood historical epics through phenomenology. In doing so, she

---

[82] Sobchack's terms for the films' relationship to history are "historical interpretation" or "mode of historicizing, of creating history" (Sobchack: "Surge and Splendor", op. cit., p. 26). However, sometimes she also writes of "historical representation" (ibid.). Yet, this last formulation is linguistically imprecise and in my opinion, not only falls behind the film theoretical tradition described previously, but also fails to keep up with Sobchack's own premises, which I will introduce below. After all, Sobchack does not seek to verify the films' historical accuracy – yet the term "representation" points in this direction.

[83] Ibid. When Sobchack writes that academic historiographies also construct narratives in order to present past events, she refers implicitly to Hayden White: Metahistory. The Historical Imagination in Nineteenth-century Europe, Baltimore 1987.

[84] She defines "history" as "an excess of temporality over any individual's participation in and comprehension of it" (Sobchack: "Surge and splendor", op. cit., p. 36) and notes that the question of what constitutes historical consciousness is itself a historical question and must therefore be historicized (ibid., p. 39).

3.2 Film and the Experience of History — 61

looks at both the films' context – their conditions of production, their marketing and their reception – and the films themselves. Sobchack de-emphasizes the latter – yet precisely in this area she raises several productive points that are worth addressing, since the two levels ultimately cannot be separated. First, she refers to these films' sensational and hyperbolic marketing campaigns, which overflow with generalizations and superlatives, and concludes that their goal is certainly not to create the most accurate representation possible of a specific epoch or event. Instead, they aim to exceed the specificity of an event. She reinforces this argument by referring to a review of NICHOLAS AND ALEXANDRA (Franklin J. Schaffner, GB 1971), a film about the Russian royal family during the February and October Revolutions, in which the film is criticized for trying to incorporate too many historical details: The tenor of the critique is that the film's fixation on concrete details inhibits the generalization and transcendence of concrete historical events that are proper to an epic. From these remarks, Sobchack concludes:

> In a paradoxical way, the suggestion here is that the Hollywood historical epic is not so much the narrative accounting of *specific historical events* as it is the narrative construction of *general historic eventfulness*.[85]

The films do not show *historical events* so much as *the production of history*. This means that the films abstract from the specific situation that is being staged, thus opening up a field on and through which the spectator can experience historicity; in this way, their oft-criticized historical imprecision fulfills a quite basic function. The films open "a temporal field,"[86] which enables spectators to experience and recognize themselves as historical subjects, as subjects with and especially in history. Sobchack clarifies this idea, which on first glance is unusually abstract for a phenomenological approach, piece by piece over the course of her essay. Drawing on Hayden White's work, she begins by explaining how the relationship of the films to the events they present can be

---

85 Ibid., p. 28.
86 Ibid., p. 29. Later in the essay, Sobchack describes this field as a "temporal field that allows us prereflectively to experience the possibility of temporal transcendence" (ibid., p. 45). The sentences that I paraphrase in the above paragraph state: "It also could be argued that this sloppiness is profoundly functional – and that it is by means of iconographic expansiveness and formal excessiveness that the Hollywood historical epic creates a field of temporality experienced as subjectively transcendent and objectively significant. The importance of the genre is not that it narrates and dramatizes historical events accurately according to the detailed stories of academic historians but rather that it opens a temporal field that creates the *general* possibility for re-cognizing oneself as a *historical subject* of a particular kind" (ibid., p. 29).

understood positively – namely, that the decisive element is not historical accuracy: Rather, the form of the Hollywood historical epic is onomatopoetic mimesis.[87] This mimesis is both the meaning and the "content of its form," another reference to White.[88] Yet what comprises the onomatopoeia of these films? What about their form (their 'resonance') recalls that which they imitate? Sobchack argues that in their excessive, extravagant form – by which she means not only the production process but also the staging strategies and the conditions of exhibition – the films repeat the work and effort that they narrate on the level of content. She sees a connection between the narrative events on one hand, and the films' production and presentation on the other. The epic form repeats the greatness and significance of the story. In a decisive move, Sobchack connects these back to the spectator's body and to excess:

> Through these means, the genre *allegorically* and *carnally* inscribes on the modal spectator a sense and meaning of being in time and human events in a manner and at a magnitude exceeding any individual temporal construction or appropriation – and, most importantly, in a manner and at a magnitude that is *intelligible as excess* to lived-body subjects in a historically specific *consumer* culture.[89]

Through the epic form, spectators experience a corporeal inscription of their consciousness that they exist in history and that this history exceeds their personal experiences, the history of their individual lives: Their excessive form gives spectators a sense of history. Spectators get a sense of their temporality, an awareness that they exist in time; but also an awareness that both before and after their own existence, there were and will be people in the world, and that the world has been influenced by these people.

This sense of history is produced by precisely those features of Hollywood epics that Sobchack has already named. According to her, the films' tendency to begin with text panels or an offscreen narrator announces that an important story from the past is about to be told. Furthermore, this kind of opening represents another form of repetition. If the film itself is already a story that stages the past, text panels or a narrator's voice tell a story within the story, one that directly addresses the spectator and thus creates a connection between the past staged in the film and the present created by it, and in doing so underscores the importance of this past for the present. For when films start with voice-over

---

[87] With the concept of mimesis, Sobchack also refers here to one of the cornerstones of Aristotle's *Poetics*. Cf. especially the first three chapters of *Poetics*: Aristotle: The Poetics of Aristotle, op. cit., pp. 4–7 (1447a–1448a).
[88] Sobchack: "Surge and Splendor", op. cit., p. 29.
[89] Ibid.

narration, according to Sobchack the role has mostly been played by the deep, sonorous, and distinctive voices of male stars. Their star status lends additional authority to their offscreen voice.

Another form of repetition – and of connection between what is shown in the film and the world of the spectator; the connection that creates a sense of history and allows spectators to experience the fact that they do not exist independently of history – is, according to Sobchack, that in their production, the films take up the topics they address and breathe new life into them in a certain way. The love story between Mark Antony and Cleopatra mirrors the love story of Richard Burton and Elizabeth Taylor, and the downfall of both empires repeats itself in the financial disaster of the film CLEOPATRA (Joseph L. Mankiewicz, US/CH/GB 1963). Of course, Sobchack does not intend to equate the phenomena, but she argues that they create a relationship between the present moment and what is shown in the film. For Sobchack, a decisive factor in these forms of repetition and the relationships that emerge between the spectators' world and what is shown in the film is – as mentioned previously – the use of stars in the films. Through their high degree of recognizability alone, they make it somewhat impossible to see the film as an accurate representation of the past. With their mere presence, they draw attention to the fact that the film is a reenactment of the past. The stars not only create distance between the time of what is shown in the film and the time of the spectator, but also demonstrate the greatness and significance of the story: "Indeed, the very presence of stars in the historical epic mimetically represents not *real historical* figures but rather the *real significance* of historical figures. Stars literally lend *magnitude* to the representation."[90]

The aforementioned opulent production values as well as the pathos-laden, orchestral soundtrack are also elements of mimetic onomatopoeia for Sobchack. The enormous number of props and extras, and the monumental studio sets and landscapes in which the films take place, emulate the significance of the narrative and reflect the degree of significance that history holds for the spectators and their existence. The films' scores elevate this opulence and importance to an extradiegetic level, which is present exclusively for the spectator and therefore functions as a further avenue of connection between the spectator and what is presented in the film.

Finally – the embodied spectator is very important here – the excessive spatial and temporal conditions of the films contribute to the spectators' consciousness of their own historicity. Compared with normal Hollywood productions,

---

90 Ibid., p. 36.

Hollywood's historical epics are unusually long; hardly any of them run under three hours. Sobchack describes the effect of this unaccustomed duration as follows:

> On the one hand, experiencing this extraordinary cinematic duration, the spectator as a body-subject is made more presently aware than is usual of his or her bodily presence – indeed, is "condemned" to the present and physically "tested" by the length of the film's duration. On the other hand, however, enduring the film in the present imprints the body with a brute sense of the possibility of transcending the present, of the literal and material capacity of human being to be tested and to continue and last through events represented as a temporal "spread staggered out in depth." This writing on the body by experience, I would argue, provides the carnal and subjective ground necessary for the constructed abstract and objective premises considered sufficient to historical reflection.[91]

With the above passage, Sobchack arrives at a concrete explanation of the quite abstract theory with which she began. The epic length of the films first leads to a heightened awareness of one's own corporeality. Yet corporeality – even if Sobchack does not pursue this at this point – is always connected with mortality and therefore one's own temporality and historicity, which become perceptible through watching generally and through watching epics specifically. For Sobchack, this is the second significant factor in the films' excessive length, how it realizes itself in spectators' perception. By quite literally sitting out the epics, the individual becomes able to grasp and experience temporal dimensions that outlast and overwhelm the individual. Enduring the excessive duration of these films, according to Sobchack, indicates the possibility and basis for the individual to experience the equally excessive temporality of history, and going further, to reflect on it.[92] The temporal excess that exceeds the individual, which constitutes history – and history is what the films are about – reappears in the films' duration, and sitting through the length of the film indicates that spectators are capable of thinking 'history' and historicity. Returning to the two temporalities of revolution analyzed in the second chapter, and connecting them with Sobchack's ideas, the temporality that Koselleck describes

---

91 Ibid., pp. 37 f. With the phrase "spread staggered out in depth," Sobchack cites Maurice Merleau-Ponty: The Visible and the Invisible, ed. by Claude Lefort, trans. by Alphonso Lingis, Evanston, IL 1968, p. 186.
92 In her characteristically playful, fresh style, Sobchack describes the connection between Hollywood historical epics and the corporeal experience of history: "thus, writing on the body of the model American spectator/consumer, the Hollywood historical epic is *transcoding* the culture's emphasis on literalism and materialism into specific carnal terms, and reprinting its version of History not only for posterity but also on our posteriors. This is, philosophically and carnally, a profound form of repetition" (ibid., p. 38).

3.2 Film and the Experience of History — 65

as the long-term structural change of revolution is the one that becomes available to experience through excessively long films about revolution.

Sobchack introduces TV mini-series as a legitimate successor to historical epics after their decline,[93] even if the former differs significantly from the epic in a number of ways. On one hand, she also sees the "*formal* construction of historical consciousness" that she finds in epic films of the 1950s and early 1960s. She refers to TV mini-series about historical events as "epic equivalents."[94] In contrast to epics, she notes, mini-series frequently place less emphasis on production values. In addition, the broadcast form of temporal excess differs. Whereas the cinematic epic is watched collectively and all at once, the mini-series is watched individually on television and fragmented into episodes.[95] Without going into more depth here on the relationship between the mini-series and the epic, I want to note that the differences identified by Sobchack between epics and mini-series can also be seen in parallel to Arendt's conception of the differences between the French and American Revolutions.[96]

If revolution is an event that stands like no other for a historic change, and if – as I argue in Chapter 2 – it enables the thinking of historical change as well as attempts to theorize that change, it is not surprising that films about revolution frequently take the form of Hollywood epics. This holds true for the films I examine later in this book. In the following pages, I attempt to show that Sobchack opens up a perspective on films that makes it possible to see these films also as giving their spectators a sense of history. In the respective chapters on the films, the next step will be to use this perspective to show *how* the films produce and open up this sense not only through their *general* form, but also through concrete strategies of staging. Sobchack shows how the global form of epics enable the *experience* of history and historicity. The following chapters will draw on Deleuze to show how films build on this basis to *think* revolution as a historical event. This work will require concrete scene analysis.

---

[93] Explaining the reasons for this decline would lead to the question of the relationship between society and successful films, as well as flops. This discussion would lead too far away from my book's subject at this point. In this vein, Sobchack cites Allen Barra: The Incredible Shrinking Epic, in: American Film 14 (5), 1989, pp. 40–45 and p. 60. Briefly, the reasons Sobchack names are: the spread of television, the end of the Hollywood studio system, the fragmentation of audience interest, as well as the domestic (civil rights movements) and foreign (Vietnam War) political crises of the US, which contradicted the homogenizing tendencies of epics (cf. Sobchack: "Surge and Splendor", op. cit., p. 40).
[94] Ibid., p. 41. Both citations can be found on this page.
[95] The possibility to broadcast the TV series more than once – or for the spectator to record it on video – emerges as a form of repetition on another level than those already discussed.
[96] This is one of my main arguments in Chapter 6 in this book.

When it comes to REDS, the connection is obvious; Sobchack herself names this film as a contemporary example of a film in the tradition of 1950s and early 1960s Hollywood epics. Here too, there is excessive length (200 minutes), the use of stars (Diane Keaton and especially Warren Beatty), extravagant production values (according to Sheldon Hall and Steve Neale, the film was part of a "risky megabuck pic trend" and was considered "mega-budgeted"[97]), and the staging of historic events (World War One and the Russian Revolution). It also exhibits the overlap of narrative and production history: the 'great man' Reed and the 'great man' Beatty, who was involved with or in charge of nearly all the central creative positions in the making of the film – an aspect that Sobchack sees critically in this case. Yet in the end, Sobchack is not able to use the film productively in her argument. While she states that it is left-leaning and well-intentioned, she bemoans the fact that the film, as mentioned just now, adheres too closely to a historiography of 'great men.' This part of Sobchack's argument, however, relies much too heavily on representation and plot – she completely neglects methods of staging or film form. In a certain way, Sobchack's mode of observing REDS takes the same shortcuts and rests on the same simple premises that she criticizes in much of the research on Hollywood epics of the 1950s and early 1960s (she also claims these films focus on the history of 'great men' – but then shows that narrative level is not what makes the films interesting).[98]

The mini-series JOHN ADAMS can also be analyzed from the perspective introduced by Sobchack. As an HBO prestige production[99] comprised of seven episodes ranging from 62 to 92 minutes in length, it clearly stands in the tradition of Hollywood historical epics, even if the ruptures noted by Sobchack still apply. Abel Gance's NAPOLÉON seems almost to exceed Sobchack's categories.

---

[97] See Sheldon Hall/Steve Neale: Epics, Spectacles, and Blockbusters. A Hollywood History, Detroit 2010, p. 232. The phrases quoted here come from *Variety*. Leger Grindon writes that the film's production cost as much as $33.5 million before distribution and marketing (cf. Leger Grindon: Shadows on the Past. Studies in the Historical Fiction Film, Philadelphia 1994, p. 180).

[98] For more on the relationship between REDS and the Hollywood epics as they are analyzed by Sobchack, as well as the attempt to make the film productive from this perspective, see Chapter 5 of this book.

[99] The series production costs totaled $100 million (cf. Brian Lowry: HBO's Radical Chic, in: Variety, 410 (5), 2008, p. 28 and p. 35, here p. 28), which led to the following result: "technically, the term 'sumptuous' almost doesn't do justice to the production [...]." Lowry places particular emphasis on the large number of speaking parts and the "massive sets," which he describes as displaying "splendid glory" (cf. ibid., p. 35). See also: "[...] technically, JOHN ADAMS is certainly sublime, *cinematic television* par excellence" (Lukas Förster: John Adams, in: Cargo, 4 (12), 2011, pp. 61f., here p. 62 [Translator's note: my translation]).

3.2 Film and the Experience of History — 67

With an original running time of six hours and 28 minutes (which, furthermore, was planned to be just the first of seven parts), its enormous crowds of extras, its costs, its triptych sequences, and enormously extravagant production values, the film outdoes 1950s and early 1960s Hollywood historical epics. The megalomania that Gance displayed during production thoroughly resembles Napoleon's own – and Gance even repeated the emperor's failure.[100]

Yet before showing how films think revolution in this framework, it is important to address the basics of embodied filmic perception in more detail. Sobchack explains these basics in her most important book on film theory.[101] One can begin by saying that the work attempts to turn away from approaches to film theory based in psychoanalysis, linguistics, or ideology critique. Sobchack is interested in forms of cinematographic communication between film and spectator beyond ideology, poetics, and rhetoric – all these subjects are set aside here and remain available for further exploration. She focuses on forms of communication that she situates on the plane of experience; or more precisely, on the plane of corporeal filmic experience, on which there is a form of "wild meaning" that appears long before any linguistic construction of meaning.[102] A central element of these forms of communication, and Sobchack's understanding of the relationship between film and spectator, is her well-known definition of film as an "expression of experience by experience."[103] This formulation means that she accords with Merleau-Ponty's assumption that in interpersonal communication – regardless of film or cinema – perception is always expression and, conversely, expression is always also perception. Further, she postulates that film is the expression of an experience through experience, that film is experience because it is an

---

[100] On this film's production history, which has been extensively researched, see Kevin Brownlow: Napoleon. Abel Gance's Classic Film, London 1983 (on the length of the original version, see p. 299, endnote 3) and Nelly Kaplan: Napoléon, London 1994 (on the plan for seven parts, see p. 16). On the various versions of the film, see also Paul Cuff: A Revolution for the Screen. Abel Gance's Napoleon, Amsterdam 2015, p. 23; on the film's international production, see ibid., p. 46. And for a more precise examination of the screenplay for the final episode of the planned series, see ibid., p. 223. For a quite effusive discussion of the circumstances of production, see also François Truffaut: Napoléon, in: id.: The Films in My Life, trans. by Leonard Mayhew, New York 1985, pp. 29–32.
[101] Cf. Vivan Sobchack: The Address of the Eye. A Phenomenology of Film Experience, Princeton 1992, p. 3. The summary that follows of Sobchack's thoughts on the connection between the film and the spectator is a re-worked version of a presentation that I gave on January 20, 2014, as part of working group 3 ("Spaces of Experience of Art") of the collaborative research center 626 "Aesthetic Experience and the Dissolution of Artistic Limits." Thanks to Sarah-Mai Dang for helpful notes and comments on the presentation.
[102] Cf. ibid, pp. 3 f.
[103] Ibid., p. 3.

68 — 3 The "Machine Which Thinks Temporally"

expression. For Sobchack, film perception should be thought as experience. Then she applies the structure of interpersonal communication to the relationship between film and spectator, because she conceives of film's perception and expression as almost directly analogous to human perception and expression.[104] The film also sees, hears, perceives and expresses what it perceives. Sobchack assumes that in the cinema there are always two modes of perception and experience that are placed into relationship with each other: the perception of the film and that of the spectator, both of which are thought as embodied subjects. She writes:

> The entailment of incarnate consciousness and the "flesh" of the world of which it is a part will be described as the basis for the origination of the general structures of cinematic signification, structures that are themselves produced in the performance of specific modes of existential and embodied communication in the film experience (that is, in the activity of vision intersubjectively connecting film and spectator with the world and each other).[105]

Significantly, the intersubjectivity discussed by Sobchack in this passage, i.e. forms of communication that occur in the cinema between the film and the spectator, are based on a mode of perception that is similarly structured in both entities. Because both perceptions have a similar structure, there can be a communicative exchange between the film and the spectator. Not only is it possible for this exchange to occur, the film cannot be thought separately from the spectator's experience. For Sobchack, filmic experience is always defined by the relationship between the film and the spectator; through the question of how the film is realized in the spectators' experience. This idea becomes clear when she writes, "a film is an act of seeing that makes itself seen, an act of hearing that makes itself heard, an act of physical and reflective movement that makes itself reflexively felt and understood."[106] She formulates this idea more precisely as follows: "Watching a film, we can see the seeing as well as the seen, hear the hearing as well as the heard, and feel the movement as well as the moved."[107] We see not just the film; the spectator sees it always already as the camera's sight. We see not only what the camera sees, but also the camera itself – and the camera's seeing, through its movements. As previously mentioned, Sobchack conceives of film as both a perceiving and an expressing body. This means that

---

104 At this point Sobchack's perspective diverges from Deleuze's, who argues convincingly that filmic perception exceeds human perception (cf. Deleuze: The Movement-Image, op. cit., p. 20: "But the sole cinematographic consciousness is not us, the spectator, nor the hero; it is the camera – sometimes human, sometimes inhuman or superhuman").
105 Sobchack: The Address of the Eye, op. cit., p. 7.
106 Ibid., pp. 3 f.
107 Ibid., p. 10.

the space perceived by the film camera (and subsequently projected into the cinema), which is perceived in film-viewing, is always also a constructed, formed, and expressing space. Film is thus not only the representation of a preexisting space, but always also the presentation of the film's own perception – and as became clear from her essay on Hollywood epics, Sobchack is aligned with Epstein and Deleuze in critiquing the idea that film represents something.

"Perception," which she paraphrases as "having sense," and expression, which she describes as "making sense,"[108] are not opposites in Sobchack's analysis; instead, they are interwoven with each other and converge in experience. They are not independent of each other yet should also not be understood as melded. (With regard to these two terms, she also writes of "reversibility.") Her sweeping criticism of the history of film theory is that it fails to recognize this dual function and instead reduces film to one of the two capacities or combines them into a single entity. She opposes conceiving of film as a "window onto the world" – this is the formula that can be used to summarize a strain of film theory which, according to Sobchack, reduces film to "perception" and which she categorizes as "realistic film theory." Yet she also opposes understanding film merely as "expression," which she characterizes as "formalism" and associates with the metaphor of the "frame." She also rejects the idea that cinema always presents a mirror image of the world, or more precisely, a reflection of hegemonic ideologies.

It is thus always important to think this duality, the relationship between perception and expression, and to do so in relation to the film as well as the spectator. For these dual elements – the body of the film and the body of the spectator, as well as the space of the film and the space of the theater in which the spectators sit – can never fully merge. Although Sobchack speaks of immersive phenomena, they never go so far as to create a synthesis of both spaces of experience. In the most important passage on this topic, Sobchack explains:

> The "Here, where eye (I) am" of the film retains its unique situation, even as it cannot maintain its perceptual privacy. Directly perceptible to the viewer as an anonymous "Here, where eye am" simultaneously available as "Here, where we see," the concretely embodied situation of the film's vision also stands *against* the viewer. It is also perceived by the viewer as a "there, where I am not," as the space consciously and bodily inhabited and lived by an "other" whose experience of being-in-the-world, however anonymous, is not precisely congruent with the viewer's own. Thus, while space and its significance are intimately shared and lived by both film and viewer, the viewer is always at some level aware of the double and reversible nature of cinematic perception, that is, of perception

---

108 Ibid., p. 13.

as expression, of perception as a process of *mediating* consciousness's relations with the world. The viewer, therefore, shares cinematic space with the film but must also negotiate it, contribute to, and perform the constitution of its experiential significance.[109]

Here, it is very important to understand that Sobchack is taking a resolute stance against film theories that seek to establish a stark opposition between spectators on the one hand and film (understood as text) on the other.[110] Yet she also rejects the possibility that there could be a merging of film and spectator. Here, she speaks of a double sense in a divided space: both in the sense of shared and separated space. Perception and perceptual space intersect, but do not come together in a synthesis.

Building on this foundation, Sobchack investigates three assumptions of film theory, questioning them and seeking to clarify their premises. First there is the centering of visuality in the cinema. She questions the assumption that every form of cinematographic communication can be traced back to seeing.[111] Second, she sets out to investigate how cinematic forms of communication are to be understood in the first place. And third, according to Sobchack, film has always been conceptualized as a "viewed object," which she does not want to take as a necessary given. She answers the first question, about the "act of viewing," in passing: She writes that, as already discussed, she is always interested in *embodied* perception, which she understands to be a "commutation of perception and expression" in both the film and the spectators."[112] Here, Sobchack insists again on the interwovenness of perception and expression. And – as already noted – this doubling of perception and expression in film and spectator is also what enables cinematographic communication. This in turn leads her to expand on the question of film as a "viewed object," that film is not only a visible and viewed object – in this context she writes of a "viewed view" of the film, but also a viewing subject.[113]

---

[109] Ibid., p. 10.
[110] Sobchack does not address the possibility of softening the opposition between text and the body through the etymology of the term *text* (web). The relationship between cinema, text, body, and event in films and film theory is examined in more detail in Sabine Nessel: Kino und Ereignis. Das Kinematografische zwischen Text und Körper, Berlin 2008.
[111] Although Sobchack does not concretely name the figures to whom she ascribes this position, it is not difficult to find passages from the history of film theory that resonate with it. For example, during his psychoanalytic phase Christian Metz wrote of the situation of the spectator in the cinema that the film is "brought into being by nothing other than the look" (Christian Metz: The Imaginary Signifier. Psychoanalysis and Cinema, trans. by Celia Britton et al., Bloomington/Indianapolis 1982, p. 93).
[112] Sobchack: The Address of the Eye, op. cit., p. 21.
[113] Ibid., pp. 21 f.

Sobchack explores her concept of embodied film experience more concretely in her essay "What My Fingers Knew."[114] There, she expands on her departure from the idea that film is a purely visual medium, once again repeatedly drawing on the philosophy of Merleau-Ponty. This departure is grounded in the synesthetic capacities of the spectator that are decisive for filmic experience. Even aside from clinical or 'pathological' cases of synesthesia, in every film spectator there is an active exchange between the senses. What is seen on the screen is also tasted, felt, and smelled – and not only in so-called 'body genres,' but on principle in every film.[115] According to Sobchack, this phenomenon is so common in everyday life that we hardly notice it. Along with synesthesia, *coenaesthesia* is also important.[116] This term refers particularly to the sensory openness and unity that is present particularly in newborns, but also in adults. Whereas synesthesia presumes an exchange occurring between senses that are separated from one another, in 'coenaesthesia' this separation does not exist to begin with.[117] Yet of course the question remains of how that which is shown on the screen makes its way to the spectator's body. Despite the references to synesthetic and 'co-aesthetic' perception, this is not quite felt in the same way as something directly present, nor are spectators touched by the bodies in the film or the body of the film as they could be by an immediately present body. How then to explain strong physical reactions to what is shown in film? On this point, Sobchack elaborates:

> However, insofar as I cannot literally touch, smell or taste the particular figure on the screen that solicits my sensual desire, my body's intentional trajectory, seeking a sensible object to fulfill this sensual solicitation, will *reverse its direction* to locate its partially frustrated sensual grasp on something more literally accessible. That more literally accessible sensual object is *my own subjectively felt lived body*. Thus, "on the rebound" from the screen – and without a reflective thought – I will reflexively turn toward my own carnal, sensual, and sensible being to touch myself touching, smell myself smelling, taste myself tasting, and, in sum, sense my own sensuality.[118]

---

114 See Vivian Sobchack: What My Fingers Knew. The Cinesthetic Subject, or Vision in the Flesh, in: id.: Carnal Thoughts. Embodiment and Moving Image Culture, Berkeley/Los Angeles/London 2004, pp. 53–84.
115 Linda Williams uses the term 'body genres' to refer to horror, melodrama, and pornography. See Linda Williams: Film Bodies: Gender, Genre, and Excess, in: Film Genre Reader III, ed. by Barry Keith Grant, Austin 2003, pp. 141–159.
116 Sobchack: What My Fingers Knew, op. cit., p. 68.
117 The term 'coenaesthesia' refers to what psychologist Daniel Stern calls 'amodal perception.' The results of Stern's research in infant development appear in a film theoretical context in Raymond Bellour: Le dépli des émotions, in: Trafic, 43, 2002, pp. 93–128.
118 Sobchack: What My Fingers Knew, op. cit., pp. 76 f.

In the absence of a counterpart toward which the sensory impressions awakened by the film could be directed, this reaction is turned in on the spectator's own body and thus acquires a somewhat diffuse quality on the one hand, while on the other hand it is further intensified. Sobchack explains this structure with reference to a famous example from Merleau-Ponty: When I touch my left hand with my right hand, I feel my left hand with my right hand. At the same time, however, I also feel my right hand with my left hand. The touched hand becomes the touching hand, and the feeling of touch becomes diffuse, no longer limited to a single hand. Yet it is also intensified, since it is doubly present. Further, it is important to underscore a point that Sobchack references, but does not elaborate: In the cinema, these feedback loops between the body of the film and the body of the spectator happen absent any conscious intellectual processing ("without a reflective thought") on the part of the spectator. Although this is a reflexive corporeal process, it precedes and cannot be equated with any conscious processing. Conscious processing of these occurrences would, on the contrary, lead to a form of becoming-aware, which would lead to more self-consciousness and ultimately interrupt the feedback loop: When we become aware of our tears, we stop crying, to use one of Sobchack's examples of this effect.[119]

Sobchack's theorization of Hollywood historical epics centers on the question of experience and the ability to experience historicity, as well as the closely related question of corporeality – and not on the films' thinking of history. This focus echoes her foundational work on the relationship between film and spectator, which privileges *experience*. She leaves aside the question of how films think, or how they make spectators think. In order to take the next step toward the thinking of films, I will engage in more detail with Deleuze's remarks on NAPOLÉON and use them to demonstrate that Gance's film can be seen as a paradigm for how films can think revolution productively. Against the background of the positions on film outlined in the preceding chapters – its qualities, its relationship to the spectator, and its historicity – NAPOLÉON will serve to further specify my proposed perspective on films about revolution.

---

119 Cf. ibid., p. 70, footnote 69.

4 NAPOLÉON: The Sublime Conceptualization of Revolution

4.1 The Mathematical Sublime and Deleuze

The Prewar French School

A scene near the end of Abel Gance's monumental film about Napoleon:[1] It shows Napoleon visiting an abandoned convent shortly before the campaign in Italy with which the film ends. Sentimental organ music plays.[2] While Napoleon stands at the pulpit, looks toward the empty pews, and lingers for a moment, the convent pews gradually fill with people, who appear in a cross-fade. Finally – also in cross-fade – the great men of the French Revolution appear. Robespierre, Danton, Saint-Just, Couthon and Marat speak to Napoleon: "Listen, Bonaparte, the French Revolution is about to speak to you." Napoleon, who at first moves about, somewhat frightened, and wants to leave the convent, pauses and returns to the pulpit. Once there, he takes his hat off and hears the revolutionaries say: "We have realized that the revolution cannot prosper without a strong authority. Will you be its leader?" Napoleon nods in agreement, a determined expression on his face. The next intertitle, which presents the revolutionaries' speech, runs: "If the Revolution does not spread beyond our frontiers, it will die at home. Will you lead it into Europe?" With his determined expression and emphatic gestures, Napoleon answers: "Yes," which also appears in an intertitle. The continuous organ music slowly grows louder; the pitch increases as well, emphasizing and intensifying the emotional atmosphere and poignancy of the scene.[3] Even this

---

[1] The time code for this scene is 01:15:11–01:20:40 (Disc 2). I refer to the DVD distributed by Arthaus which appeared in 2012 with a length of 222 minutes. The Blu-ray edition released by the British Film Institute in late November 2016, which includes newly discovered material, different tinting, and a different score, could unfortunately not serve as the basis of my analysis. The theses presented in the following pages, however, could also have been derived from the longer version. On the extremely complex situation of the film's material and distribution, see Kevin Brownlow: Napoleon. Abel Gance's Classic Film, London 1983; Nelly Kaplan wrote in 1994 that there were more than twenty different versions of the film. Cf. Nelly Kaplan: Napoléon, London 1994, p. 9.
[2] The score in the version of the film I reference was composed by Carmine Coppola.
[3] The scene goes even a bit further: Napoleon is ordered to report his plans for the future. He answers that he wants to conquer neighboring countries and create a universal republic of a united Europe. Most importantly for my argument, in service to this task, Saint-Just declares Napoleon to be the "direct heir" of the French Revolution.

https://doi.org/10.1515/9783110754704-004

brief summary of the scene clearly shows that in its diegesis, the film NAPOLÉON leaves no room to doubt Napoleon's identification with the French Revolution. In the film, Bonaparte is a consequence and consummator of the Revolution. In a certain sense, the Revolution culminates in him.

This film becomes thoroughly obvious when one adopts an Epsteinian perspective on revolution films. Epstein himself saw his arguments realized and further developed in Gance's films. The latter's "great works," according to Epstein, "had triumphantly paved the way to quality for French cinema."[4] Epstein credits Gance with "science and boldness" and writes of the "studied singularity" of his images.[5] For Epstein, this phenomenon peaks in the thesis that Gance laid bare the essence of cinema with his films: "[...] one saw [...] discoveries, brief yet dazzling, of what the cinema alone, and no other technique, is capable of representing."[6] Elsewhere, he characterizes Gance as "our master, one and all"[7] and underscores the immense influence of Gance's films on his own cinematic works.[8]

---

4 Jean Epstein: Mémoires inachevées, in: id.: Écrits sur le cinéma. 1921–1953. Édition chronologique en deux volumes. Vol. I: 1921–1947, Paris 1974, pp. 27–57, here p. 30 [Translator's note: my translation].
5 Ibid., p. 33 [Translator's note: my translation].
6 Ibid., p. 34 [Translator's note: my translation]. Here, I am not attempting to problematize the question of essence in artistic genres, though I think that work is necessary; cf. André Bazin: In Defense of Mixed Cinema, in: id.: What Is Cinema?, Vol. 1, ed. and trans. by Hugh Gray, Berkeley/Los Angeles/London 2004, pp. 53–75. From a contemporary perspective, to problematize this question would mean first and foremost to historicize it (for Jacques Rancière, the aesthetic regime of art is determined by dissolving the question of essence in art, which also explains his critique of the term modernity); see Jacques Rancière: The Politics of Aesthetics. The Distribution of the Sensible, ed. and trans. by Gabriel Rockhill, London et al. 2013, pp. 15 ff. One would still have to consider, however, how to handle the question of medium specificity.
7 Jean Epstein: On Certain Characteristics of *Photogénie*, trans. by Tom Milne, in: Jean Epstein. Critical Essays and New Translations, ed. by Sarah Keller/Jason N. Paul, Amsterdam 2012, pp. 292–296, here p. 294. One can also find references to Epstein in Gance's theoretical work. Gance characterizes cinema as "a synthesis of movement, space, and time" (Abel Gance: Qu'est-ce que le cinématographe? Un sixième art!, in: Ciné-journal, 185 (9), 1912, p. 10 [Translator's note: my translation]) and writes that film enables us to see the world in a totally new light, thanks in part to slow motion and time-lapse; see Abel Gance: Le temps de l'image est venu!, in: L'art cinématographique, Vol. II, ed. by Léon-Pierre Quint et al., Paris 1927, pp. 83–102, here pp. 85 f. The text is accessible at: Die Zeit des Bildes ist angebrochen! Französische Intellektuelle, Künstler und Filmkritiker über das Kino. Website zum Buch. Hg. v. Margrit Tröhler und Jörg Schweinitz: https://www.film.uzh.ch/de/research/publications/einzel/zeit-des-bildes.html [last accessed 18 May 2022].
8 See Jean Epstein: Bilan de fin de muet, in: Écrits sur le cinéma I, op. cit., pp. 229–237, here pp. 235 f. Interestingly, Epstein was quite restrained on the subject of NAPOLÉON, as Kevin Brownlow states; see Brownlow: Napoleon, op. cit., p. 159. See also the hymn of praise Epstein

It is thus unsurprising when Deleuze, whose proximity to Epstein is demonstrated in the previous chapter, writes that Gance was "the recognised leader"[9] of the prewar French school.[10] Yet how does Deleuze come to this conclusion? What interests him, in the wake of Epstein, about prewar French cinema, and how does Gance become so important for Deleuze as well? In order to answer these questions, the first order of business is to establish that Deleuze differentiates the prewar French cinema from American, Russian, and German cinema of the same era. The decisive criteria for his taxonomy are the different montage compositions that inform each school. While he describes American composition as organic, Russian as dialectic, and German as intensive, the French school is characterized by quantitative composition. More precisely, much as for Epstein, it is the quantity of *movement* that is central to this school. According to Deleuze, the goal of this composition was to achieve maximum movement. Deleuze returns explicitly to the concept of *photogénie* and sees in it the difference between photography and the film image. In his understanding, *photogénie* occurs in an image that has been 'majored' by movement. Working with mathematical concepts, Deleuze specifies how the image is 'majored' by movement, how the maximum quantity of movement can be achieved:

> What seems to characterise the French school – in this sense Cartesian – is that it simultaneously raised the calculation beyond its empirical condition, to make it into a sort of 'algebra' – to use Gance's word – and made the result of this each time the maximum possible quantity of movement as a function of all the variables, or the form of that which goes beyond the organic.[11]

This claim requires some explanation: By 'calculation,' Deleuze means the metric relations between shots, the rhythm of montage. He defines the relevant factors, the 'variables' referenced in the above passage, as the composition of the visual field, the distribution of moving and fixed objects, the angle of framing, the lens, the shot duration as well as the tinting and the atmosphere of the shot. The objective is to achieve the maximum possible quantity of movement through the

---

sings to Gance in Jean Epstein: Abel Gance, in: Écrits sur le cinéma I, op. cit., pp. 173–177, an essay published in September 1927, five months after the premiere of NAPOLÉON, that does not mention the film.
9 Gilles Deleuze: Cinema 1. The Movement-Image, trans. by Hugh Tomlinson/Barbara Habberjam, Minneapolis 1986, p. 40. For the following pages, see ibid., pp. 40–48.
10 I am concerned here with the *movement formations* in the films that Deleuze includes in this category. A more extensive (film) historical contextualization can be found in Richard Abel's work, who suggests the term 'narrative avant-garde' for these films. See Richard Abel: French Cinema. The First Wave, 1915–1929, Princeton 1987, pp. 279–294.
11 Deleuze: The Movement-Image, op. cit., p. 44.

relationship between all these factors. Deleuze characterizes this maximum as *relative*. Maximum movement emerges from the *relation* between shots and cannot be seen as absolute. This relative maximum can be achieved both through very fast movement (Deleuze's example for this is Gance's LA ROUE, FR 1923) and through a decelerated, infinitely stretched movement (the example here is Epstein's LA CHUTE DE LA MAISON USHER).

This relative maximum must be distinguished, albeit not separated (the two aspects are "strictly inseparable and implied each other, presupposed each other from the beginning"[12]) from the *absolute* maximum quantity of movement. Here, the focus is no longer contained within the movement of an ensemble; instead, the movement is of a changing whole.[13] To clarify his definition of absolute movement, of which the first example he names is Gance's NAPOLÉON, Deleuze draws on Kant's mathematical sublime. He offers a precise summary of the concept:

> Kant said that as long as the numerical unit of measurement is homogeneous, one can easily go on to infinity, but only abstractly. On the other hand, when the unit of measurement is variable, the imagination quickly runs up against a limit: beyond a short sequence it is no longer capable of *comprehending* the set of magnitudes or movements that it successively apprehends. Nevertheless, Thought, the Soul, by virtue of a demand proper to it, must understand the set of movements in Nature or the Universe *as a whole*. This latter is what Kant calls the mathematical sublime: the imagination devotes itself to apprehending relative movements, and in so doing quickly exhausts its forces in converting the units of measurement. But thought must attain that which surpasses all imagination, that is, the set of movements as whole, absolute maximum of movement, absolute movement which is in itself identical to the incommensurable or the measureless, the gigantic, the immense: canopy of the heavens or limitless sea.[14]

In this passage, Deleuze names all the essential points of the Kantian sublime, yet they require a bit more explanation. Kant discusses the sublime in his *Critique of Judgement*, in which he is primarily concerned with the question of beauty, because for him the sublime – like the beautiful – is an aesthetic judgment.[15] He begins his examination of the sublime by comparing the beautiful

---

12 Ibid., p. 45.
13 On the whole, see ibid., pp. 8 ff.; on ensembles and their relation to the whole, see pp. 12 ff.
14 Ibid., p. 46. Deleuze briefly discusses the Kantian sublime in Gilles Deleuze: Kant's Critical Philosophy. The Doctrine of the Faculties, trans. by Hugh Tomlinson/Barbara Habberjam, London/New York 2008, pp. 42 ff.
15 In the following pages, I am not attempting to situate the sublime in Kant's philosophy (for an overview of this question, see Michaël Fœssel: Analytik des Erhabenen (§§ 23–29), in: Immanuel Kant. Kritik der Urteilskraft, ed. by Otfried Höffe, Berlin 2008, pp. 99–119, here especially pp. 99–102) or even to discuss it. My sole objective is to reconstruct and explicate the

with the sublime. Both are ends in themselves; both assume a reflective judgment, rather than one determined by logic or the senses. That is, the sublime is neither a question of the purely sensory relationship of human perception to an object (for example, 'the stone is warm' or 'in touching the stone I sense warmth'[16]), nor a logical deduction that happens a priori without sensory perception (for which mathematical problems are the classic example). Reflective judgment (on which the feeling of the sublime is based) occupies a liminal position between these two forms of judgment. It is based on perception and is thus a form of sensory judgment. Yet the reflective level still comes into play, and with it – as distinct from pure sensory judgment – the question of generality. To clarify this description with some examples: The judgment 'oysters are tasty' is a purely sensory judgment and therefore, according to Kant, has no claim to generality.[17] If, however, one describes something as beautiful or sublime, one makes a claim to generality, as *sensus communis*.[18] The pleasure in reflexive judgment is based neither in a sensation like that of enjoyment (as is the case in sensory judgment), nor in a particular notion such as the idea of goodness. Yet the beautiful and the sublime, or more precisely the pleasure they generate, cannot be disentangled from concepts, but must be understood in relation to them. It is rather a question of reconciling the capacity for representation (the imaginative faculty) with the capacity for understanding (beauty) or reason (sublimity) – although Kant relativizes this reconciliation with regard to the sublime.

Kant then moves on to enumerating the distinctions between the beautiful and the sublime. The categorization I mentioned, of the sublime in the realm of reason and not the realm of understanding, is based on the idea that the sublime – in contrast to the beautiful – can also be found in formless, limitless objects. When it comes to the sublime, pleasure is bound up in quantity, not quality. In addition –

---

themes addressed by Deleuze. Kant formulates his first, still pre-critical thoughts on the sublime in Immanuel Kant: Observations on the Feeling of the Beautiful and Sublime, in: Observations on the Feeling of the Beautiful and Sublime and Other Writings, ed./trans. by Patrick Frierson and Paul Guyer, Cambridge 2011, pp. 9–62. On the following, however, see Immanuel Kant: Critique of Judgement, trans. by J.H. Bernard, New York 1951, pp. 82 ff. (B 7 ff.).

16 An overview of the various forms of judgment in Kant's work can be found in Thomas Hilgers: Was ist ein ästhetisches Urteil?, in: Affekt und Urteil, ed. by id. et al., Paderborn 2015, pp. 23–48, here pp. 23 f. and pp. 35 ff. This is also the source for the reference to the warm stone.

17 I take the oyster example from Arendt; see Hannah Arendt: Lectures on Kant's Political Philosophy, ed. by Ronald Beiner, Chicago 1992, p. 66.

18 On the *sensus communis*, see Kant: Critique of Judgement, op. cit., pp. 74 ff. (B 64 ff.). In the case of the sublime, Kant limits the claim to generality and the role of the *sensus communis*, but does not withdraw them completely.

and importantly – desire emerges only indirectly in the feeling of sublimity. There is always an interplay between attraction and revulsion, between a temporary suspension of life force and an immediate intensification of life force. Building on this dynamic, Kant identifies the most important difference between the beautiful and the sublime as the fact that judgment of an object's beauty cannot be separated from the object's form. By contrast, an object is often referred to as sublime even if, indeed especially when, its form appears counter-purposive.[19] Even more so than with beauty, which cannot be linked exclusively to the object (it would be a great misunderstanding to characterize Kant's work as a normative study in art), the sublime is situated in the observing subject rather than the object. Kant explains this idea as follows:

> Thus the wide ocean, disturbed by the storm, cannot be called sublime. Its aspect is horrible; and the mind must be already filled with manifold ideas if it is to be determined by such an intuition to a feeling itself sublime, as it is incited to abandon sensibility and to busy itself with ideas that involve higher purposiveness.[20]

Kant describes the route from the object – for example the horrible ocean, or more in the realm of the mathematical sublime, the sky – to the feeling of the sublime in the subject. In order to evoke the feeling of the sublime, the object must possess either immensity (in the case of the mathematical sublime) or force (in the case of the dynamic sublime). These qualities enable the impression of sublimity to arise in the subject (Kant emphasizes repeatedly that the sublime is not a quality of an object, but lies "in us"[21]). This immensity must be absolute, independent of any comparison. One arrives at this impression through the aesthetic estimation of magnitude, which Kant differentiates from the mathematical estimation of magnitude. Mathematical, logical estimation compares the magnitude with other magnitudes and categorizes it accordingly, with the help of the intellect. This process does not evoke a feeling of the sublime, which can only occur in an aesthetic estimation of magnitude. The latter is an intuitive estimation that takes priority over mathematical estimation. In aesthetic estimation, and the resulting feeling of the sublime, perception and comprehension diverge from one another. We can no longer get an overview of that which we perceive. Imagination reaches its limits; the object appears infinite, overwhelms us, and exceeds our imaginative capacity. Yet according to Kant – and here desire comes into play – the impression of the sublime emerges precisely when we draw on ideas and reason (or more specifically,

---

19 See Kant: Critique of Judgement, op. cit., p. 83 (B 76).
20 Ibid., p. 84 (B 77).
21 Ibid., p. 83 (B 76).

we draw on "reason, the faculty of ideas"[22]) to resist the magnitude of the object, which at first overwhelms us, and to think beyond what is available to the senses. Ultimately, the feeling of the sublime is a form of superiority to that which (in imprecise speech) is called sublime. Although this counter-purposive object may overwhelm us at first, we can proceed to observe it; it pleases us in spite of itself, we do not have to submit to it. We can rise above that which exceeds every measure of the senses, and take a stand against it. Even more: In the pleasurable feeling of the sublime, our power of judgment is based on reason and its ideas – through the sublime, we are led away from sensory observation[23] and stimulated to think. At the same time, however, Kant refers to the failure of imagination. For Kant, ideas cannot be represented, only thought. The failure of imagination is a constitutive element of the sublime. Kant even speaks of a "conflict"[24] between imagination (which is overwhelmed) and reason, which produces the subjective purposiveness of *Gemütskräfte*.

This doubling of superiority and failure can also be found in the more precise definition of the pleasure experienced in the sublime, for this pleasure is similarly ambivalent and volatile: "[...] as the mind is not merely attracted by the object but is ever being alternately repelled, the satisfaction in the sublime does not so much involve a positive pleasure as admiration or respect, which rather deserves to be called negative pleasure."[25] Thus for Kant the first step, of being overwhelmed, is not only related to admiration [*Achtung*],[26] but also described as "astonishment that borders upon terror," "dread," and "holy awe."[27]

Kant connects the next step, the pleasure that follows the intervention of reason and the emerging feeling of the sublime, with a particular affect:[28] the

---

22 Ibid., p. 106 (B 112).
23 Kant also characterizes the biblical commandment banning images of God as sublime; see ibid., p. 115 (B 124).
24 Kant: Critique of Judgement, p. 97 (B 99). For Lyotard, this conflict is the most important characteristic of the sublime. Cf. Fœssel: Analytik des Erhabenen, op. cit., p. 118. On Lyotard, see Jean-François Lyotard: Lessons on the Analytic of the Sublime, trans. by Elizabeth Rottenberg, Stanford 1994, pp. 123 ff. When referring to the sublime, Deleuze also remarks that reason cannot be reconciled with it. Cf. Deleuze: Kant's Critical Philosophy, op. cit., pp. 51 f.
25 Kant: Critique of Judegment, op. cit., p. 83 (B 75 f.).
26 On the role of admiration [*Achtung*] in Kant's philosophy of the sublime, see Fœssel: Analytik des Erhabenen, op. cit., pp. 115 ff. A more detailed, less general discussion, more focused on the relationship between admiration and reason, is in Judith Mohrmann: Affekt und Revolution. Politisches Handeln nach Arendt und Kant, Frankfurt/Main/New York 2015, pp. 128 ff.
27 Kant: Critique of Judgement, op. cit., p. 109 (B 117).
28 In a brief explanation, Kant defines affect as "related [...] to feeling," "stormy and unpremeditated" (as distinct from passions), see ibid., p. 112 n14 (B 121); on this point, see also Jean-

affect of enthusiasm. He defines the latter as "the idea of the good conjoined with [strong, in original] affection,"[29] and asserts that no great deed could possibly take place without enthusiasm. Kant does qualify affect as problematic insofar as it is blind and opposed to human freedom. Yet on the other hand, he emphasizes, "aesthetically, enthusiasm is sublime, because it is a tension of forces produced by ideas, which give an impulse to the mind that operates far more powerfully and lastingly than the impulse arising from sensible representations."[30] Even beyond enthusiasm, for Kant, "every affection of the strenuous kind (viz. that excites the consciousness of our power to overcome every obstacle – *animi strenui*) is aesthetically sublime."[31] In the sublime too, the vanishing point of observing is acting, but observing does not necessarily lead to acting. In sum, Kant's sublime reveals a connection between aesthetic modes of observation, reason (i.e. ideas), and affect, particularly enthusiasm, which enables acting.[32]

Thus, Kant traces an arc between enthusiasm and revolution. For him, enthusiasm is the affect felt by spectators of the French Revolution, and only through their enthusiastic reception did the French Revolution become an event of world-historical significance. The event of the French Revolution itself is not the decisive element or the expression of human progress for Kant; instead, this understanding emerges only in the enthused public.[33] Thus in Kant's work, enthusiasm becomes a connector between revolution and the sublime.

Several parallels are immediately obvious between the Kantian concept of the sublime, film, Sobchack's theses on the historical epic, and Arendt's writings on revolution. With regard to film and cinema, on a basic level there is the coincidence that the Kantian sublime is a theory of the spectator. The sublime is first realized in the spectator who looks at something. Ultimately, Kant writes that the spectator of the sublime experiences a feeling of desire – and there is hardly any

---

Christophe Merle: Affekt, in: Kant-Lexikon, ed. by Marcus Willaschek et al., Berlin/Boston 2015, pp. 26 f.; with this definition, Kant's concept of affect can be reconciled with Deleuze's.
29 Kant: Critique of Judgement, op. cit., p. 112 (B 121).
30 Ibid., pp. 112 f. (B 121).
31 Ibid., p. 113 (B 122).
32 For Judith Mohrmann, enthusiasm and admiration (which I mentioned earlier) are not only the two central affects in the conceptualization of the sublime, but also two possible explanations within Kantian philosophy for how one moves from thinking to acting. According to Mohrmann, in both admiration and enthusiasm, there is a becoming-affective of reason. This development not only resolves the dichotomy between reason and affect, but also the division between thinking and acting; for in becoming affective, reason also becomes practical. See Mohrmann: Affekt und Revolution, op. cit., especially pp. 128 ff.
33 See Immanuel Kant: The Conflict of the Faculties, trans. by Mary J. Gregor, Lincoln 1992, pp. 153–157.

area of film theory that does not center the spectator's aesthetic pleasure.[34] Furthermore, the spectator in the theory of the sublime and the film spectator are arranged in a quite similar order: The spectator of the sublime must be at a safe distance from the object (if we are about to drown, the horrible ocean cannot awaken the feeling of the sublime). In the cinema, this safe distance is always already given by the radical separation between the onscreen world and the auditorium – this is another common theme in the history of film theory.[35] Leaving aside general film theory and turning to historical films on the premises introduced by

---

[34] Through Kant's emphasis on the oscillation between attraction and revulsion, and particularly his discussion of 'negative desire,' the concept of the sublime seems reconcilable with approaches to film theory that stress sadistic pleasure in the film spectator, and with approaches that stress masochistic pleasure. The paradigmatic work on sadistic pleasure is Laura Mulvey: Visual Pleasure and Narrative Cinema, in: Screen, 16 (3), 1975, pp. 6–18; on masochistic pleasure see Gaylyn Studlar: In the Realm of Pleasure. Von Sternberg, Dietrich, and the Masochistic Aesthetic, Urbana et al. 1988; and Kaja Silverman: Male Subjectivity at the Margins, New York/London 1992; for a work that distances itself from psychoanalytic theory and relates masochistic pleasure to the spectator's body, see Steven Shaviro: The Cinematic Body, Minneapolis 1993. On this point see also Sabine Nessel: Kino und Ereignis. Das Kinematografische zwischen Text und Körper, Berlin 2008, pp. 37 ff., and Thomas Morsch: Medienästhetik des Films. Verkörperte Wahrnehmung und ästhetische Erfahrung im Kino, Paderborn 2011, pp. 40 ff. Thomas Morsch himself strictly differentiates his thoughts on corporeality in filmic experience from the aesthetic sublime, since he understands the latter (a bit too narrowly in my opinion) as an aesthetic of mastery and reflection; see ibid., pp. 104 f., and Thomas Morsch: Filmische Erfahrung im Spannungsfeld zwischen Körper, Sinnlichkeit und Ästhetik, in: montage AV, 19 (1), 2010, pp. 55–77, here pp. 61 ff. On the basic structure of the film spectator's aesthetic pleasure in sentimental theater and melodrama, see Hermann Kappelhoff: Matrix der Gefühle. Das Kino, das Melodrama und das Theater der Empfindsamkeit, Berlin 2004, pp. 77 ff.

[35] Miriam Hansen draws attention to this consonance between the theory of the sublime and the cinema: See Miriam Hansen: Dinosaurier sehen und nicht gefressen werden. Kino als Ort der Gewalt-Wahrnehmung bei Benjamin, Kracauer und Spielberg, in: Auge und Affekt. Wahrnehmung und Interaktion, ed. by Gertrud Koch, Frankfurt/Main 1995, pp. 249–271, here pp. 252 f. For a foundational text on the dissociation of spaces in the cinema, see Albert Michotte van den Berck: Le caractère de 'réalité' des projections cinématographiques, in: Revue internationale de filmologie, 3/4, 1948, pp. 249–261, here p. 256; building on this text and addressing the question of fiction, Christian Metz opines on this point in Christian Metz: On the Impression of Reality in the Cinema, in: Film Language. A Semiotics of the Cinema, trans. by Michael Taylor, Chicago 1974, pp. 3–15, here pp. 9–11; Metz revisits this question in his psychoanalytic phase and observes it from this perspective in Christian Metz: The Imaginary Signifier. Psychoanalysis and Cinema, trans. by Celia Britton et al., Bloomington/Indianapolis 1982, pp. 61 ff. On the relationship between the cinema and the theory of the sublime, see also Jihae Chung: Das Erhabene im Kinofilm. Ästhetik eines gemischten Gefühls, Marburg 2016, pp. 101 ff.

Sobchack, it is worth noting that the historical films she discusses approach sublimity on the basis of their temporal scope alone: The spectator eventually overcomes what seems (phenomenologically speaking) to be an endless runtime. Arendt also addresses the sense of being overwhelmed in her book on revolution, when she writes that the French Revolution appeared to its participants, and especially to its spectators, as an irresistible movement. All these points are important when exploring the question of Abel Gance's NAPOLÉON as a revolution film.

Although it goes unaddressed by Deleuze, there is a possible objection to applying the Kantian sublime to cinema that merits discussion. In his theory of the sublime – as in his theory of beauty – Kant clearly focuses on nature. He gives two reasons for this approach: On the one hand, the sublime in art can only ever attempt to imitate the sublime in nature, and the former therefore orients itself toward the latter.[36] It is necessary either to expand Kant's concept of art or to discuss whether Kant maintained this understanding of art or perhaps expanded on it himself.[37] On the other hand, as an aesthetic judgment, the sublime is bound up with pure [zweckfreie] observation. A purposive observation of nature or human culture (which would result in a teleological judgment) can never evoke the feeling of the sublime, according to Kant. In works of art as well, both the form and the size are often determined by a human purpose, he claims.[38] Yet nature too can be observed based on purposive premises (for example when one sees the stars in the sky as points of orientation[39]). One must liberate oneself from this mode of observation with regard to nature as well. Finally, both the sublime in nature and the sublime in art depend on the manner of observation and not the object itself.[40] The difference is thus a matter of degree (in the case of art objects it is more difficult to observe them without the notion of ends) rather than principle.

To come back to Deleuze: how does he find his way from the Kantian sublime back to his philosophy of film and to NAPOLÉON? First, he identifies the sublime with the whole. He writes:

> This is the second aspect of time: it is no longer the interval as variable present [with this phrase, Deleuze alludes to the relative maximum of movement, H.B.], but the fundamentally

---

36 See Kant: Critique of Judgement, op. cit., p. 83 (B 76).
37 Jihae Chung argues that this is not the case, and that Kant postulates in his concept of genius that genius can exceed and manipulate [verarbeiten] nature. Cf. Chung: Das Erhabene im Kinofilm, op. cit., pp. 51 f.
38 See Kant: Critique of Judgement, op. cit., p. 91 (B 88 f.).
39 Ibid., p. 110 (B 118 f.).
40 On the potential for different ways of observing a work of art, see Jacques Rancière: Aesthetics as Politics, in: id.: Aesthetics and Its Discontents, trans. by Steve Corcoran, Cambridge/Malden 2009, pp. 19–44, here pp. 28 ff.

open whole as the immensity of future and past. It is no longer time as succession of movements, and of their units, but time as simultaneism and simultaneity (for simultaneity, no less than succession, belongs to time; it is time as whole). It is this ideal of simultaneism which has constantly haunted French cinema [...].⁴¹

According to Deleuze, one reaches this whole, the sublime, through the absolute quantity of movement that exceeds the imagination's capacity. And the example he selects to demonstrate this phenomenon is NAPOLÉON. Not only does this film reach the relative maximum of movement through forms of accelerated montage, Deleuze also finds concrete examples of the absolute quantity of movement. He sees this movement achieved first through Polyvision, the triple screen deployed by the film, and also through its superimpositions:

> By superimposing a very large number of superimpressions (sixteen at times), by introducing little temporal shifts between them, and by adding some and removing others, Gance is perfectly aware that the spectator will not see what is superimposed: the imagination is, as it were, surpassed, saturated, quickly reaching its limit. But Gance relies on an effect of all these superimpressions in the soul, on the constitution of a rhythm of added and subtracted values, which presents to the soul the idea of a whole as the feeling of measurelessness and immensity.⁴²

Accordingly, Deleuze summarizes: "In short, with Gance the French school invents a cinema of the sublime."⁴³ It is worth going into more depth on Deleuze's brief reference to superimpositions with concrete reference to the film, after

---

41 Deleuze: The Movement-Image, op. cit., p. 46. On this point, see also: "[...] the whole has become the simultaneous, the measureless, the immense, which reduces imagination to impotence and confronts it with its own limit, giving birth in the spirit to the pure thought of a quantity of absolute movement which expresses its whole history or change, its universe. This is exactly Kant's mathematical sublime" (ibid., p. 48). Deleuze repeats this identification of the sublime with the whole when he speaks of an absolute out-of-field [*hors-champ*] that refers all movement to a changing whole, which he in turn connects with time and which urges us to think the sublime; Gilles Deleuze: Cinema 2. The Time-Image, trans. by Hugh Tomlinson/Robert Galeta, London/New York 1989, p. 229. Yet it is important to consider that this characterization of the whole follows from the movement-image. When it comes to the time-image, his concept of the whole shifts. The whole is replaced by an interstice that inserts itself between the shots: It becomes a liminal space; see ibid., p. 173, p. 181, and especially pp. 204 ff.
42 Deleuze: The Movement-Image, op. cit., pp. 47 f. The significance of the spectator in Deleuze's cinema books is a subject of debate. According to Raymond Bellour, the spectator is minimally present in these books, leading him to rely on Deleuze's book on Leibniz in order to find a Deleuzian spectator-subject; see Raymond Bellour: Le dépli des émotions, in: Trafic, 43, 2002, pp. 93–128, here p. 99. Yet the above passage (while perhaps not generally applicable) and the reference to the Kantian sublime reveal that at least when it comes to NAPOLÉON, the spectator plays an immense role in Deleuze's theorization.
43 Deleuze: The Movement-Image, op. cit., p. 48.

84 — 4 Napoléon: The Sublime Conceptualization of Revolution

which I will connect this technique to the theory of revolution as well as the decisive question for Arendt: the form of movement in a revolution.

The Snowball Fight

Close analysis of individual scenes from Napoléon will benefit from a few introductory remarks on the film's affective flow, the macro-structure into which respective scenes fit. Not only through its great length, Napoléon sets out to overwhelm the spectator. Attention to the film's 'affective flow' reveals a number of scenes that approach the aesthetic of the sublime. The film begins with a prologue that shows an episode from Napoleon's childhood at a boarding school. Then the film deals with Napoleon and the French Revolution, as well as his military ascent. Next the film turns to the epoch of the Terror, the end of the great figures of the Revolution, Napoleon's second ascent, as well as the love story between Napoleon and Josephine de Beauharnais. The film ends with a staging of the campaign in Italy.

Both the prologue and the main part of the film can be described as a constant alternation between overwhelming scenes with excessive movement and relatively peaceful scenes. The prologue opens amidst an overwhelming scene that might be understood as paradigmatic, the snowball fight that will be analyzed in this section. A classroom scene follows that instills some calm, before the staging of a pillow fight divides the screen first into four, then nine different frames, each of which shows unrestrained movement figurations. This alternation between overwhelming movement and relative calm recurs throughout the rest of the film. Even the love story follows this scheme: Calmer segments alternate with the staging of a roaring party whose quality of movement hardly ranks behind the action scenes. And this constant alternation, this up and (relative) down, is also necessary for the overwhelming scenes to have their full effect. Only through variation and temporary relief, and against this background, does it become possible to experience the conflict between overwhelm and mastery required for the sublime.

Before diving into the snowball fight scene in the prologue, a few remarks on the film character of the roughly 11-year-old Napoleon (played by Vladimir Roudenko): Napoleon is immediately introduced as a General in the first shots of the film. In a snowball fight at his boarding school, he leads his team in an attempt to capture the flag of the opposing team, whose two leaders are introduced as his antagonists. In uniform and two-corned hat, the young Napoleon already appears in the mold of the commander he will become. Furthermore, over the course of the prologue, other characters repeatedly predict a great and eminent future for the young Napoleon in the intertitles. Roudenko's performance reinforces his closeness to the future Napoleon. His head is usually held aloft, evoking a sense of pride that is very unusual for a child. With blustery, emphatic gestures that have nothing childlike about them, and instead seem determined and imperious, he influences his environment and – even in everyday situations – quiets his schoolmates in the style of a general with military authority. This superimposition of the future Napoleon onto the younger version of the character becomes quite clear in a brief classroom scene at the beginning of the film. Here, the overlay consists not only in gesture and image composition, but also in the narrative content. The topic of instruction is the climate of islands. First the instructor draws an outline of Corsica on the chalkboard and characterizes it as a semi-civilized island. Napoleon starts, rises from his chair and stares into the distance with an insistent posture. As a consequence of this intervention from his pupil, the teacher characterizes Corsica as the most beautiful island in the world. When the instructor subsequently draws St. Helena on the board, Napoleon stops taking notes, his face darkens – and with it the entire screen, as the scene fades to black.[44]

This scene shows the second displacement that occurs in this film: Not only *is* Napoleon the French Revolution; the young Napoleon *is* already the old Napoleon. Drawing on the image types developed by Deleuze, many of the images of young Napoleon can be understood as crystal images, which unite several temporal layers within them.[45] Through a temporal substitution, the young Napoleon thus also embodies the French Revolution, or more precisely: He embodies what the film supposes the Revolution to be.

Through the interplay of cinematography,[46] *image composition, and performance, the scene analyzed in the following pages, which shows the young Napoleon as a general in a snowball fight, stages an image of the sublime as a movement that is at first overwhelming, and subsequently mastered.*[47]

---

44 The timecode of this scene is 00:12:28–00:14:37 (Disc 1).
45 Put briefly, the young Napoleon is already a walking crystal-image based on his gestures alone. Yet this element only speaks to one of the two forms of crystal-image. On the crystal-image and its two types, see Deleuze: The Time-Image, op. cit., pp. 68–97 and Oliver Fahle: Zeitspaltungen. Gedächtnis und Erinnerung bei Gilles Deleuze, in: montage AV, 11 (1), 2002, pp. 97–112. With regard to these images, Fahle writes of time as the simultaneity of the present of the present and the present of the future; cf. ibid., p. 104.
46 The formal category 'cinematography' also includes montage and the rhythm of montage.
47 The timecode of this scene is 00:06:27–00:10:37 (Disc 1).

In the scene's first expressive movement unit (EMU),[48] the cinematography, image composition, and constellation of characters are the dominant formal levels; they stage an image of a hectic battle that is at once clear and confusing. The use of long shots and medium close-ups create an overview of the action and the progression of the snowball fight. This sense of having an overview is reinforced by the relatively long shot duration (relative to this scene in the film). This overview, however, is disrupted when the camera crosses the 180-degree line in the middle of the EMU, impeding the viewer's sense of spatial orientation. Furthermore, the camera movement makes the visual field more dynamic, without creating a sense for the spectator of having lost his overview.

The beginning of the scene's second EMU is signaled through the use of multiple exposures on the level of image composition and steadily accelerating cuts. It begins with shot 33 and uses cinematography, image composition, and performance to create an overwhelming image that transforms into a sublime image, that is an image of constant, fragile mastery of something overwhelming. The EMU oscillates between overwhelming the spectator and images of mastery. For the second EMU not only presents more, faster, busier, and more confusing movements; through the massive use of superimpositions, it also multiples the layering of the image, and thus of movement. The main reason for the resulting impression of being overpowered, however, is the editing frequency, which progressively increases over the course of the EMU, climaxing with a shot change at every frame. From the spectator's perspective, this technique has the effect of a cross-fade, which contains both aspects of the sublime: the experience of being overwhelmed, as well as gaining mastery.

First EMU 00:00:00:00–00:00:58:15[49]
Through the interplay of cinematography, image composition, and constellation of characters, the EMU stages an image of the snowball fight that while hectic, still alternates between moments of clarity and confusion, and is presented as a

---

[48] On the concept of expressive movement, see Hermann Kappelhoff: Front Lines of Community. Hollywood Between War and Democracy, trans. by Daniel Hendrickson, Berlin/Boston 2018, pp. 115 ff.; as well as Hermann Kappelhoff/Jan-Hendrik Bakels: Das Zuschauergefühl. Möglichkeiten qualitativer Medienanalyse, in: zfm – Zeitschrift für Medienwissenschaft, 5 (2), 2011, pp. 78–95.

[49] The timecodes of the EMUs start with the beginning of the relevant scene and are accurate to the frame. When shots are labeled with a number in the scenic analyses, these numbers are always based on the scene in question; that is, the numbering of shots starts with the beginning of the given timecode.

mixture of hasty, backwards movements, alternating between stabilizing and destabilizing spatial orientation.

The EMU begins with a medium shot that shows Napoleon and his team behind a snow barricade. The barricade of the opposing team is also established in a long shot so that no confusion arises about their respective spatial locations. Similarly, the beginning of the first attack – in which Napoleon storms out of his barricade and rushes toward the enemy camp – is easy to follow. A pan to the left, following the quickly moving figure, already serves to make the scene more dynamic. This effect is further intensified by a jump cut during Napoleon's run, which results in a shift in focal length from an American shot to a long shot. This dynamization continues in the following shots with increasingly lively movement among the boys – that is, movement *within* the image – and also more and more hectic movement *of* the image: The camera shakes restlessly. The first significant challenge to spatial orientation comes after Napoleon has overcome his enemy and drags him back to his camp. The camera jumps its axis: While Napoleon at first drags the other boy to screen right, we see – after a shot showing Napoleon's older antagonist preparing to rush to his younger companion's aid – Napoleon dragging the figure to screen left. The fistfight that follows between Napoleon and his opponents is once again characterized by quite quick and hectic movements from the combatants, who are shown in closeup and American shots, and through the camera movement that seeks to follow them. After the end of the struggle (Napoleon defeats both his opponents one after the other, which is additionally dynamized through a jump cut), the quality of movement calms down again, and the spatial situation becomes clearer. In a long shot, Napoleon runs back to his team and his camp, and at the end of the EMU both of his opponents sit on the ground, two dark figures surrounded by nothing other than white snow.

Second EMU: 00:00:58:16–00:04:01:24
In the interplay of cinematography, image composition, and performance, the EMU stages the sublime and sublimity in the form of oscillation between an overwhelming image and a mastered one.

The second EMU occupies the longer and more important part of the scene. It begins – and here it already becomes clear that from now on, the dynamics will reach an entirely new level – with a quick and jerky tracking shot to the left, across countless boys who break forth from their barricade, moving on a diagonal to the camera's trajectory. They stumble at first, then run more and more confidently. Next, Napoleon appears with the scullion, who is clearly situated apart from the playfield, and whom Napoleon quickly leaves. The protagonist, who with this shot has also been established as off the field, will be further removed from the events on the 'battlefield' over the course of the EMU without ever being completely separated from it. He is spatially separated, yet remains connected with the events of the snowball fight. This phenomenon occurs at first through superimpositions. Just a few shots into this second EMU, a static long shot shows a background with a slightly high angle that suggests an overview. This impression, however, is contradicted by the extremely disorganized and bustling movement in the shot. The image field is dominated by the many figures who appear in the image and throw snowballs at each other. Some stand on or in front of the barricade, which is centered in the image in terms of both depth and height. Other figures stand behind the barricade. Some boys throw snowballs, others fall down: There is so much movement in the image that the viewer cannot follow individual figures. In the shot foreground, there is a superimposition of Napoleon's face: He looks slightly to the right, so his face appears in semi-profile. He gets a faceful of snow, which he quickly shakes off. He blinks frequently. The principle of this image composition (in the background the confusion and chaos of the snowball fight and in the foreground, withdrawn as a superimposition, Napoleon's head) will recur repeatedly over the course of this EMU.

A second visual strategy that removes Napoleon from the chaos of the battle consists in showing him massively multiplied in a liminal space. These shots work with a countless number of exposures of Napoleon.[50] Some of these exposures show only his face; in others he can be seen from the waist up. The exposures appear to be located in a dark space that has no recognizable connection to the diegetic space; it is a kind of non-space. Almost the entire surface of the image is filled with exposures of Napoleon, which flicker like ghosts. The movements of all these Napoleons are quite reduced – that is, there are no sweeping movements to be seen, and most motion only involves his head and a snowball-throwing arm, which can be identified, but not assigned to a specific, or even to his, body. Napoleon is presented not as a steadfast participant amidst the tumult, but as the director of the battle. At the beginning of the EMU there is a constant alternation between shots that overlay Napoleon's face over the action of the snowball fight, and the mass exposures that stage Napoleon in his own space (shots 32–54).

---

50 Deleuze is likely thinking of these shots when he writes of the unimaginable number of multiple exposures in NAPOLÉON, which he relates to the absolute quality of movement, the sublime, simultaneity, and to time as the whole.

After a fast and quite immersive tracking shot forward through tussling youths into the depth of the image, a third variant emerges that removes Napoleon from the action of the snowball fight and – most important in this context – from the movements of the battle while simultaneously situating him in relation to them. Close-ups show Napoleon's face from chin to brow. At the very beginning of the first close-up, he shakes his head vehemently, then looks to the left and appears in profile; he is lit from behind, generating a bright iris around his profile. The edges of the frame (particularly the sides) are shrouded by a silvery grey matte so that only a narrow oval opening remains in the center of the image. The image composition is thus extremely concentrated on Napoleon's face. This appears again in the dark liminal space, or non-space.

Shots of this type, in which Napoleon looks around and continues to speak (that is, to give commands), subsequently alternate with shots showing scenes from the snowball fight. Now the editing frequency comes to absolutely dominate the EMU and the scene: It is obvious, even upon first viewing the scene, that the frequency steadily increases.[51] Yet it is not only the editing frequency that increases; the movement of the shots showing the snowball fight become more and more confusing. It quickly becomes impossible to recognize any concrete figures or objects with the naked eye. Due to the extremely quick shots and the fast, vehement pans, the viewer can make out only grey and white surfaces. The acceleration montage continues to the point where the shot changes with every frame. The result of this technique is the perception of superimposition: Napoleon's face observes events on the battlefield that appear to the spectator only as an abstract, visual roar. He gives orders, takes control: He has mastered the movement that overwhelms the spectator.

After this mixture of chaos and overwhelm (the battle) and the staging of an overview (Napoleon's face), after the climax of the acceleration montage, there comes a shot in which Napoleon appears from the chest up in the left half of the

---

51 Furthermore, a frame-by-frame analysis shows that the close-ups of Napoleon's face in particular were precisely counted and follow a logic of intensification and reduction: They are at first twenty (occasionally nineteen) frames long (this goes for the first twenty shots of this kind); after three further shots with a length of sixteen, seventeen, and nineteen frames, they drop to a duration of nine frames (here too there are a few exceptions), before they can only be seen for six frames (five times in a row). Then they have a length of five frames (four times in a row) and are then reduced to four frames (for six shots). For four further shots, they are only three frames long. After the shift to a length of two frames, at the climax of the acceleration montage, they can be seen only one frame at a time. The shots showing the battle also constantly decrease in length. There too, regularity and repetition can be identified in the shot length. These, however, are not quite as regular and consecutive as the closeups of Napoleon's face. Regarding this acceleration montage, see shots 60–224.

frame. He has crossed his arms over his chest. His body is turned to the right of the camera, but because he has turned his head to the left, he looks toward the camera. This shot has a noticeably longer duration (almost six seconds), signaling that the acceleration montage is over and the battle has been won. The dynamic of the acceleration montage, however, continues in the next shots through quick tracking shots on the numerous running children. Only as Napoleon plants his flag in the snow does the camera come to rest, and the EMU ends with relatively long shots with relatively clear visual composition and spatial orientation, which come as a relief after the excessive movement of the earlier sequence.

Looking at this analysis in the context of Deleuze's theory of film, with regard to film's relation to the Kantian sublime, it becomes clear that the viewer's imaginative capacity is overwhelmed not only by the multiple exposures, but also by the movements that can no longer be synthesized into a unified entity. More precisely: This scene also divides the sublime. This division can be seen in the second EMU, in the alternation between the abstract visual roar of the battle and the close-ups of Napoleon's face as he takes command. Here, the spectator's perception takes on the role held by imagination in Kant: to be overwhelmed. Napoleon takes over the role of reason: to maintain a view of the whole and to synthesize the overwhelming movement. Thus, what could be described as sublime in this scene has nothing to do with the psychology of the characters. It would simply be false to claim that the character of Napoleon experiences the sublime. The character is never overwhelmed, neither in his perception nor his imagination. Yet the sublime is also not entirely contained in the images of the battle. The wild camera movements with which the battle is staged generate a sense of being overpowered and overwhelmed – it becomes impossible to follow the plot. Yet it would also be a misinterpretation of the Kantian sublime to search for it *within* the images. For the Kantian sublime is precisely that which lies beyond the image and representation, and which compels us to think this beyond. The question is now what sort of thinking this scene inspires.

To this end, it is helpful to revisit the way in which Napoleon is staged in the scene's second EMU: through affection-images. Deleuze defines affect as "a motor tendency on a sensitive nerve"[52] or "'a kind of motor tendency on a sensible nerve', that is, a motor effort on an immobilised receptive plate."[53] This definition becomes a bit more concrete when one considers that for Deleuze the close-up of a face is the paradigmatic affection-image. Here, too, are the sensitive nerve and

---

52 Deleuze: The Movement-Image, op. cit., p. 87.
53 Ibid., p. 66. Here Deleuze cites Henri Bergson: Matter and Memory, trans. by Nancy Margaret Paul and W. Scott Palmer, Mineola, NY 2004, pp. 61–63.

the motor tendency or motor effort (the facial expression). Importantly for the context of the scene analyzed here, for Deleuze the affection-image stands between perception and action. That is, the affection-image is characterized by an interruption of movement, an interruption of the plot.[54] Affect and the affection-image are what occurs between perception and action, forming an interval and suspending motion.[55] This suspension of motion is intensified by the separation from diegetic space that results from a close-up, as Deleuze underscores with reference to Béla Balázs.[56] The close-ups of Napoleon's face fulfill precisely this function that Deleuze assigns to affection-images: Through their neutral background and the silvery-grey matte, they are severed even more markedly from the diegetic space of the snowball fight. It is thus filmic staging qua affection-images that lets Napoleon appear to be removed from the excessive movement taking place on the battlefield and to be positioned as a general.

Connecting the above analysis with Arendt's theses on the French Revolution and its cardinal problem, that in the eyes of its spectators it appeared to be an irresistible, uncontrollable movement, the relationship to the film seems obvious. When it comes to describing the problem, the film is much in line with Arendt. This scene as well is about mastering and controlling an irresistible movement that sweeps up everything in its path and overpowers individual people. The answer that the film gives to this problem is that Napoleon is capable of it: Napoleon can master and control the overwhelming motion.[57]

In the sections that follow, I will first undertake a closer examination of how Deleuze defines the relationship between film and thinking, in order to then show how this film (also in later scenes) stages Napoleon as the master of the irresistible and intoxicating movement formation of the Revolution. And even though the contemporary reception after the premiere did not include accusations of

---

[54] Deleuze would speak of the interruption of the sensory-motor system.
[55] To round out the definition of affection, it is worth noting that affect refers to a quality that cannot be equated with individual, psychological emotion. Affection is much more impersonal; it does not belong to the individual subject, but rather places the subject into relation with the world (on affect and the affection-image, see Deleuze: The Movement-Image, op. cit., pp. 87–122).
[56] The text to which Deleuze refers is *Der Geist des Films* [*The Spirit of Film*], available in English translation in Béla Balázs: Béla Balázs. Early Film Theory. Visible Man and the Spirit of Film, ed. by Erica Carter, trans. by Rodney Livingstone. New York/Oxford 2010, pp. 91–234.
[57] There is one more detail that connects the snowball fight, as it is staged by the film, with the French Revolution as it is theorized by Arendt and Kant: The snowball fight obtains its significance only from the commentary of its observers, the scullion, and the head of the boarding school who watches from a safe position behind a glass window, both of whom are edited (in close-up!) into the snowball fight.

fascist tendencies in the film, and though this reproach itself arouses the suspicion of a retrospective, teleological historiography that fails to grasp the film, the speculation still exists that the film is devoted to a fascistic *Führer* cult.[58] It will therefore be important to examine how the film relates to the character Napoleon and why this relationship does not signify a turn toward fascism. On the basis of the scenic analyses above, however, it should already be clear how mistaken it would be to accuse the film of having a fascist *aesthetic*.[59] The excessive movements that overwhelm and overpower the spectator's perception are directly opposed to the aesthetic associated with Leni Riefenstahl's TRIUMPH DES WILLENS (DE 1935), for instance, where strictly organized military troops march in file past the camera. The geometric order of Riefenstahl's gaze – which adopts and suggests Hitler's gaze[60] and that ultimately does not overwhelm the imagination, but rather confirms it which means that this staging of the gaze does not result in an aesthetic of the sublime in the strict sense (or that it reduces the aesthetic of the sublime to the aspect of mastery) – stands in stark contrast to the disorder, chaos, and overwhelming of the spectator's perception in Gance's film. The political value of an aesthetic articulation of the sublime is thoroughly determined by *how* it is staged and cannot be reduced to the context of the film.[61]

---

[58] On the lack of accusations of fascism by contemporary audiences of the film, see Brownlow: Napoleon, op. cit., pp. 159 f.; according to Brownlow the film was not even popular among fascists. Wolfgang Koller, however, found a positive review in the National Socialist publication *Angriff*; cf. Wolfgang Koller: Historienkino im Zeitalter der Weltkriege. Die Revolutions- und Napoleonischen Kriege in der europäischen Erinnerung, Paderborn 2013, pp. 111 f. Critiquing a retrospective, teleological approach to film history is one of the basic principles of New Film History; cf. Thomas Elsaesser: Filmgeschichte und frühes Kino. Archäologie eines Medienwandels, Munich 2002, p. 21.

[59] For example, see Peter Pappas: The Superimposition of Vision. 'Napoleon' and the Meaning of Fascist Art, in: Cinéaste, 11 (2), 1981, pp. 4–13. Pappas's argumentation falters, however, on two of his premises: First, he defines fascist art as muddled (a claim that is difficult to reconcile with Riefenstahl's films or Speer's architecture); second, for him fascism is the political expression of madness, and therefore the definitional opposite of the Enlightenment. In this way, he lags behind the basic premise of Adorno and Horkheimer's *Dialectic of Enlightenment*; cf. Theodor W. Adorno/Max Horkheimer: Dialectic of Enlightenment, trans. by John Cumming, London/New York 1997.

[60] On the translation of Hitler's position into a spectatorial illusion in Riefenstahl's work, see Kappelhoff: Front Lines of Community, op. cit., p. 55.

[61] Jihae Chung argues that in the case of TRIUMPH DES WILLENS, the film's historical context renders its sublime aesthetic unpleasant for a contemporary viewer; see Chung: Das Erhabene im Kinofilm, op. cit., p. 233. By contrast, Kappelhoff argues that the political content of a film can already be inferred from its formal staging; for a contrast between a democratic and a fascist propaganda film see Kappelhoff: Front Lines of Community, op. cit., pp. 48 ff. In the case of NAPOLÉON, looking at the film's context, understood as an expression of the director's

A political discussion of the sublime, however, cannot be neglected: For Kant, an anti-egalitarian moment is inherent in the sublime. In our judgment of the sublime, he writes, "[...] we cannot promise ourselves so easily the accordance of others"[62] as we can with the beautiful, for which we (correctly, in Kant's view) demand the agreement of all.[63] In order to pass judgment on the sublime, Kant claims, it is necessary to be cultured. To the "uneducated man," the same object would simply be terrifying: "So the good, and indeed intelligent, Savoyard peasant [...] unhesitatingly called all lovers of snow-mountains fools."[64] The sublime is a mark of distinction: It distinguishes people as participants in culture. Accordingly, as Fœssel puts it: "There is no *sensus communis* of the sublime."[65] Yet this does not mean that the sublime is unreachable for some; in principle, anyone could experience it:

> But although the judgement upon the sublime in nature needs culture (more than the judgement upon the beautiful), it is not therefore primarily produced by culture and introduced in a merely conventional way into society. Rather has it its root in human nature, even in that which, alike with common understanding, we can impute to and expect of everyone, viz. in the tendency to the feeling for (practical) ideas, i.e. to what is moral.[66]

According to Kant, the *capacity* for the sublime is thus universal, but its realization is determined by culture. That means that even the Savoyard peasant *could* experience the feeling of the sublime, since he also has the capacity for moral feeling. Seen from this angle, the sublime reveals who *is allowed to participate* in culture: In other words, the Savoyard peasant is not an uncultured idiot, but rather one who is excluded from culture. Who is capable of experiencing the sublime is thus not a natural constant, but historically contingent.[67] With that,

---

point of view, complicates attempts not to let the film be subsumed by fascism; after all, Gance dedicated the original version of his 1941 film VÉNUS AVEUGLE (FR 1941) to Philippe Pétain. Cf. Jean-Pierre Jeancolas: Abel Gance entre Napoléon et Philippe Pétain, in: Positif, 256 (6), 1982, pp. 17–21, here p. 21.
62 Kant: Critique of Judgement, op. cit., p. 104 (B 110).
63 Cf. ibid., p. 48 ff. (B 21 ff.) and pp. 74 ff. (B 64 ff.).
64 Both quotations are on ibid., p. 105 (B 111).
65 Fœssel: Analytik des Erhabenen, op. cit., p. 118 [Translator's note: my translation].
66 Kant: Critique of Judgement, op. cit., p. 105 (B 111 f.).
67 Seen from this perspective, the sublime can be related to the *sensus communis* after all – if one understands it in Arendt's interpretation rather than Fœssel's. For Arendt, the *sensus communis* is not a natural constant, but always arises from a particular context. Cf. especially the translator Ursula Ludz's note in Hannah Arendt: Das Urteilen. Texte zu Kants Politischer Philosophie. Dritter Teil zu 'Vom Leben des Geistes', ed. by Ronald Beiner, Munich/Zurich 2012, p. 237, footnote 155. Kappelhoff theorizes the Arendtian notion of *sensus communis* in Kappelhoff: Front Lines of Community, op. cit., pp. 344 ff.

the sublime loses its necessarily anti-egalitarian character. The sublime instead becomes a locus of negotiation for who counts as a full member of society. Arendt's theory of revolution and Kant's theory of the sublime share an interest in the mastery of an overwhelming situation; here, a second correspondence between the sublime and revolution arises. A revolution in the Arendtian sense is always focused on the *new* foundation of freedom, premised on a universally accepted gesture; the sublime, too, is characterized by the fact that it is both historically contingent and makes a claim to universality.[68] Both revolution and the sublime ask who belongs to the circle of those participating in freedom or culture. A successful revolution leads to an expansion of this circle – and that is the central demand for a sublime aesthetic of revolution.

4.2 The Thinking of Images and Deleuze

How to Think With Images?

In *Cinema 2: The Time-Image*, Deleuze returns to his theorization of the sublime in the context of the relationship between cinema and thought; in doing so, he also returns to Abel Gance's film about revolution.[69] With reference to the first film theorists, Eisenstein and Epstein, he goes back to the argument already introduced in relation to Epstein, that in the cinematic image movement is an immediate given, and this movement is automatic and inherent to the image. Movement does not require an intellect that animates it, nor is it dependent on any moving body or object. The conclusion that Deleuze draws from this premise is immense in scope: "It is only when movement becomes automatic that the artistic essence of the image is realized: *producing a shock to thought, communicating vibrations to the cortex, touching the nervous and cerebral system directly.*"[70] The automatic movement of cinematic images confronts the spectator with a shock that forces thought: a cognitive shock.[71] The shock of cinematic images

---

[68] On the thesis that revolution brough historical contingency into the realm of the political, see the second chapter of this book. On the universal claim of revolution, see: "[...] both [the French and the American Revolution, H.B.] prided themselves on having ushered in a new era for all mankind, on being events which would concern all men qua men, no matter where they lived, what their circumstances were, or what nationality they possessed" (Arendt: On Revolution, op. cit., p. 53).

[69] On the following, see Deleuze: The Time-Image, op. cit., pp. 156 ff.

[70] Ibid., p. 156.

[71] The argument that thought originates in an external shock or compulsion (and not from the subject's interior, as conceived by Descartes) is also central to the conclusion of Part I of

unleashed the capacity[72] for thought in the masses of the cinema public. Taking the argument a step further, Deleuze brings this shock that forces thought – which lies not in the power of the represented content, but solely in the composition and movement of the image – into conversation with the sublime:

> Something was in play, in a *sublime* conception of cinema. In fact, what constitutes the sublime is that the imagination suffers a shock which pushes it to the limit and forces thought to think the whole as intellectual totality which goes beyond the imagination.[73]

In order to clarify and illustrate the relationship between film images and thought, which, as is clear from the passage cited above, is expressed through a general claim about the sublime, Deleuze analyzes three instances from Eisenstein's writings on film. He postulates that they apply to the classical cinema in general, the cinema of the movement-image. The first moment goes from the percept to the concept. This movement ultimately describes Eisenstein's notion of intellectual montage. Intellectual montage occupies the highest level in Eisenstein's theory of montage. Intellectual montage builds on metric, rhythmic, tonal, and overtonal montage.[74] A metric montage is determined by the absolute duration of the shots, so precise as to be measurable by a stopwatch. In this form, tension is created by accelerating the elements of the montage. This category of montage, however, is broadly dominant in character, and deploys an unrefined motor effect that sets the spectator in motion only externally. In rhythmic montage, Eisenstein's second category, movement *within* the image is significant. Here, the content of the shot becomes important as well. How much and what movement is in the shot?

Deleuze's study on Proust (cf. Gilles Deleuze: Proust and Signs. The Complete Text, trans. by Richard Howard, Minneapolis 2000, pp. 94–102; on Descartes, see René Descartes: Meditations on First Philosophy. With Selections from the Objections and Replies, trans. by Michael Moriarty, Oxford 2008, p. 13 ff.).

72 Deleuze cites Heidegger to distinguish the capacity for thought from the possibility of thought: "Man can think in the sense that he has the possibility to do so. This possibility alone, however, is no guarantee to us that we are capable of thinking" (Heidegger: What is Thinking?, qtd. in Deleuze: The Time-Image, op. cit., p. 156).

73 Ibid., p. 157. See also: "The cinematographic image must have a shock effect on thought, and force thought to think itself as much as thinking the whole. This is the very definition of the sublime" (ibid., p. 158).

74 On the following see Sergei Eisenstein: Methods of Montage, in: Film Form. Essays in Film Theory, trans. by Jay Leyda, San Diego/New York 1977, pp. 72–83. My brief reconstruction of Eisenstein's categories of montage is already much more detailed than Deleuze's extremely concise summary. For the levels of montage up to intellectual montage, which are a central point of reference for the concept of expressive movement, and how they relate to cinematic thinking, cf. Hermann Kappelhoff: The Politics and Poetics of Cinematic Realism, trans. by Daniel Hendrickson, New York 2015, pp. 30 ff.

Eisenstein describes the effect of this montage type as "primitive-emotive."⁷⁵ The spectator no longer experiences movement alone, but also emotion; yet the emotion is still primitive, not sophisticated. In the third montage category, tonal montage, Eisenstein expands on the concept of movement. Here, he identifies all forms of fluctuation and intensity that emerge from a montage. These include e.g., changes to brightness, depth of field, or shapes that can be seen in the image – are the elements angular or curved? All these elements, however, are just as rule-bound as metric montage, and by no means subjective. The next level of montage is the overtonal montage, in which not only the dominant formal level of a shot is relevant but also the secondary stimuli. While the form of a tonal montage is guided by its dominant, the overtone montage relies on "the collective calculation of all the piece's [tonal, H.B.] appeals."⁷⁶ These emerge only in the dynamics of a cinematic *process*. The overtone exists only in time, in the fourth dimension; it is a temporal phenomenon and cannot be identified in a single, arrested image. Thus, the overtone montage is first realized in the spectator's perception – Eisenstein characterizes this phenomenon as a dialectical leap and a transformation of quantity into quality.⁷⁷ Intellectual montage builds on this foundation. Whereas the first four levels of montage center on formal conflicts that are supposed to have an emotional impact on the spectator, here the focus is on conflict in intellectual effects and overtones. Intellectual montage centers the movement of thought: The spectators are supposed to be rationally persuaded.⁷⁸ A problematic element of this form of montage, however, is that here Eisenstein reduces the cinematic images to their represented content.⁷⁹

The second instance highlighted by Deleuze of thinking with images is particularly important for this book, since he once again uses NAPOLÉON as an example to demonstrate his point. This second instance cannot be separated from the first, yet does not directly follow from it; instead, it can be understood as a correlate, as Deleuze insists. It traces an inverted path from the concept to affect and from thought to the image. Deleuze characterizes this movement as follows:

---

75 Eisenstein: Methods of Montage, op. cit., p. 80.
76 Ibid., p. 78.
77 On the dialectical leap and the transformation of quantity into quality, see Friedrich Engels: Herr Eugen Dühring's Revolution in Science, in: Karl Marx/id.: MECW 25. Engels, London 2010, pp. 5–309, here pp. 110 ff.
78 As an example, Eisenstein offers a scene from his film OCTOBER (SU 1928) in which the expression "for God and fatherland" is followed by a series of images of various deities, ending with a wooden idol. The montage is supposed to demonstrate how empty this expression is.
79 On this critique of intellectual montage, see Kappelhoff: The Politics and Poetics of Cinematic Realism, op. cit., pp. 26 f., and Balázs: Early Film Theory, op. cit., pp. 149–151.

In this second moment, we no longer go from the movement-image to the clear thinking of the whole that it expresses; we go from a thinking of the whole which is presupposed and obscure to the agitated, mixed-up images which express it. The whole is no longer the logos which unifies the parts, but the drunkenness, the pathos which bathes them and spreads out in them.[80]

This thinking in images, which according to Deleuze embodies an unconscious concept and thereby shocks the spectator, manifests in rhetorical figures such as metaphor. Here, too, Deleuze acknowledges the importance of Epstein and his exploration of the possibilities for staging metaphor in film.[81] It is thus no wonder that Deleuze discusses Abel Gance at this point, given that Epstein considered Gance a pioneer of the relationship between film and metaphor: "Mr. Abel Gance was the first to create visual metaphors."[82] Somewhat concealed in an endnote, Deleuze remarks: "Gance and L'Herbier lay equal claim to a metaphorical montage: the scene of the Convention and the storm, in *Napoleon*, the scene of the Stock Market and the sky, in *Money*."[83] Before moving into an analysis of the scene mentioned by Deleuze, I want to take a closer look at the relationship between cinema and metaphor: How do films stage metaphors, and how do films think with metaphors? Deleuze's own explications on metaphor are vague and obscure. Moreover, they are quite focused on the represented content. A deeper explanation of the relationship between film and metaphor can be found in Kappelhoff and Müller.[84]

While metaphors are primarily understood as linguistic events, they can also easily be recognized in forms of visual language as boundary-crossing phenomena. Following this approach, Cornelia Müller and Hermann Kappelhoff have developed a method for analyzing metaphors in film. The starting point of their work is George Lakoff and Mark Johnson's definition of metaphor as "understanding and experiencing one kind of thing in terms of another."[85] In their model, Kappelhoff and Müller modify this definition in a few ways: One of their central assumptions is that the basic understanding of metaphor can be situated on an affective and corporeal level. Accordingly, comprehension is not situated on the same level as

---

[80] Deleuze: The Time-Image, op. cit., p. 159.
[81] Cf. ibid., p. 308, endnote 6.
[82] Jean Epstein: Cinema and Modern Literature, trans. by Audrey Brunetaux/Sarah Keller, in: Jean Epstein. Critical Essays and New Translations, ed. by Sarah Keller/Jason N. Paul, Amsterdam 2012, pp. 271–276, here p. 274.
[83] Deleuze: The Time-Image, op. cit., p. 308, endnote 8.
[84] See Hermann Kappelhoff/Cornelia Müller: Embodied Meaning Construction. Multimodal Metaphor and Expressive Movement in Speech, Gesture, and in Feature Film, in: Metaphor and the Social World, 2 (1), 2011, pp. 121–153.
[85] Qtd. in ibid., p. 122.

affective and corporeal experience; instead, experience is the basis for comprehension. Furthermore, they assume that metaphors can be realized through multiple modalities. They do not limit themselves to metaphors that are articulated only through speech – rather, they give equal weight to the interplay between e.g., speech and gesture, as would occur in interpersonal communication.

With regard to film, the construction of metaphor is even more complex, since it is created 'multimodally,' i.e., under the influence of all formal levels. Not only the lines, verbal expressions, and gestures of the actors, but also camera movement, editing rhythm, music, and other auditory elements as well as the synesthetic effects created for the spectator through the combination of these formal levels can contribute to metaphors' construction. This is also the reason why it makes sense to draw on film in order to engage with metaphor: If the comprehension of metaphors is grounded in embodied, affective experience, film is an effective medium for staging them. That is to say, insofar as metaphors are necessary to understand the significance of revolutions – I have already noted the foundational importance of metaphor in the theory of revolution – films are very well suited to show us what revolutions are or could be, and how they can be understood. In so doing – according to Kappelhoff and Müller – films do not limit themselves to staging familiar metaphors. Just as every linguistic metaphor is only a metaphor in a given context,[86] each film forms the dynamic context for the metaphors that exist within it.

The third moment, for which Deleuze once again relies heavily on Eisenstein, also cannot be separated from the other two, but is contained within them. Deleuze defines this third moment as "action-thought," which describes "*the relation between man and the world*, between man and nature, the sensory-motor unity."[87] With reference to Bazin, Deleuze defines nature as the object of the cinema, meaning cinema has a special capacity to show man's reaction to nature and his unity with it.[88] Thus cinema endows humanity and nature with unity; Deleuze extends this unity to encompass the individual and the masses. The masses become the collective subject of the cinema and the cinema becomes an art of the masses. The cinema does not address individuals (particular people), but rather an individuated mass, a mass that becomes "dividual," i.e., indivisible, yet not homogeneous.[89] Deleuze summarizes the three levels as follows:

---

86 Cf. Gerhard Kurz: Metapher, Allegorie, Symbol, Göttingen 2004, p. 14.
87 Deleuze: The Time-Image, op. cit., p. 161.
88 Deleuze refers here to André Bazin: Theater and Cinema, in: id.: What is Cinema?, op. cit., pp. 76–124, here pp. 100–107.
89 Cf. Deleuze: The Time-Image, op. cit., pp. 161 f. For a brief explanation of the Dividual, which is defined by the fact that it cannot be divided without changing its qualities, see Deleuze: The Movement-Image, op. cit., pp. 14 f.

It is indeed true that the three relationships between cinema and thought are encountered together everywhere in the cinema of the movement-image: *the relationship with a whole which can only be thought in a higher awareness, the relationship with a thought which can only be shaped in the subconscious unfolding of images, the sensory-motor relationship between world and man, nature and thought.* Critical thought, hypnotic thought, action-thought.[90]

All three levels pertain to the relationship between cinema and thought and can be productive for exploring how films think revolution. The second level, of course, is particularly interesting, since as already noted, Deleuze names Abel Gance's NAPOLÉON as an explicit example of metaphor. Yet here too, the question arises of how to understand Deleuze's observation concretely and analytically, with which staging strategies it operates and what effects result therefrom.

Revolution as Storm

The scene is placed toward the end of the film's first half.[91] It shows Napoleon after he has stolen the French flag from Corsica; he flees his pursuers in a boat on the open sea and finds himself in a storm.[92] By cross-cutting with the tumultuous scenes in the National Convention, where the great men of the French Revolution – Marat, Danton, and Robespierre – face increasing difficulties, the film draws a parallel between the two events. *In the interplay between camera movement,*

---

90 Deleuze: The Time-Image, op. cit., p. 163.
91 The timecode is 01:05:00–01:12:03 (Disc 1).
92 He uses the purloined Tricolor as a sail. He has taken the flag from the Corsican regime with the explanation they would be unworthy of it, which doubtlessly exaggerates its importance as a nationalist symbol. Yet through Napoleon's use of the flag as a sail, the film can be distinguished from fascist films – and from the work of Eisenstein. Compare a scene from Veit Harlan's historical film DER GROSSE KÖNIG (DE 1942) about Friedrich II, which is easy to recognize as fascist propaganda: A wounded soldier needs a doctor, and there is a search for bandages. The protagonist Louise wants to use the Prussian flag for this purpose, and is immediately rebuked by the surrounding soldiers that the flag must never be used as a bandage. Instead, they remove bandages from a dead soldier (timecode: 00:10:26–00:11:23). In Eisenstein's THE GENERAL LINE (SU 1929) the following scene occurs: A newly purchased tractor breaks down and is leaking fluid. The driver wants to fix the problem by stopping the leak with a flag; Marfa, the film's protagonist, forbids this and instead tears off a piece of her skirt, which leaves part of her underskirt visible – a moment of subtle eroticism in the film (timecode: 01:44:48–01:50:33). For both Harlan and Eisenstein, the flag has a cult value that prohibits any practical use; in NAPOLÉON, by contrast, the flag can be used pragmatically beyond its value as a cult object. In this comparison, it is worth noting Harlan and Eisenstein's different approach to gender relations.

constellation of characters, and image composition, the film stages the image of an overwhelming storm as increasing dynamization of movement figurations.

The beginning of the scene (EMU 1) is dominated by uniform movements *in* the frame, i.e., on the level of image composition and constellation of characters. These elements are dominant throughout EMU 1. Although no uniform vector of movement can be determined, there is still only one vector per shot. This relatively clear form of movement relations is complicated with the beginning of the second EMU, which introduces movement in multiple different directions within each shot, leading to a diversification of movements. These different directions also take place on the level of image composition and constellation of characters. In contrast to the first EMU, constellation of characters is the dominant. The transition to the third EMU comes when the camera emerges as a movement factor. This shift leads to further multiplication and diversification of movements. Yet there is a clearly discernible pattern to the camera movement: swinging, wave-like motion. This formal element is a decisive factor in the scene's project of staging the Revolution as a storm.

The entire scene is grounded in the fact that the shots showing Napoleon in the storm at sea are tinted blue, and the shots showing the events at the Convention are tinted red. The constant and, over the course of the three EMUs, increasingly frequent alternation between blue and red has a dynamizing effect on perception and makes the scene more turbulent.

First EMU: 00:00:00:00–00:01:00:09
Through image composition, constellation of characters, and cinematography, the EMU stages an image of crackling tension as the collision between self-contained movements in different directions.

Although the first EMU of the scene already displays a fair amount of movement, generating relatively high tension, it is still dominated by shots in which movement is unidirectional and in which there is a single dominant movement per shot, whether it is Napoleon's boat, the passing clouds, Napoleon's gaze, the water swirling around his boat, the roaring waves and their foam, the public at the Convention or Robespierre's gestures during his speech at the Convention. This impression of (relative) order is reinforced by relatively long camera distances (American shots, medium shots, and long shots predominate), as well as open image composition. With three exceptions, the shots are static with no camera movement. In addition, the first EMU is clearly divided into a blue-tinted half (the first ten shots) and a red-tinted half (the second ten shots).

Yet the movements in the various shots often differ in direction – meaning the movements do not appear uniform, even if there is one main direction of movement per shot. Napoleon sails to the left into the depths of the image; a few shots later, the water disturbed by the boat moves to the right; the clouds also move to the right; and the breaking waves move frontally toward the camera. Similarly, in several shots Robespierre gesticulates directly toward the camera. In American, straight, static shots, he occupies the center of the image and gives a lecture. He stands and appears in medium closeup. He wears a white wig and a quite voluminous white scarf that reaches to his belly button. Behind him sits a man who is partly cut off by the frame. To his right and left (next to each of his hands) sit two other men whose faces can be seen from the nose up. Robespierre opens his mouth wide: He is yelling. Again and again, he raises his arm quickly and energetically, then points toward the audience, i.e., toward the camera, contributing significantly to the image of crackling tension staged in the EMU. In the second half of the EMU, the audience reactions grow stronger: They jump up and gesticulate with increasing vehemence, more and more wildly. However, these audience movements still seem like a uniform movement in this EMU.

Second EMU: 00:01:00:10–00:02:27:00
In the interplay of constellation of characters, image composition, and cinematography, the second EMU stages an image of increasing chaos as a diversification of movement directions.

The second EMU begins with a panoramic shot showing the entire convention hall where Robespierre speaks. He can just be made out, a quite small figure at the bottom center of the frame. The audience is arranged in three tiers. Most are bustling about in the highest tier. In the center of the image stand two large lamps, one on the right and one on the left. At the beginning of the shot, there is a large banner in the upper right edge of the frame, and on the upper left edge a column; two flags hang in the top center. After a smooth pan to the left, the column stands in the center of the image. The room seems quite large and dominant, the people very small. The camera movements that occur in this shot, the pan to the left and a later pan back to the right, are both smooth; they do not increase the sense of dynamism or chaos, but rather serve to give a spatial overview of the hall. The change in movement quality from the first EMU occurs much more in the constellation of characters. The change begins at the very end of this shot, when a sudden commotion erupts in the audience. This change continues in the next shot, when an incalculable number of people appear in a crowd that extends beyond the edges of the frame. Many of them are in motion, creating a quite hectic and lively impression. These two aspects of the shots showing the crowd at the convention – the lively, disorderly, chaotic movement of the figures and a shot that fails to give an overview since it does not capture the action in its entirety – dominate the rest of the EMU and continue to intensify over its course. This quality holds true not only for the action in the convention, but also for the shots of Napoleon in the storm – the alternation between the two locations occurs more frequently than in the first EMU – which are marked by increasing dynamism and chaos. The waves get larger and larger, the foam sprays higher (sometimes the camera even dips under the water, and the entire image is covered in seafoam – as in the last shot of the EMU), making it harder and harder to get an overview of the action; the rain, too, falls harder and harder, bringing more movement and another direction of movement into play. The shots of the big names of the Revolution – Danton and Marat in particular – are also characterized by more unrest in the background and exaggerated gestures: Marat breathes heavily, cries out, opens his eyes wide, and waves a pistol around as he gesticulates wildly. The camera movements are still quite reduced in this EMU. In the shots of Napoleon and the boat, they are restricted to a gentle shaking, which adds a degree of intensity to the feeling of uncontrolled movement that is primarily created by the constellation of characters. In the shots showing the events at the convention, the camera largely remains still and only pans slightly, foreshadowing the swinging movements that become dominant in the next EMU.

Third EMU: 00:02:27:01–00:06:41:15
In the third EMU in this scene, the interplay of cinematography, image composition, and constellation of characters stage an image of the storm as a swinging motion that comes to encompass all the chaotic movements.

With this EMU, the camera – particularly its dynamics – become the scene's dominant formal element. Whereas the camera was mostly static earlier on, the third EMU, the last and longest of the scene, begins with a highly dynamic shot. Danton speaks and gesticulates while Marat stands beside him. In the background are several other figures. Danton runs his hand through his hair and then, as so many other speakers in this scene have done, points toward the audience and the camera. Marat appears stubborn and determined, his face revealing no emotion. He gazes forward and is lit only from the left. Meanwhile, the camera makes a swinging motion: It tracks forward (coming so close to Danton that for a moment he nearly fills the entire frame) and back again, and turns (with a slight pan) to the left and then forward again. Then it tracks back again with a pan to the right, then forward again to the right. When the camera arrives at Danton and Marat, it is at a slightly low angle; otherwise, eye level shots predominate. This wavelike oscillating movement becomes the primary formal principle of this EMU. Again and again, the camera tracks forward and then, sometimes a few shots later, back again. Or it pans to the left and to the right, as well as down and up. With these swinging movements, which are frequently paired with a restless, shaky motion, the camera captures and provides structure for the extremely busy, chaotic movement of the figures – which are more intense still than in the previous EMU. This form climaxes when the oscillations no longer occur through tracking or panning shots, but with a crane. The camera flies and swings above the tumult. First forward, then three shots later back, and again forward, again three shots before moving back, then again forward. The shots of Napoleon in the storm – the alternation between the two plot threads is even more frequent – are also marked by chaotic movements in differing directions, as well as surging wavelike motion.

In addition, the film begins to use superimpositions between the two scenarios. In terms of narrative logic, this technique again signals the merging of both storms. With regard to the scene's form, the effect further diversifies movement; now both the tumultuous, chaotic movement at the convention and the equally tumultuous, but swelling and wavelike movement of the sea appear in a *single* image. For instance, in Shot 92, one image layer shows Danton, Robespierre, and Marat in medium shot. Marat wants to walk to the right, but his movement is interrupted by Robespierre. Robespierre and Danton turn toward each other and begin to argue. They are surrounded by hustle and bustle. On a second image layer, the swelling sea and isolated foam can be made out in superimpositions; Napoleon's ship appears twice on the left edge of the frame. In a way, the water washes around Robespierre, Marat, and Danton, unifying the chaotic, hectic movements and the wavelike movements.

There are also three shots with superimpositions that represent both the climax and the close of the EMU. In these shots, there are three or even four different image layers. They are both the climax, because all the forms of movement in the scene come together again and completely overpower the spectator's perception: the flying seesaw of the camera, the surging tumult at the convention, the ship that sways on the sea's waves, and the heroes of the French Revolution with their exaggerated speech and gestures toward the camera. These three shots, however, are also the conclusion of the EMU, since in contrast to the previous shots they are significantly longer (8 seconds, 16 frames; 10 seconds, 24 frames; 18 seconds, 17 frames); with them, the growth logic of movement development in the scene fades away and comes to an end.

If one connects the formal staging analyzed above with the content of the scene, two central points emerge. First, the metaphor that Deleuze recognizes in this scene – the Revolution as storm[93] – is realized not only through the use of text[94] and a parallel montage. Both of these techniques are encompassed by Eisenstein's category of intellectual montage. Yet the scene functions better as an example of how the *film* thinks than as an Eisensteinian intellectual montage. The decisive point in this scene is that the metaphor manifests in *qualities of movement*. The swelling of the sea waves becomes the swinging of the camera that shows the tumult at the Convention, and is thus – drawing on Sobchack's phenomenological theory of embodied filmic experience[95] – viscerally experienced by the spectator. The Revolution as a storm is staged not only through intertitles or other signs, but inscribes itself directly into the spectator's body. The Revolution is a revolution in precisely the sense intended by Goethe when he used the word: Watching the scenes, a person can become 'ill' from the swaying of the camera.

In terms of content – this is the second point I want to introduce here – in this scene Napoleon is once again, as in the snowball fight, the one person who resists irresistible motion.[96] Here, the movement is less amorphous than in the snowball fight and instead has the structure of a storm. Yet it still has the quality of an unstoppable, unmanageable movement, which sweeps up the giants of the Revolution and threatens to lead to the demise of the Revolution itself. And not only Danton, Marat, and Robespierre, but also the spectators are carried away by this motion. Only Napoleon is capable of withstanding it. Even though this scene is difficult to reconcile with a fascist aesthetic, on the level of content it raises the suspicion that it feeds into a fascistic glorification of Napoleon.[97] In order to

---

[93] Arendt had already recounted the importance of this metaphor for spectators of the Revolution.
[94] Describing the storm that Napoleon sails into, the intertitles read: "A dangerous sirocco gradually builds up." Referring to the events at the Convention, the following intertitle appears: "That same night, at the same time, another mighty storm was unleashed at the Convention".
[95] Sobchack's phenomenological film theory is also the basis for experiencing audiovisual metaphor in Kappelhoff and Müller.
[96] See the intertitle: "Thus all the giants of the Revolution were swept, one after the other, into the raging whirlpool of the Reign of Terror." See as well "And a man, the defiant sport of the ocean, his tricolour sail opening to the wind of the Revolution, was being triumphantly carried to the Heights of History".
[97] Heinz-Peter Preußer concludes in his discussion of this scene that it performs a fascistic glorification of Napoleon. However, he decouples the interpretation of content from the way in which the scene is staged, and thus in my opinion limits its complexity and inner tension. Cf.

more fully comprehend the role assigned by the film to Napoleon and to answer the question of whether the critique of the film as fascistic is justified, I will first examine how Arendt answers the question of authority in a revolution. In a second step, I will investigate the staging of Napoleon as a character and connect it to Arendt's work.

4.3 The Authority of State Foundation

The Revolution and the Question of New Beginnings

Alongside 'power' and 'violence,'[98] 'authority' is the third central concept for Arendt when it comes to understanding the Revolution, its rationale, and its course. In her essay "On Violence," Arendt defines 'authority' as a quality that can be granted to an individual person, an institution, or an office. Its trademark is the unquestioning recognition of authority by those who must obey. When authority has to start debating or using violence, it has already lost respect and therefore its authority. In this sense, the most dangerous opponents of authority are contempt and ridicule.[99]

Arendt makes it clear that these conceptual distinctions are not merely empty abstractions when she blames the inglorious end of the French Revolution on the confusion and mixing of these three terms (this is not to say that all three concepts stand independently alongside each other: 'power [Macht]' and 'violence [Gewalt]' are opposites, while 'power' and 'authority' are closely linked to each other[100]). First, there was confusion between 'power' and 'violence,' as the actors of the French Revolution did not distinguish between the two. They understood 'power' as "a 'natural' force whose source and origin lay outside the political realm, a force which in its very violence had been released by the Revolution and like a hurricane had swept away all institutions of the *ancien régime*." And further: "This

---

Heinz-Peter Preußer: Massen im Monumentalfilm – Überwältigungsstrategien des Genrekinos. Versuch einer Typologie aus der Theorie des Erhabenen, in: Masse Mensch. Das ‚Wir' – sprachlich behauptet, ästhetisch inszeniert, ed. by Andrea Jäger/Gerd Antos/Malcolm H. Dunn, Halle 2006, pp. 308–325, here p. 312.

98 For Arendt, 'power' is the human capacity to join with others. In this sense, a powerful person is someone who is backed by a number of other people. Thus, for Arendt 'power' is a political phenomenon, whereas 'violence' means the end of politics. Arendt understands a government's loss of power – which can certainly lead to violence – as a necessary condition for a revolution. On this point, see section 2.2.
99 Cf. Hannah Arendt: Macht und Gewalt, Munich/Zurich 2013, pp. 46 f.
100 Cf. Arendt: On Revolution, op. cit., pp. 153 f.

force was experienced as superhuman in its strength."[101] Arendt distinguishes this approach from the American Revolution: "The men of the American Revolution, on the contrary, understood by power the very opposite of a pre-political natural violence. To them, power came into being when and where people would get together and bind themselves through promises, covenants, and mutual pledges."[102] The problem of confusing 'power' with 'violence' thus did not exist in the American Revolution. Yet the question still had not been answered of how this power is to be won and sustainably installed. Arendt writes: "Neither compact nor promise upon which compacts rest are sufficient to assure perpetuity, that is, to bestow upon the affairs of men that measure of stability without which they would be unable to build a world for their posterity, destined and designed to outlast their own mortal lives."[103] She calls this the "problem of authority."[104] The problem poses itself in every form of new beginning and is particularly natural in the founding of a polity – whether or not it takes the form of a state – since it is a question of *beginning*, of something *new*. If the foundation can be fully derived from the old formation, there would be nothing new. After a certain point, a new beginning was the demand of both the American and French Revolutions. This was precisely the point that made them world-historical events, and that led to a breakthrough in the theorizing of history, which had been running in circles. Following Arendt, one can say that a revolution without a new foundation is no revolution.

When one is unable to call on what has come before, how does one legitimize a foundation? And how can the new foundation be protected from being swept away by the next political generation? This problem is not easily solved, given that it presents a *petitio principii*, which Arendt describes as follows:

> [T]hose who get together to constitute a new government are themselves unconstitutional, that is, they have no authority to do what they have set out to achieve. [...] And with this problem, which appeared as the urgent need for some absolute, the men of the American Revolution found themselves no less confronted than their colleagues in France.[105]

The responses to this problem were quite different in the French and the American Revolutions. What they had in common, however, was that the protagonists of each attempted to solve the problem by invoking a divine, transcendent

---

101 Ibid., p. 181.
102 Ibid. Arendt derives this theory of power in the American Revolution, founded on mutual promises, from the pilgrims' *Mayflower Compact*. Cf. ibid., p. 167 and p. 173. On the central importance of promises in Arendt's work, see: "There is an element of the world-building capacity of man in the human faculty of making and keeping promises" (ibid., p. 175).
103 Ibid., p. 182.
104 Ibid.
105 Ibid., pp. 183 f.

authority.[106] While this approach does not solve the problem with finality, as Arendt correctly implies, but only displaces it to a different plane (the question of how the otherworldly, religious authority legitimizes itself is not answered here, and instead is referred to a realm that exceeds man and human reason[107]), it is worth noting and understanding that in both revolutions of modernity the solution to the problem of authority was sought in the realm of religion and the absolute, even if – I will go into more detail on this point – Arendt does not consider this to have been the only legitimization strategy in the American Revolution. In the French Revolution, according to Arendt, the strategy was expressed in three ways. First, there was a "deification of the people" with respect to their *volonté générale*.[108] According to Arendt, this phenomenon came from the divine right of kings under absolute monarchy. There too the deification of the ruler resulted in an identification – and with it a short circuit – of 'power,' 'violence,' and 'authority;' a short circuit that recurred in the Revolution. Arendt argues that the mystification was pushed even further when the French Revolution ultimately stopped calling on the general will of the people as a source of authority for constitutional laws, and, this is the second manifestation, turned instead to "the revolutionary process [...] itself."[109] With that turn, however, the Revolution had become the unstoppable process that led to the death of freedom and thereby to the end of the Revolution. Thus, with regard to the question of authority as well, the problem of the French Revolution lies in its movement formation. As the third manifestation of religious authority as a solution to the problem of authority, Arendt names Robespierre's 'Cult of the Supreme Being.' This attempt to introduce a new religion, and thereby to endow the Revolution and its laws with legitimacy and authority, also failed. Arendt writes of the "ridiculousness of the enterprise" and the "circus clown" that had stepped onto the stage of the Revolution.[110] As already noted, vulnerability to ridicule signals the death of any authority.

---

106 Of course, this is unsurprising, since all the theorists on whom the men of the revolution relied – with the exception of Montesquieu, as Arendt underscores – invoke a divine authority when it comes time to justify new foundations. Cf. ibid., pp. 185 f.
107 On this point, see ibid., p. 207.
108 Ibid., p. 183. There is not room here for a detailed discussion of the relationship of the French revolutionaries – especially Robespierre and Saint-Just – with Rousseau. For Arendt's explanation of the role of *volonté générale* in the French Revolution, cf. ibid., pp. 76–79. For Rousseau's influence on Arendt herself and her theorization of the French Revolution, cf. Mohrmann: Affekt und Revolution, op. cit., pp. 27 ff.
109 Arendt: On Revolution, op. cit., p. 183.
110 Cf. ibid., p. 184.

Yet the actors of the American Revolution also saw the necessity of appealing to a higher, absolute power, in order to authorize the Revolution and to protect the relations created by it. They also sought an "Immortal Legislator."[111] This approach, Arendt argues, was grounded not in religion, but in political conviction. They were interested not in proclaiming belief in a Christian god – as students of the Enlightenment they pursued the separation of politics and religion, of worldly matters from the church – but in the long-term protection of what they had achieved. Furthermore, in America – as in France – the reference to religion was an attempt to provide a direction for the morality of the people.[112]

Yet it is not only in the American Revolution's direct appeal to a religious, otherworldly authority – the preamble to the Declaration of Independence refers to 'nature's God' – that Arendt sees the attempt to solve the problem of authority.[113] In Jefferson's famous phrase with which the Declaration begins, "We hold these truths to be self-evident," she uncovers traces of a claim to an absolute and therefore apolitical sphere. She refers to the paradoxical structure of this phrase: How did they *agree* on self-evident truths? The phrase "We hold," which is based on an agreement and is thus necessarily somewhat relative, stands in contrast to compulsorily evident truths that would not require any agreement. For Arendt, Jefferson's statement is a hybrid of two different kinds of reasoning: On the one hand, political reasoning through consensus and agreement; on the other – here she sees traces of the religious and absolute sphere – reasoning through the axiomatic truths of mathematical theorems or 'laws.' This phrase, then, imposes the realm of mathematics onto the realm of politics. For Arendt, its legitimacy is of course a fallacy. The truths that had been agreed upon in the American Revolution by no means have the same evidence and compulsory character as mathematical equations like 'two times two is four.' According to Arendt, this fallacy comes from confusing understanding [*Verstand*] with reason [*Vernunft*]. They believed that they could impose the character of mathematical equations that compel human logic on the lawmaking capacity of moral reasoning. Furthermore, this fallacy was an attempt to solve the problem of authority:

> The authority of self-evident truth may be less powerful than the authority of an 'avenging God', but it certainly still bears clear signs of divine origin; such truths are, as Jefferson wrote in the original draft of the Declaration of Independence, 'sacred and undeniable'.[114]

---

111 Ibid., p. 184. Arendt borrows this phrase from Robespierre.
112 Cf. ibid., p. 191.
113 On the following, see ibid., pp. 192–194.
114 Ibid., p. 194.

4.3 The Authority of State Foundation — 109

Thus, Arendt also finds in the American Revolution an attempt – both direct and indirect – to solve the problem of authority through the sphere of transcendence and the absolute. Yet she takes care to underscore that it is not the only possible form this solution can take. This form is by no means universal, but can be historicized; this is a decisive point. Antiquity, by which she means both the Greeks and the Romans, had no difficulty getting by without appealing to an immortal legislator.[115] In Greece, she writes, it was common for the lawgiver to be a stranger from outside the community. This demonstrates only that legislation was seen as something prepolitical, comparable to e.g., the building of city walls: Both were a necessary condition for the community to exist, but not part of its political life. "The Greek legislator was outside the body politic, but he was not above it and he was not divine."[116] According to Arendt, an important characteristic of Greek law was that they had limited spatial validity; they were in no way intended to be absolute, and therefore had no need for transcendent justification.[117]

The Romans also had no need for an absolute authority to justify their laws. According to Arendt, they were even familiar with the idea that an ethnically homogeneous tribe could live together without laws. Only when they began to conquer other peoples and tribes did laws become necessary, since the Romans were not interested in the brute domination of other peoples. In Arendt's account, the Romans were only satisfied when their former enemies became friends or allies. The expansion of the Roman Empire was not motivated by the desire for power or conquest. Rather, the goal was to extend the network of the Roman confederation to the ends of the Earth. Laws emerged from the need to regulate the coexistence of different peoples, and were therefore regarded neither as a prepolitical fact, nor as a phenomenon that required divinity.

It is precisely the influence of the Romans and their concept of authority – which unites foundation, expansion, and protection – that makes the American Revolution so important and meaningful to Arendt.[118] According to her, the authority of the American Revolution and its laws did not rely solely on the appeal

---

115 On the following, see ibid., pp. 186–188.
116 Ibid., p. 186.
117 In the history of revolutions, according to Arendt, "[t]he only trace we find of this [ancient, H.B.] notion of the Legislator's role and status" (ibid., p. 187) is in a suggestion by Robespierre. She thus cannot be reproached for taking an overly generalized approach to the two revolutions of modernity.
118 On the immense influence of the Roman Republic on the American Revolution, see ibid., p. 203. In the following, however, I am interested only in the minimal significance of absolute power for the authority of laws, which according to Arendt followed the Roman example, and not in an extensive reconstruction of Arendt's arguments concerning the American Revolution's relationship to the Roman Republic.

to divine power – and in this way it resembled the Roman Republic. Beyond this appeal, the authority of laws came from acting, from the act of foundation itself and the consciousness of new beginnings – and this is ultimately the more important foundation strategy in Arendt's analysis. On the basis of the existential fact of "natality," every person has the capacity to begin anew. It is this fact that forms the basis for authority.[119] To Arendt it seems that

> [t]he very fact that the men of the American Revolution thought of themselves as 'founders' indicates the extent to which they must have known that it would be the act of foundation itself, rather than an Immortal Legislator or self-evident truth or any other transcendent, transmundane source, which eventually would become the fountain of authority in the new body politic.[120]

She goes on to connect the question of authority with the movement formation of the Revolution: The American Revolution

> did not break out but was made by men in common deliberation and on the strength of mutual pledges. The principle which came to light during those fateful years when the foundations were laid – not by the strength of one architect but by the combined power of the many – was the interconnected principle of mutual promise and common deliberation; and the event itself decided indeed, as Hamilton had insisted, that men 'are really capable […] of establishing good government from reflection and choice', that they are not 'forever destined to depend for their political constitutions on accident and force'.[121]

Arendt does not omit the fact that the foundational strategies of the American Revolution included appealing to a transcendent power, but she sees the Revolution as ultimately providing a quite different answer to the problem of authority. Unlike the political theorists of modernity, who legitimized laws with the authority of an otherworldly power, but also unlike the French Revolution, where this divine authority was transferred onto the people and their universal will, the decisive factor in the American Revolution lay in the fact that authority

---

119 This is not the proper place for a more detailed discussion of the philosophical background that leads Arendt to this statement. It is worth noting, however, that with this emphasis on the simple act of new foundation, Arendt wades into possibly problematic, decisionist waters. For a brief overview of decisionism and the particularly problematic form it took in the work of Heidegger, see Hasso Hofmann: Dezision, Dezisionismus, in: Historisches Wörterbuch der Philosophie. Vol. 2: D–F, ed. by Joachim Ritter, Darmstadt 1972, pp. 159–161. Also relevant in this context, however, is Eva Geulen's remark that for Arendt (in contrast to Badiou), foundation is not subjective, and instead always occurs as a collective act and a mutual promise. Cf. Eva Geulen: Gründung und Gesetzgebung bei Badiou, Agamben und Arendt, in: Hannah Arendt und Giorgio Agamben. Parallelen, Perspektiven, Kontroversen, ed. by id./Kai Kauffmann/Georg Mein, Munich 2008, pp. 59–74, here p. 66.
120 Arendt: On Revolution, op. cit., p. 204.
121 Ibid., pp. 213 f.

originated in acting itself, in the consciously planned and controlled new beginning. Thus, in the American Revolution as well, the answer to the problem of authority is formulated through the Revolution's quality of movement. What answers do audiovisual stagings give to this problem? In the following pages, I seek to explore this question in more depth with scenes from NAPOLÉON.

The Question of Authority

Does Abel Gance's film discover its own unique answer to the question of authority? Or can it be related to the solutions that manifest in the French and American Revolutions? If one takes the premise seriously that in the film, Napoleon is the heir, the leader, and the embodiment of the Revolution. These questions can only be answered by examining how the film stages the character 'Napoleon.' In the preceding chapters I have shown that the film stages Napoleon as the one, who is capable of controlling the inexorable process of the Revolution, of resisting and managing its unstoppable movement.

In addition, as I will attempt to show here, the film separates Napoleon not only from the uncontrollable movement, but also from the uncontrolled violence of the people. The second scene after the film's prologue[122] shows events that an intertitle dates to 10 August.[123] The entire scene is tinted red and characterized by consistent low-key lighting with many shadows and hard contrasts, creating a tense, highly dramatic, and increasingly infernal mood. The score consists of solemn organ music, which heightens the atmosphere even further.

Napoleon's room is shown in long shot – a messy apartment with a large desk on the right side of the image. In front of the desk, in the right background, is a large, open window, through which only blurry movements can be made out in this first shot. Four shots later, the following events occur in a shadow play on Napoleon's wall: With the camera angle tilted 90 degrees to the right creating a slightly alienated perspective that makes it difficult to recognize what is happening,

---

[122] The first scene after the prologue shows the arrival of the 'Marseillaise' in Paris; Napoleon, speaking with the song's composer, Rouget de Lisle, predicts that the hymn will have a great future.

[123] The reference is to 10 August 1792. This was the day of the storming of the Tuileries and the radicalization of the revolutionary process. The scene's timecode is 00:32:50–00:39:00 (Disc 1). This is another scene which shows many plot levels in parallel and aims to overwhelm the spectator using an acceleration montage. It also deploys metaphor on multiple levels (the Revolution as a melting pot that dissolves the monarchy and forges the republic). In the following, however, I am interested in only one aspect of this scene: how the staging differentiates Napoleon from the violence in the streets.

human shapes march past. They carry scythes, spears, pitchforks. The shadow play suggests that Napoleon is watching the violence on the streets like a cinema spectator. The spatial distinction between the spectator (Napoleon) and the action (implied violence) is certainly not as radical and dichotomous as in the cinema. The sequence's focus on spatial differentiation, however, can be traced through the rest of the scene. Napoleon sits in his room and writes.[124] Two moments reinforce the spatial – and consequently, the narrative – separation between Napoleon and the violence. Once again, we see a long shot of Napoleon's room. This time, the camera is placed somewhat closer to Napoleon's desk, so that it is centered in the image with Napoleon seated at it. Behind it, we can now clearly see the wide-open window. In front of the railings that are visible through the bottom third of the window, the tips of scythes, pitchforks, and spears march by. At the very end of the shot, the head of a female giant appears at the bottom edge of the window. The next shot shows Napoleon in closeup; he has interrupted his writing, but still holds the quill in his hand; he looks up and to the left. He blinks and recoils a bit. He appears surprised – he, too, seems irritated by the head in front of his window.[125] The following shot complements the point-of-view construction that has thus been introduced: In a slightly high-angle closeup,[126] we see the head behind the window railings. Left of the head are burning torches, which push the atmosphere further into the infernal realm. The head itself is recognizably a woman's head, but its lack of facial expression or pupils in the eyes make it seem strangely artificial. Another cut follows, to a closeup of Napoleon. Again, he looks to the left.[127] He blinks quickly and stands up. The next shot shows him in a medium shot, running to the window to get a closer view of this strange head. Then the head appears again in closeup; while it was largely motionless in the previous shot (only turning slightly), now it rises higher in the air – and turns out to be a severed head on a spike. The next shot shows Napoleon's reaction: In a closeup, he quickly looks up, stares into the distance, and breathes heavily. In this shot sequence, Napoleon is not just a spectator who observes the disorderly, uncontrolled revolutionary violence in a separate space; he is so far removed

---

124 On the level of content, as well, the scene distances Napoleon from the revolutionary mob: The intertitles that show Napoleon's notes explicitly critique their violence.
125 With the last remark, I of course do not intend to make any statements about the character's psychology. Instead I am interested in describing how the scene builds suspense.
126 The shot thus offers a deviant reproduction of Napoleon's point-of-view. If one assumes the spatial organization established by the long shot that came two shots earlier, Napoleon sits higher and further away from the window.
127 This cut completes the classical point-of-view construction as theorized by Edward Branigan. See Edward Branigan: Point of View in the Cinema. A Theory of Narration and Subjectivity in Classical Film, Berlin/Boston 2012.

from this violence that he has to look a second time and more closely in order to get an overview of the situation.

Shortly thereafter, in a sequence that continues to be quite clearly constructed as his point-of-view, Napoleon sees two men scale the façade and clamber onto his window railing, in order to secure a rope there that a man can tie onto. A closeup shows Napoleon's face, his gaze drifting downward. Then a cut to another closeup – a point-of-view shot of Napoleon's gaze at the pistol that is lying on the desk. Slowly and hesitantly, from the right edge of the frame, Napoleon's hand appears and approaches the pistol. Yet just before the hand grabs for the gun, it balls into a fist and its forward motion ceases. Napoleon does not intervene; he does not take part in the violence; he remains a spectator. The next shot, a closeup, shows the blood-smeared hand of one of the men on the railing, holding onto the structure. A long shot that captures the entire room reveals Napoleon sitting at his desk, his head lowered. He leans his head onto his left arm, resting his elbow on the table. A medium shot follows of his torso and face. Slowly, he raises his head and upper body, and looks up. Yet the next shot shows not the bloody hand, but rather a poster with a slogan proclaiming the rights of man and citizen. A smooth rightward pan to the window contrasts the words with the lynching in the streets. A thrice-repeated rapid alternation follows between the closeup on the bloody hand and the shot showing the declaration of the rights of man and citizen. The alternation ends with a closeup of Napoleon, who breathes heavily and stares ahead without expression, then with an abrupt, quick movement slumps forward and lays his head down. Here too, Napoleon is clearly distanced from the events on the street.

Yet if this fictional staging of the French Revolution distances Napoleon so much from the people, from their *volonté générale*, and the revolutionary process that lend the authority to legitimize the new polity in Arendt's account of the historical French Revolution, where does the film locate the source of Napoleon's authority? Or to put it another way: how does Napoleon become the film's solution to the problem of authority, and how can that happen without the film becoming the fascist concoction that it is often considered to be? The answer is: Napoleon is both idolized and dismissed. More concretely, he is staged as a messiah who keeps his distance.

This staging occurs on multiple levels and in different ways. Even a fleeting glance at the film reveals that over the course of the film Napoleon's face, shown repeatedly in closeups with supplementary lighting from behind, is surrounded by a halo. This 'elevation' resonates with the way in which the young Napoleon at the beginning of the film already possesses all attributes of the future, adult Napoleon. Art historical depictions of the Christ child repeatedly endow him with the attributes of the adult Jesus; for example, when the year-old child gives a benediction, as has been the case in devotional images since the fourteenth century.[128] The clearest illustration of this strategy in the film's staging of Napoleon first appears at the end of the film, which is staged as a triptych.[129]

Gance planned Polyvision in the form of triptych sequences: To the left and right of the screen on which the film was to be shown in the cinema, there were supposed to be two more screens. Therefore, the projection booth also had to contain three projectors. At multiple points in the film, the two supplemental projectors were supposed to start up and project a threefold image.[130] These triptych sequences created a temporary *expansion* of the screen and the frame.[131] Deleuze also puts these sequences into conversation with the whole and the sublime for Deleuze is thinking of precisely these sequences when he writes about Gance's achieving a maximum of movement. With three different screens, according to Deleuze, Gance presents the simultaneity of three different perspectives on the same scene, or of three different scenes. This simultaneity is liberated from the interval and directed towards "the image as the absolute movement of the whole which changes."[132] In this way, the triptych sequences also gesture toward the sublime.

Yet how do the triptych sequences relate to the argument that the film stages Napoleon as a messiah? The history of visual art supports this argument insofar as triptychs were long restricted to altars and reserved for images of saints or

---

128 See the entry: "Christuskind", in: Lexikon der Kunst. Architektur, bildende Kunst, angewandte Kunst, Industrieformgestaltung, Kunsttheorie. Vol. I: A-F, ed. by Ludger Alscher et al., Leipzig 1973, pp. 449 f., here p. 449.
129 My earliest thoughts on this point can be found in Hanno Berger: Revolution, Metapher und 'Napoléon', in: Überschreitungen. Beiträge zur Theoretisierung von Inszenierungs- und Aufführungspraxis [e-book], ed. by Nicole Haitzinger/Franziska Kollinger, Munich 2016, pp. 22–29.
130 For practical reasons, screenings in this format were quite rare. Hardly any exhibitors had three projectors and three screens, or the space necessary to install them (on the problems that the film encountered immediately after its premiere, see Brownlow: Napoleon, op. cit., pp. 161 ff.). It also creates an irresolvable disparity between the historical cinema experience and DVD reception: On the DVD, the images in these sequences are smaller, and the overpowering effect can only be inferred.
131 For this reason, I find the argument that Gance's triptych format represents an early form of Cinemascope to be too simplistic. Whereas Cinemascope is a permanent change to the size of the visual field, the triptych sequences imply this field's variability. On the argument that I am countering, see Preußer: Massen im Monumentalfilm, op. cit., p. 313; Epstein also tends in this direction in Epstein: Bilan de fin de muet, op. cit., pp. 235 f. On the idea that in Gance's work the triptych can be seen as a form of variability of the visual field, see Deleuze: The Movement-Image, op. cit., p. 13.
132 Deleuze: The Movement-Image, op. cit., p. 49.

other sacred themes.[133] Yet if the film merely staged Napoleon as a messiah, it would run the risk of becoming fascistic propaganda, and would make the same mistake that Arendt attributes to the historical French Revolution. While the latter engaged in a deification of the people that led to the death of the Revolution, the deification of Napoleon has just as little to do with the basic principles of the Revolution, freedom, and novelty. It is therefore crucial to interrogate the concrete forms of staging in which triptychs appear. These scenes also support the argument that the film stages Napoleon as a messiah, yet they add an important twist. The film ends with Napoleon's Italian campaign. In a triptych sequence, Napoleon gives an address to his troops to boost their morale.[134] The scene uses the triptych format not only to extend the visual field and create a continuous image,[135] but also to place disparate images – i.e., images that are not spatially connected – next to each other. From the outset of his address, Napoleon is spatially removed – he stands on top of a mountain, more or less in the clouds, while his troops are camped at its base. Napoleon can be seen in a medium closeup. In the frames to his left and right are clouds that are not easily recognizable as cloud formations, but instead form a monochrome and depthless field. Napoleon thus finds himself once again in an abstract non-space. This separation of Napoleon from the rest of the diegetic world intensifies over the course of the scene through increasingly close shots. Napoleon appears in long shot at the beginning of the scene; by its end, there are only extreme closeups of his face. This constant approach by the camera repeats a theme that recurs repeatedly throughout the film: Namely, that Napoleon becomes more and more detached from any spatial context, and increasingly liberated from his environment. Only at the end of the sequence is he reconnected with that environment by three very brief shots.

The separation of Napoleon from his spatial context is reinforced by the fact that he is filmed from different angles, and that he looks sometimes to the left, sometimes to the right. This violation of the 180-degree rule obfuscates the spatial situation of both Napoleon and the soldiers he addresses. Furthermore, the triple screen divides the viewer's perspective, and the disparate lines of sight on the screens intensify the sense of spatial disorientation and dissociation in the spectator's perception. This impression is further augmented by the confusing nature of the crowd shots.

---

133 See Wolfgang Pilz: Das Triptychon als Kompositions- und Erzählform in der deutschen Tafelmalerei von den Anfängen bis zur Dürerzeit, Munich 1970, p. 16.
134 The timecode of this scene is 01:15:11–01:20:40 (Disc 2).
135 Nonetheless, in between the shots in which the images are supposed to extend seamlessly from the central screen to the left and the right, there is a small gap, a small crack between the images.

There are thus multiple staging strategies that lead to Napoleon's detachment from his environment as a sort of ethereal being.[136] He leaves the realm of men, and it is only a slight exaggeration to say that the film thereby makes him into a foundational myth, whose concrete connection to the nation he founded is severed: He disappears into the clouds. One could perhaps speculate that the reason why Gance was unable to film the subsequent films about Napoleon that he had planned was not the first film's lack of success, insufficient funds, or some other extrinsic reason; rather, it was an intrinsic consequence of the character's staging at the end of the first part. As a figure removed from the world, Napoleon can no longer determine the fate of the nation or the process of the Revolution. Herein lies the difference between the film's deification of Napoleon and the deification of the people's general will that Arendt discusses in her account of the French Revolution. In Gance's film, Napoleon functions as a mythical founding father, without whom foundation would hardly have been possible,[137] yet not as a figure who foretells the course of the Revolution or the nation. Separation from the rest of the diegetic world endows this figure with authority, but does not equip him with power or force.

4.4 After 1945: How Do We Look at Revolution Films With and Against Deleuze?

For Deleuze, after World War II it is impossible to draw on the analytical models for understanding the relationship between film and thought that he developed with reference to Eisenstein, Epstein, and NAPOLÉON. "How strangely," he writes, "the great declarations, of Eisenstein, of Gance, ring today."[138] The hope for cinema as a mass art and new form of thought are gone, he argues. Gance's sublimity was adopted by mediocre authors, displaced from the level of the image itself to the level of what is represented in the image, and thereby profaned. Although this reference to the mediocrity of many postwar films can be

---

136 To distinguish the film from an audiovisual staging of fascism in this point as well: Eight years later, in TRIUMPH DES WILLENS, Leni Riefenstahl would stage Hitler similarly, yet completely differently in one crucial aspect. Her film begins with Hitler in an airplane above the clouds over Nuremberg that subsequently lands there (timecode: 00:02:13–00:06:27). While Hitler descends from the clouds and lands, coming closer and closer to the rest of the world, Napoleon disappears into the clouds and the staging removes him progressively further from his environment.
137 As noted previously, for Arendt the American Revolution is the great exception as the new foundation that primarily (if not exclusively) justifies refoundation through the act of foundation itself.
138 Deleuze: The Time-Image, op. cit., p. 164.

4.4 After 1945: How Do We Look at Revolution Films With and Against Deleuze?

refuted and problematized as a conceited form of cinephilia,[139] there is another reason that has destroyed Deleuze's faith in cinema and its capacity to stimulate thought among the masses. This reason is, as Deleuze himself writes, far more important:

> [...] the mass-art, the treatment of masses, which should not have been separable from an accession of the masses to the status of true subject, has degenerated into state propaganda and manipulation, into a kind of fascism which brought together Hitler and Hollywood, Hollywood and Hitler. The spiritual automaton became fascist man. As Serge Daney says, what has brought the whole cinema of the movement-image into question are 'the great political *mises-en-scene,* state propaganda turned *tableaux vivants,* the first handlings of masses of humans', and their backdrop, the camps. This was the death-knell for the ambitions of 'the old cinema': not, or not only, the mediocrity and vulgarity of current production but rather Leni Riefenstahl, who was not mediocre.[140]

A cinema that has faith in the masses, and attempts to move them toward political change by inspiring them to think, seems impossible after World War II – as Deleuze justifiably argues.[141] Furthermore, to him the ways in which the relationship between film and thinking can be theorized with Eisenstein (who also stands in for Gance and Epstein) have become obsolete. Yet Deleuze sees a way

---

139 I do not intend to argue that every form of cinephilia is automatically conceited. On the question of cinephilia, its problems, and its contemporary potential, see Thomas Elsaesser: Cinephilia or the Uses of Disenchantment, in: Cinephilia. Movies, Love and Memory, ed. by Marijke de Valck/Malte Hagener, Amsterdam 2005, pp. 27–43.

140 Deleuze: The Time-Image, op. cit., p. 164. Deleuze cites Serge Daney: La rampe. Cahier critique 1970–1982, Paris 1983, p. 72. On the end of belief in the cinema as a democratic mass art, see also: "But a great many factors were to compromise this belief: the rise of Hitler, which gave cinema as its object not the masses become subject but the masses subjected; Stalinism, which replaced the unanimism of peoples with the tyrannical unity of a party; the break-up of the American people, who could no longer believe themselves to be either the melting-pot of peoples past or the seed of a people to come [...]" (ibid., p. 216). These remarks culminate in Deleuze's famous argument that the people are missing from modern cinema.

141 Deleuze sees the future of political cinema not in monumental epics about revolution, but in the minoritarian films of the so-called 'third world' (see ibid., p. 217); on the concept of minority and its political significance in Deleuze's philosophy, see especially Gilles Deleuze/Félix Guattari: Kafka. Toward a Minor Literature, trans. by Dana Polan, Minneapolis 1986, pp. 16 ff., as well as Gilles Deleuze/Félix Guattari: A Thousand Plateaus. Capitalism and Schizophrenia, trans. by Brian Massumi, Minneapolis 1987, pp. 232 ff., and Gilles Deleuze: Control and Becoming, in: Negotiations, 1972–1990, trans. by Martin Joughin, New York 1995, pp. 169–176. I have further traced this thread in Deleuze's thought on the political potential of film, putting it into conversation with Pedro Costa's NO QUARTO DA VANDA (PT 2000) and questions of genre theory in Hanno Berger: Das Minoritäre als Genre der Revolution, in: Prekäre Genres. Zur Ästhetik peripherer, apokrypher und liminaler Gattungen, ed. by id./Frédéric Döhl/Thomas Morsch, Bielefeld 2015, pp. 51–64.

out of this situation in Antonin Artaud, even if the latter himself only believed in film and its potential for a brief euphoric moment.[142] At first, Artaud took a position similar to Eisenstein's: that the cinema has a direct effect on the brain and causes a shock that forces thought.[143] Yet despite these similarities with Eisenstein's theories on the relationship between film and thought, which are apparent in Artaud's work upon first glance, there is "something quite different"[144] about the two positions. For Artaud, the argument does not lead to thinking the Whole with cinema (in this passage, the Whole can be interpreted as the sublime); instead, it points toward a break, a rupture:

> It might be said that Artaud turns round Eisenstein's argument: if it is true that thought depends on a shock which gives birth to it (the nerve, the brain matter), it can only think one thing, *the fact that we are not yet thinking*, the powerlessness to think the whole and to think oneself, thought which is always fossilized, dislocated, collapsed.[145]

Ultimately, the goal of Artaud's argument is "the presence of an unthinkable in thought."[146] This phenomenon is precisely what manifests in good postwar cinema, according to Deleuze. He traces this manifestation back to the interruption of the sensory-motor system, which he sees as fundamentally determinative for postwar cinema, and which, as he explains at this point, is also a break on a higher level of the bond between man and the world: "The sensory-motor break makes man a seer who finds himself struck by something intolerable in the world, and confronted by something unthinkable in thought."[147] If the link between man and the world is broken, according to Deleuze it is the task of the cinema to restore the *faith* in this link. Because we no longer believe in this world, the cinema must return our faith to us.[148] It must film not the world, but rather belief in the world, in order to restore this belief to us. Yet with regard to the question of what world we should have faith in, Deleuze is unequivocal:

---

142 Worth mentioning is not only his collaboration with Germaine Dulac on LA COQUILLE ET LE CLERGYMAN (FR 1928), from which he later distanced himself, but also that Artaud plays the role of Marat in NAPOLÉON.
143 Cf. a direct quotation from Artaud: "There is also a kind of physical intoxication which the rotation of the images communicates directly to the brain" (Antonin Artaud: Sorcery and the Cinema, in: The Avant-Garde Film. A Reader of Theory and Criticism, ed. by P. Adams Sitney, New York 1978, pp. 49 f., here p. 49).
144 Deleuze: The Time-Image, op. cit., p. 166.
145 Ibid., p. 167.
146 Ibid., p. 168.
147 Ibid., p. 169.
148 This thesis is fundamental to the ontology of film in Josef Früchtl: Vertrauen in die Welt. Eine Philosophie des Films, Munich 2013.

"Belief is no longer addressed to a different or transformed world." Shortly after this statement, he elaborates:

> What is certain is that believing is no longer believing in another world, or in a transformed world. It is only, it is simply believing in the body. It is giving discourse to the body, and, for this purpose, reaching the body before discourses, before words, before things are named: the 'first name', and even before the first name. Artaud said the same thing, believe in the *flesh* [...].[149]

This idea appears again further down the same page in a very elegant formulation: "We need an ethic or a faith, which makes fools laugh; it is not a need to believe in something else, but a need to believe in this world, of which fools are a part."[150] It would be a misunderstanding, however, to accuse Deleuze of having a conservative political agenda for this reason. His relationship to political change and utopia is more complex, as is revealed by the work he co-authored with Félix Guattari, *What is Philosophy?* With regard to the utopias introduced by Ernst Bloch in *The Principle of Hope*, they distinguish between authoritarian utopias of transcendence and libertarian, revolutionary, immanent utopias. The revolutionary utopias are characterized on the one hand by their endless movement (they have no definitive form); on the other hand, however, they are always connected with concrete circumstances and specific oppressed forces. The idea is to pursue these immanent utopias.[151] Deleuze's rejection of a transformed world is thus not as sweeping as it might appear to be in some sentences of *Cinema 2: The Time-Image*.

Applying Deleuze's thoughts on NAPOLÉON to films that deal with revolution and were made after World War II seems problematic in another way as well. For Deleuze, postwar cinema is characterized not only through the sensory-motor break and the resulting consequences, but also by the rejection of cinematic staging of rhetorical figures like metaphor. Whereas Deleuze sees this staging as closely bound up with montage, he understands the increasing significance of depth of field in modern cinema (for whom his principal witness is Orson Welles) as a turn away from metaphor. Instead of operating metaphorically or metonymically, films now think (particularly in Pasolini's case) "theorematically."[152]

---

149 Deleuze: The Time-Image, op. cit., pp. 172 f.
150 Ibid., p. 173.
151 See Gilles Deleuze/Félix Guattari: What is Philosophy?, trans. by Hugh Tomlinson/Graham Burchell, New York 1994, pp. 99 f. With regard to Bloch, see Ernst Bloch: The Principle of Hope. Vol. 1–3, trans. by Neville Plaice/Stephen Plaice/Paul Knight, Cambridge, MA 1995.
152 With this term, Deleuze means that the films' thought is now more oriented toward mathematical, geometrical proofs, and the mathematical processes of problems and theorems. Cf. Deleuze: The Time-Image, op. cit., pp. 173 f. On the significance of depth of field,

How – in spite of his own protestations – can one productively relate Deleuze's theories on NAPOLÉON to postwar revolution films? How can these films be analyzed with regard to the sublime and metaphor? Is that even possible? A first argument exists on a very basic, empirical level: In the postwar cinema too, there are still action-images. Deleuze must therefore incorporate a qualitative judgment of taste and a normative element in order to make his argument relevant. With the inclusion of such an element, however, he runs the risk of distorting his perspective on the films.[153] For the question of whether films after World War II are still capable of stimulating thought, staging the sublime, or maintaining the belief in a transformed world, which does not lose sight of belief in the body – all without falling prey to a fascist aesthetic – cannot be determined in advance, but only on the level of the films themselves. Ultimately, therefore, I agree with Cavell's postulation that it is impossible to know beforehand what films are capable of; instead, only films themselves can define the medium of film, its possibilities and qualities.[154]

Besides this argument against Deleuze, which responds to his objections on a different level rather than theoretically parrying them, there is a basic point that seems to establish the legitimacy of revolution films for reflecting on political transformation after World War II. With Kant and Arendt, I was able to show in the second chapter that revolutionary *acts* were not the decisive factors for the effectiveness of the two modern revolutions; instead, it was commentating spectators who made the French Revolution into an event of world-historical significance, and their absence that became the downfall of the American Revolution. The notion that after World War II, revolution films that foreground action-thought – the third form of cinematic thought identified by Deleuze – have become impossible, is not a death sentence for revolution films. To put Arendt and Kant into conversation with Deleuze, in the postwar period it is important to turn to revolution films that do not attempt to mobilize the masses like the films of Eisenstein, but rather that stage revolution in an observational and commenting mode. After all, this is the level on which the success or failure of a revolution is decided.

---

which occupies the background of this discussion, see André Bazin: The Evolution of the Language of Cinema, in: id.: What Is Cinema?, op. cit., pp. 23–40. On the importance of problem and theorem, see Gilles Deleuze: Difference and Repetition, trans. by Paul Patton, London 2004, pp. 196 ff.

153 For a discussion of the various positions that can be found in Deleuze's writings on judgment, see Alexander García Düttmann: Das Urteil in der Kunst, in: Affekt und Urteil, op. cit., pp. 63–73, here pp. 63 ff.

154 Cf. Stanley Cavell: The World Viewed. Reflections on the Ontology of Film – Enlarged Edition, Cambridge, MA/London 1979, pp. 29 ff.

In the following chapters, I will examine this notion via two case studies. The question of the sublime remains a point of reference. Both audiovisual stagings can be regarded as a reaction to the limits and possibilities of the sublime after the Second World War. With regard to REDS, I will show how even after the war, it remained possible to create an aesthetic that is deeply related to the sublime. JOHN ADAMS, by contrast, should be understood as a turn away from the sublime; with this mini-series I will show what other possibilities exist for staging political transformation. The question of audiovisual metaphor as a possibility for thinking film will also remain in view. For Deleuze may have been too quick to exclude this figure in advance: Here too, it is only possible to determine on the level of the films themselves to what extent these types of stagings can be productive in post-World War II cinema – particularly if one lets go of Deleuze's overly narrow concept of metaphor in and through film.

5 REDS: The Russian Revolution in Hollywood

5.1 Situating the Film Historically

"I Was Hoping for a Happy Ending"

There is an anecdote about the film REDS that is sometimes invoked as paradigmatic of its political content or the reception thereof: On 7 December 1981, a few days after its nationwide premiere in the United States, there was a gala screening of the film at the White House, attended by the director, the star Warren Beatty, his co-star Diane Keaton, thirty other members of the cast and crew, and the Republican President Ronald Reagan. After the screening, the conservative anti-communist Reagan had only praise for the film. His sole criticism was that he would have liked to see a happy ending.[1]

If a film about the Bolshevik Revolution and the history of the American Communist Party could be so enthusiastically received by Reagan, argues the film historian Leger Grindon, it is evidence that in the film, at least contradictory forces are at work. And if, like Grindon, one examines the film's fifteen-year production history, it seems to confirm the existence of these forces.[2] As early as the mid-1960s, Beatty was toying with the idea of making a film about John Reed's life. Yet only with the success of BONNIE AND CLYDE (Arthur Penn, US 1967), which he co-produced, did he achieve the reputation and influence he needed to make this project a reality. He met with the Russian director Sergei Bondarchuk,[3] completed a treatment in 1969 and a step outline (the next step in Hollywood screenplay development) in 1971. Yet during these years, film work receded into the background for Beatty as he became increasingly politically engaged. In 1968 he

---

[1] On this anecdote, see Leger Grindon: Shadows on the Past. Studies in the Historical Fiction Film, Philadelphia 1994, p. 179.
[2] On the following, see Grindon's painstakingly researched production history in ibid., pp. 181–190.
[3] Bondarchuk was also working on a film about Reed's life and attempted – unsuccessfully – to convince Beatty to play the lead role. The result of Bondarchuk's work is the two-part RED BELLS PART I: MEXICO ON FIRE (SU/MX/IT 1982), and RED BELLS PART II: I SAW THE BIRTH OF A NEW WORLD (SU/MX/IT 1983). The first film, however, is about the Mexican Revolution, and Reed appears only at the very end. The second addresses some of the same events as Beatty's film. A comparison suggests itself between the two films' different stagings of gender relations and could make the argument that the Soviet production is clearly more repressive. One could also compare Beatty's and Bondarchuk's films with another film about John Reed: REED, MÉXICO INSURGENTE (Paul Leduc, MX 1973). A few arguments on these three films can be found in Robert A. Rosenstone: History on Film/Film on History, Harlow 2006, pp. 97 ff.

https://doi.org/10.1515/9783110754704-005

supported Robert Kennedy's campaign for the presidency; after the latter's assassination, he pushed for stronger gun control measures; and three years later, in 1971, he joined the presidential campaign of George McGovern, serving as not only a PR ambassador but also a political strategist. Only after McGovern's defeat in 1972 did he return to the film business.

Although he resumed work on the Reed biopic, meeting with Reed's contemporaries as well as the historian Robert Rosenstone, who was working on a biography about Reed,[4] he did not begin production of the film. Grindon suspects the reasons for this delay were pragmatic: After only one successful film, Beatty did not yet have the reputation necessary to acquire sufficient funding for the project. Grindon speculates further that Beatty wanted to get more directorial experience, and that his political work in the preceding years had dampened his belief in the possibility of changing the world. As a result, he turned away from the revolutionary Reed and instead wrote and starred in the film SHAMPOO (Hal Ashby, US 1975). Here, Beatty plays a hairdresser whose clothing, hairstyle, and lifestyle are clearly anchored in the hippie movement and counterculture. Even as he attempts to borrow money from banks or an investor to start his own beauty salon, he is simultaneously preoccupied with coordinating his relationships with three different sexual partners to whom he feels differing degrees of emotional connection. The film has a political component through the fact that the story unfolds on 5 November 1968 – the day that Richard Nixon was elected President of the United States. News about the election runs constantly on TV or the radio,[5] and at the end of the film all the protagonists and subplots come together at an election party. What is clear even from this brief summary is that the film engages both with hippie counterculture and the "New Left" political movement, of which Grindon argues that John Reed is a forerunner. With these elements, SHAMPOO speaks to the relationship between cultural (specifically sexual) and political revolution, a relationship that is also one of the central themes of REDS. Beatty's work on the latter film intensified after SHAMPOO finished production, as he continued work on the screenplay in collaboration with the British playwright Trevor Griffiths. The

---

4 See Robert A. Rosenstone: Romantic Revolutionary. A Biography of John Reed, Cambridge, MA 1990. Rosenstone is also named as a "Historical Consultant" in the film's end credits. This did not stop him, however, from penning a harshly critical review of the film. See Robert A. Rosenstone: Reds as History, in: Reviews in American History, 10 (3), 1982, pp. 297–310. Later, Rosenstone takes on a much less critical stance toward the film; see Rosenstone: History on Film/Film on History, op. cit., pp. 103 ff.
5 The second political theme that comes into the film through news reports is the Vietnam War.

Marxist Griffiths was known for plays that engaged with the experience of the proletariat, and thus led to the expectation of an explicitly political film about Reed's life. Yet despite Griffith's support, as well as Rosenstone's on the historical research, work on the film was put off again, and Beatty turned to the film HEAVEN CAN WAIT (US 1978), which came to cinemas in 1978 and in which he not only played the lead role, but also co-directed (with Buck Henry) and co-wrote the screenplay with Elaine May.[6] Unlike in REDS or SHAMPOO, here political questions recede entirely into the background. In the mode of romantic comedy, the film tells the story of a football player who dies in a car accident and learns in Heaven that his death was an error. He comes back to Earth in the body of another person, falls in love with the adversary of the man whose body he now occupies, and tries in this body to get onto another professional football team. The film was a commercial success and increased the studios' faith in Beatty's ability to deliver profitable films. Furthermore, it was becoming more pressing to begin production on REDS, as Beatty wanted to incorporate interviews with historical contemporaries into the film, and they would not live much longer. Thus in 1978 Beatty once again resumed intensive work on the film. Yet the political situation had fundamentally changed since the early 1970s: The counterculture had failed to make lasting changes, the political efforts of the New Left had not led to any significant transformation of American society, and President Jimmy Carter had – according to Grindon – also been unable to inspire any widespread sense of optimism. The conditions of the time in which the film was actually made were thus quite different from the conditions of the late 1960s, when Beatty began to conceive of the project in the wake of BONNIE AND CLYDE's success.

Grindon's thesis is that these doubts, divisions and uncertainties within the political Left at the end of the 1970s also appear in the film: Rather than focusing on a consistent look at Reed's life, Beatty attempted to please everyone, which made the film incoherent. According to Grindon, this is evident from the development of the screenplay. After Beatty and Griffiths completed a first draft, the manuscript was sent to Robert Towne, the co-writer of SHAMPOO, and Elaine May, the co-writer of HEAVEN CAN WAIT. Both sent back detailed edits, which Beatty and Griffiths incorporated. Concretely, the changes led to the political events losing weight in favor of foregrounding the love story between John Reed and Louise Bryant. The dialogue became more contemporary and lost its historical character. After another response from Towne and May, Beatty and Griffiths

---

6 Grindon does not mention Beatty's lead role in the 1975 film THE FORTUNE (Mike Nichols, US 1975), probably because Beatty did not take on any role behind the camera in this film.

revised the screenplay again, which ultimately led to Griffiths leaving the production. According to his statements, the changes were made purely on commercial grounds, and were no longer rooted in the historical figures or the historical situation.[7] In this history of how Beatty's screenplay evolved over the course of the 1970s, Grindon sees decreasing political commitment and growing commercial efforts. He postulates the opposition between political ambitions (represented by Griffiths) and commercial interests (represented by the Hollywood writers Towne and May), which led to a heavier emphasis on the love story at the cost of neglecting historical and political analysis. He sees this aspect of the production history as reflective of the general political development of the United States in the 1970s. Here too, the furor of the 1960s died away, and there was a general retreat from the political into the private sphere.

The question, however, is whether this dichotomy between love story and political history, as well as the resolution of this dichotomy in favor of the private love story, actually occur in the film in the way Grindon describes.[8] On the level of theory alone, at least three objections arise to Grindon's reconstruction of the film's emergence and the thesis he derives from it. First, the argument is quite tailored to the historical personage of Beatty, and somewhat resembles the 'great men' approach to history. Second, it is quite teleological: Everything points toward the finished film, and every step along the way is interpreted as leading to or delaying this final product.[9] Finally, the idea can be disputed that the film mirrors a more generalized turn away from the political radicalism of the 1960s and the social reality of the late 1970s and early 1980s. Taken literally, the mirror metaphor means that a mirror can only reflect what stands in front of it and is already visible. That would mean that even before seeing the film, the viewer already knows – or believes to know – what is in it. The viewer finds this in the film and is ultimately no wiser after seeing it than before.[10] Yet these arguments merely call Grindon's thesis into question. An answer can only be provided by turning to the film itself. Yet first I will introduce the movement

---

7 On this subject, see also Mick Eaton/Trevor Griffiths: History to Hollywood. Mick Eaton Talks to Trevor Griffiths, in: Screen, 23 (2), 1982, pp. 61–70.
8 Grindon refines his thesis by dividing it across the two parts of the film: The first half, he argues, is the film that emerged in the late 1960s, while the second half can be attributed to the late 1970s. See Grindon: Shadows of the Past, op. cit., pp. 194 f.
9 For a critique of this historiographical approach, see Thomas Elsaesser: Filmgeschichte und frühes Kino. Archäologie eines Medienwandels, Munich 2002, pp. 20–46.
10 On this critique of the mirror thesis and its foundational metaphor, see Michael Lück: Poetiken der Demokratie?, in: Rabbit Eye – Zeitschrift für Filmforschung, 4, 2012, pp. 35–47, here p. 40. Lück refers in this essay to David Bordwell: Historical Poetics of Cinema, in: The Cinematic Text. Methods and Approaches, ed. by R. Barton Palmer, New York 1989, pp. 369–398.

figurations of the film historical context of REDS. If NAPOLÉON was embedded in a cinema that, according to Deleuze, sought a maximum quantity of movement, the question arises what the films around REDS were seeking and how this film should be situated in light thereof.

The Not-So-New-Anymore Hollywood

If one looks at the themes and cast of the film (Warren Beatty, Diane Keaton, Jack Nicholson), it is immediately apparent that REDS is in proximity to the New Hollywood Cinema. Yet what movement figurations characterize this cinema? Hauke Lehmann researches this question in his study *Affect Poetics of the New Hollywood: Suspense, Paranoia, and Melancholy*.[11] His argument on this matter is:

> [...] the films of New Hollywood follow a strategy aimed at *challenging and overwhelming* the spectator, with respect to the affective-corporeal act of perception. They attack the various demarcations that ensure the integrity and stability of the spectatorial position with respect to a film's perception.[12]

This challenging and overwhelming of the spectator in New Hollywood films, writes Lehmann, can be immediately traced back to two aspects that define this school of cinema: shock and freedom.[13] Shock refers to the novelty that emerges from the New Hollywood Cinema, which cannot be reduced to the influences and creative conditions of the films. The shock is produced by the "tearing of the boundaries previously separating expressive and aesthetic registers."[14] Freedom refers first to freedom from the Hays Code. In another sense, however, it also refers to the expansion of formal tools on every level of the cinema (camera, acting, light, montage, sound, and music) as well as the turn away from homogeneous political approaches. The combination of the two terms, the "shock of freedom," then refers to a spectatorial experience

> characterized by the irresolvable contradiction between a new diversity of emotional experience and the more or less violent undermining of the embodied viewing position.

---

11 See Hauke Lehmann: Affect Poetics of the New Hollywood. Suspense, Paranoia, and Melancholy, trans. by James Lattimer, Berlin/Boston 2020.
12 Ibid., p. 10.
13 See ibid., pp. 9–12 and pp. 43 f. Lehmann takes the terms from Stefan Kanfer: Hollywood. The Shock of Freedom in Films, in: Time Magazine, 8 December 1967.
14 Lehmann: Affect Poetics of the New Hollywood, op. cit., p. 10.

This is the conflict that arises when the use of a greater range of more differentiated, expressive registers is combined with a strategy of the deliberate shattering of boundaries.[15]

According to Lehmann, this dynamic manifests in the spectatorial experience of New Hollywood films in three affective modes: suspense, paranoia, and melancholy. As already noted, Lehmann is critical of the homogenization of New Hollywood films and does not propose these three affective modes as such. Yet all three have in common that they address the spectator both as active and as passive; they address the spectator's capacity to feel and perceive, but they also attack and wound. For Lehmann, the common denominator of affect-poetic understandings of New Hollywood lies in the "*splitting of the spectator* in terms of affective experience."[16] This splitting is realized as a "short circuit [...] connecting two different modalities of vision," he adds in a clarifying remark.[17]

Even a superficial viewing of REDS reveals that the film's relationship to the New Hollywood cinema is ambivalent. On the one hand, the film seems quite close to New Hollywood. In particular the lead actor, co-screenwriter, and director Warren Beatty, through his role as Clyde Barrow in BONNIE AND CLYDE – a film that is "generally regarded as spearheading New Hollywood"[18] – is associated with the movement more than almost any other figure. The themes that define the film – the counterculture of New York's Greenwich Village and the wish for a radical change to society – seem related to the term New Hollywood. On the other hand, Beatty's film maintains a certain distance from the earlier movement. Purely chronologically speaking, New Hollywood usually refers to American cinema between 1967 and 1976.[19] Even on this primary and quite banal level, it is clear that despite its proximity to New Hollywood, REDS cannot be simply categorized within it: It comes a few years too late. Further, the film's opulent – following Sobchack's essay on Hollywood epics, one might say extravagant – production values distance it somewhat from New Hollywood Cinema. It is no coincidence that Sobchack discusses the film in an essay that deals primarily with Hollywood epics of the 1950s and 1960s. The New Hollywood Cinema emerged shortly after the collapse of the Hollywood studio system and was

---

15 Ibid., p. 12.
16 Ibid.
17 Ibid., p. 8.
18 Ibid., p. 5. REDS shares not only a lead actor with BONNIE AND CLYDE, but also one of its editors, Dede Allen. The other editor of REDS was Craig McKay.
19 On the status of research into New Hollywood Cinema and different approaches to its periodization, see ibid., pp. 27–36. Lehman dates the end of New Hollywood Cinema to 1980.

characterized by small, independent productions.[20] And putting the staging of REDS into conversation with the defining movement figurations of New Hollywood Cinema reveals no clear analogy. But how does REDS *relate* to the movement figurations of New Hollywood? Even if it is difficult to relate Lehmann's affective modes of suspense, paranoia, and melancholy to this film, its connection with New Hollywood is strong enough – namely, with regard to the previously named keywords of shock and freedom, as well as the splitting of the spectator through challenging and overwhelming. The answer to the question of how precisely the film corresponds to these concepts, or to what extent it departs from them – and what significance that correspondence or departure has – can only come from an observation of the film itself.

5.2 Revolution

The Gaze on Revolution

"Paramount Pictures Presents" – in white letters against a black background, the phrase appears and the film begins. After the text fades and only the black image remains, music starts: a high, cheerful, springy melody played on a piano, whose quick rhythm immediately evokes life at the beginning of the twentieth century, and particularly the Bohemian lifestyle of some Americans in this era. The song is the "Dill Pickles Rag," composed by Charles Leslie Johnson in 1906.[21] More than almost any other style, ragtime music stands for turn-of-the-century optimism. A commonly repeated story about the derivation of the name assumes that the composite term 'ragtime' is made up of the technical term 'time' for

---

[20] On the economic background of New Hollywood, see Geoff King: New Hollywood Cinema. An Introduction, New York 2002, pp. 24 ff. I do not mean to assert that New Hollywood Cinema was simply a consequence of the collapse of the Hollywood studio system. This thesis would lag behind Lehmann's approach, which correctly comes out against an overly simple determination of film history by economic conditions (cf. Lehmann: Affect Poetics of the New Hollywood, op. cit., p. 3).

[21] See the entry "Dill Pickles" in Ingeborg Harer: Ragtime. Versuch einer Typologie, Tutzing 1989, p. 159. Vincent Canby notes the "Scott Joplin ragtime tune" that opens the film (see Vincent Canby: Beatty's "Reds," with Diane Keaton, in: The New York Times, 4 December 1981). The name Scott Joplin, however, functions more as a stand-in for the genre of the piece than a reference to the composer. Joplin is "the outstanding composer of the piano ragtime phenomenon;" see Jürgen Hunkemöller: Ragtime, in: Die Musik in Geschichte und Gegenwart. Allgemeine Enzyklopädie der Musik. Sachteil 8 Quer–Swi, ed. by Friedrich Blume/Ludwig Finscher, Kassel et al. 1998, pp. 57–68, here p. 63 [Translator's note: my translation].

rhythm, and that 'rag' can be traced back to the adjective 'ragged,' characterizing this music as a form of irregular, disorderly, torn, or tattered rhythms. This description fits with the fact that its primary marker is syncopation.[22] Even if this origin story stands on uncertain footing,[23] it offers a fitting description of the experience of listening to a ragtime composition. Especially since the syncopation indeed applies to notated ragtime compositions.[24] Thus even before the film's first images, it opens with a shift in rhythm, and with it a particular form of temporality. It is a time that is torn, out of whack, in which new freedoms arise. The use of this music introduces the first central theme of the film (and one of the central themes of this book): time and how it is modulated.

While 'ragtime,' 'ragged time,' plays on the soundtrack, first the film's title and then the names of actors appear against a black background, followed by a list of names under the heading 'Witnesses.' The music becomes quieter, retreats into the background, and gradually fades until it disappears entirely. Next comes a male voice that is not paired with any image – the opening credits continue – but whose advanced age clearly comes across. The voice is uncertain, cracked, a bit hoarse: "Was that in 1913 or 17? I can't remember now. I'm

---

22 See ibid., p. 58. See also Jürgen Hunkemöller: Was Ist Ragtime?, in: Archiv für Musikwissenschaft, 42 (2), 1985, pp. 69–86. In the context of my work, it is also worth noting that Hunkemöller credits the film THE STING (George Roy Hill, US 1973) – a classic of the New Hollywood Cinema – with the renewed popularity of this music in the late 1970s and early 1980s. Here too, REDS stands in the tradition of New Hollywood. Interestingly, the same year as REDS, 1981, also saw the film RAGTIME (Miloš Forman, US) come out. The latter takes place in pre-World War I US and like REDS, was supposed to feature Emma Goldman. The scenes with Goldman, however, were cut. See the comparison of the two films in Arthur Schlesinger Jr.: History and the Imagination. Ragtime and Reds, in: American Heritage, 33 (3), 1982, pp. 42 f. Schlesinger writes: "Ragtime's theme – the dangerous tensions building up under the syncopated cheeriness of American society before the First World War – predicts the revolutionary explosions of Reds" (ibid., p. 42). Yet RAGTIME's central point of reference for rebellion (and possible revolution) escapes him: The main plot about the character Coalhouse Walker Jr. is an adaptation of Kleist's novella *Michael Kohlhaas*. David Thomson's comparison of the two films also overlooks this connection, see David Thomson: Redtime, in: Film Comment, 18 (1), 1982, pp. 11–16.
23 See Hunkemöller: Ragtime, op. cit., p. 58. The author writes that "etymologically and grammatically, the foundations are lacking for this derivation" (ibid. [Translator's note: my translation]). Furthermore, syncopation does not encompass all the rhythmic particularities of this musical style. According to Hunkemöller, the term 'ragtime' can be traced back to a dance from Sudan with the name 'rag.' Here, however, I am only interested in the fact that the derivation gives an adequate description of the impression made by the music.
24 Cf. ibid.

beginning to forget all the people that I used to know, see?"[25] Another voice enters, also that of an old man: "Do I remember Louise Bryant? Why, of course, I couldn't forget her if I tried." After this line, the first image of the film appears: against a black background, in closeup, the face of an older woman with grey hair and wrinkled skin; located on the right edge of the frame, the right half of her face remains in shadow.[26] Wearing a black sweater and black earrings, she is both modestly clothed and modestly staged. Through this restrained staging, the focus is not on her or her appearance, but rather on what she says: "I can't ... I might sort of scratch my memory, but not at the moment. You know, things go and come back again." After a cut, an old man with grey hair, a bald spot, moustache and round glasses, also shot in closeup against a black background and located on the right edge of the frame: "It was Christopher Street, and I was thinking about another street down there instead, until it came back that it was Christopher Street. Sometimes I have lapses like that." After another cut, another old woman, whose countless wrinkles give an especially strong impression of a life lived to the fullest: "I'd forgotten all about them. Were they socialists? I guess they must've been, but I don't think they were of any importance. I don't remember them at all." The next witness: "I know that Jack went around with Mabel Dodge, and then he went around with another gal, and then he went around with Louise Bryant. I know there were shifts back and forth, but it never occurred to me ... It never impinged on my own personal life. I like baseball." More takes follow of witnesses who recall Louise Bryant and John Reed – or try to – and provide first impressions of them. With the witnesses, who are given prominent place at the film's opening, and in particular with the first voices cited here, the film introduces four more themes that concern and define it.

The use of witnesses whose age and experience are clearly visible and audible, as well as their attempt to report on the film's protagonists and historical context, addresses not only the passage of time, but also the film's second theme, which is closely related to the first (and is also one of the central topics

---

25 Lines from the film are cited based on the English subtitle track on the DVD version of the film. The timecode for these and the following citations is 00:01:24–00:02:50 (Disc 1).
26 Jonathan Rosenbaum compares the lighting of these shots with those in portraits by the photographer Richard Avedon. See Jonathan Rosenbaum: Jack Reed's Christmas Puppy. Reflections on REDS, in: Sight and Sound, 51 (2), 1982, pp. 110–113, here p. 111; the cinematographer's notes on the style he sought to create can be found in Vittorio Storaro: Photographic Aims – Reds, in: American Cinematographer, 63 (5), 1982, p. 487 and p. 490.

of film theory): the question of memory and historiography.[27] The mention of Christopher Street, which both today and at the time of the film's appearance is usually heard with the addendum 'Day,' also invokes the emancipatory LGBT movement. More generally speaking, Christopher Street brings up the question of sexuality and gender relations – a point that will become closely connected with the question of political revolution over the course of the film. Finally, the film's first voices introduce the relationship between the private and the political. One of the witnesses refuses to draw a connection between his and Reed's life on the basis that he likes baseball. The question of the relationship between the private and the political is the film's fourth central motif. Furthermore, it is important that the viewer at first hears only the witnesses speaking, and that the film's first four-and-a-half minutes include no images of the diegetic world. This strategy endows language and speech with eminent significance.[28] Looking to Sobchack's discussion of 1950s and 1960s Hollywood epics, an interesting mixture emerges of resemblance and divergence. Just like the earlier epics, REDS also begins with a voice that brings the events that will be narrated in the film into the spectator's present. In direct contrast to the epics of preceding years, however, this voice is not the deep, authoritative voice of a male star, but anonymous, frail, uncertain, and quavering. The film clearly references the scheme of old Hollywood epics only to further undermine it by using multiple voices, creating polyphony both on the level of timbre as well as that of opinion and perspective. With this opening, REDS thus embraces and breaks with the tradition of Hollywood epics. The function of language and speech is the fifth thematic complex to which the film repeatedly returns in connection with its other themes. The characters, especially the politicians in the film, are constantly shown as speakers. As in Arendt's work, in the film man is a political being because he is a speaking being: Reed and Bryant work as journalists, and as such are in St. Petersburg/Leningrad during the October Revolution; speech (writing), work, art, and revolution are all introduced here. With that, on the level of content alone the film displays an affinity with the perspective on

---

[27] Historio-*graphy* – the *writing* of history – is not meant literally (i.e., lexically). I follow Sobchack in moving away from understanding film as text.

[28] For Deleuze, the autonomy of sound, and of speech acts in particular, is an important characteristic of modern cinema: the speech act "turns in on itself; it is no longer a dependant or something which is part of the visual image; it becomes a completely separate sound image; it takes on a cinematographic autonomy and cinema becomes truly audio visual" (Gilles Deleuze: Cinema 2. The Time-Image, trans. by Hugh Tomlinson/Robert Galeta, London/New York 1989, p. 243). With this reference, I do not mean to argue that this film is in every way a modern film in Deleuze's sense; yet it can be stated that it works with the stylistic tools of this cinema and is not a pure pastiche of 1950s Hollywood cinema.

revolution developed in this book. It is not about revolutionaries, but about journalists who report on the Revolution. Just as for Kant and Arendt, for the film the decisive element of a revolution lies not in the acts of revolutionaries, but on the level of the public that sees and comments on it.

Thus, even before the diegetic world is revealed, the film establishes its primary accents through the use of ragtime music and contemporary witnesses. No wonder, then, that the use of and interaction with historical witnesses are frequently highlighted in the literature on the film.[29] The opening and closing credits give 32 names; some of them are totally unknown people who met John Reed and/or Louise Bryant over the course of their life, but some are famous personalities like the writer Henry Miller (whose presence alone gives prominent emphasis to the theme of sexual revolution). The witnesses – not only Miller, though particularly explicitly in his case – represent the sense of upheaval [*Aufbruchszeit*] and the bohemian lifestyle of New York, and especially Greenwich Village, in the 1900s and 1910s. Already through the use of witnesses, the film is recognizable as a reflection on New Hollywood Cinema, one that looks back on the preceding decade (in film) from a critical distance. With the witnesses, the film immediately expresses that the New Hollywood movement, or more generally the youth and counterculture of the late 1960s and early 1970s did not invent youth and protest culture, but are part of a much longer history. Yet no names appear with the faces; the film does not categorize or identify the witnesses. It refuses to create a hierarchy between the various statements, and instead lets equality rule. On the witnesses and the way in which they are staged, Grindon argues in brief:

> Because the appearance of the witnesses precedes the first image of the fictive world, they seem a generating force. The dark surroundings, weathered faces, and untrained voices draw a sharp line between their reminiscence and the detailed panorama of the period drama […]. The abstract nature of the setting, a completely dark, uninhabited space, makes it appear as if they speak from a common position, but one that is apart from the world. They hover over and intrude upon the fictive world at will, like spirits who

---

29 See the voices discussed by Grindon: Shadows on the Past, op. cit., pp. 210 ff. See also Thomson: Redtime, op. cit., p. 16; Jim Beaver: Reds, in: Films in Review, 33 (2), 1982, pp. 112 f., here p. 112; Edward Buscombe: Making Love and Revolution. Edward Buscombe Reviews the Reviews of "Reds", in: Screen, 23 (2), 1982, pp. 71–75, here p. 73; Rosenbaum: Jack Reed's Christmas Puppy, op. cit., pp. 111 f.; Richard Combs: Reds, in: Monthly Film Bulletin, 49 (3), 1982, pp. 47 f., here p. 48; Jon Silberg: Reds, in: American Cinematographer, 88 (5), 2007, p. 10 and p. 12; Olivier Eyquem: Reds, in: Positif, 256 (6), 1982, pp. 59 f., here p. 60; Milton Cantor: Review, in: The American Historical Review, 87 (5), 1982, pp. 1482–1484, here p. 1483; Rosenstone: Reds as History, op. cit., pp. 300 f.; a few remarks on the background of the takes of witnesses can be found in Eaton/Griffiths: History to Hollywood, op. cit., p. 62.

comment upon, but cannot change, the fate of men and women. Their collective voice animates a play between character and chorus, story and discourse, memory and history. Their voices close the film as the final credits unroll. Framing the story as they do, the witnesses resemble a Greek chorus, as noted by many commentators, probably beginning with Vincent Canby.[30]

Grindon establishes an opposition between 'history' and 'memory.'[31] This difference, which is introduced by the witnesses, becomes the film's cardinal problem for Grindon. Here he agrees with Rosenstone, who was, as previously noted, the film's 'historical consultant.' Grindon and Rosenstone understand 'memory' to refer to the witnesses' statements: They remember the historical events, or try to, and in doing so sometimes contradict each other. The decisive point for Grindon is that most of the contradictions that arise between the statements, and "appear" to lend the film a certain complexity, are unambiguously resolved through the fictional representation of events:

> The drama generally resolves the ambiguity of the testimony rather than embellishing its complexity [...]. In spite of the framing device established by the witnesses, 'Reds' gives its fiction decisive authority.[32]

The hierarchy ascribed to the film and Grindon's critique thereof are justified by the fact that the witnesses' statements not only contradict each other, but are also often followed by images that 'correct' the statements, thereby undermining them.[33] Rosenstone goes even a step further in his critique of the use of witnesses. For him, the film presents an *equivalence* between 'history' and 'memory.' The witnesses are used on the one hand as sources who deliver information about the historical personages. On the other hand, with their forgetfulness and contradictions, they stand for a deep relativization of historiography: "[...] the

---

30 Grindon: Shadows on the Past, op. cit., pp. 213 f. Grindon references Vincent Canby: Beatty's "Reds," with Diane Keaton, op. cit.
31 He does not go into more depth on the difference introduced by Émile Benveniste between 'story' and 'discourse,' which is also interesting for film theory. On these terms, see Christian Metz: The Imaginary Signifier. Psychoanalysis and Cinema, trans. by Celia Britton et al., Bloomington/Indianapolis 1982, pp. 89 ff.; a Hegelian definition of 'story,' i.e., the narrative style of so-called classical Hollywood cinema, can be found in Hermann Kappelhoff: Matrix der Gefühle. Das Kino, das Melodrama und das Theater der Empfindsamkeit, Berlin 2004., pp. 54 f. Because Grindon does not define these terms, which are quite differently conceived in different contexts, and also does not relate them more clearly to the film, it is difficult to understand what he intends to do by naming this opposition at this point. On the various meanings of these terms, see David Bordwell: Narration in the Fiction Film, London 1988, pp. 21 f.
32 Grindon: Shadows on the Past, op. cit., pp. 214 f.
33 Cf. ibid., p. 214.

Witnesses ultimately suggest that nobody can know the truth about Reed and Bryant. Thus, the filmmaker can tell us whatever story he wishes (and history be damned!)."[34] If historical truth cannot be achieved, one version of history is as good as any other, to offer a pointed summary of the position that Rosenstone ascribes to the film, and for which he reproaches it.

These critiques of the film, however, are unsatisfactory for two reasons: First, one could respond to Grindon quite simply that chronology does not necessarily imply hierarchy, but that the witnesses instead – precisely through their polyphony – relativize the authority of the fictional images. Second – and this is certainly the weightier objection – Grindon and Rosenstone's judgments hold the film to standards that it lacks or that are inappropriate for it. Indeed, Grindon himself postulates that there is a difference "between the representation of history in the cinema and the representation of history in scholarship,"[35] yet he does not conclude that he should treat the film any differently than he would a schoolbook. Instead, he makes the following remarks on the use of witnesses:

> The witnesses themselves offer memories, not history, but in the carefully shaped chorus *the filmmakers attempt to evoke history* [emphasis mine] – the spectacle of 1916–20 and the personal histories of the protagonists. The filmmakers constructed their narrative history in the drama and enlisted the witnesses to bolster it.[36]

With his assertion that the filmmakers "attempt to evoke history," Grindon unnecessarily limits his perspective on the film.[37]

---

34 Rosenstone: Reds as History, op. cit., p. 301.
35 Grindon: Shadows on the Past, op. cit., p. 220.
36 Ibid.
37 The fact that this assumption can be justified as Grindon himself does, by referring to an interview with Beatty in which the latter states that his film depicts an era of American history that should be familiar to every schoolchild (cf. ibid., p. 218 f.), does not make it any more plausible. Here, Grindon commits only one of the many possible intentional fallacies. On the concept of the intentional fallacy – developed in literary theory – see William Kurtz Wimsatt Jr./Monroe Curtis Beardsley: The Intentional Fallacy, in: The Sewanee Review, 54, 1946, pp. 468–488. For a polemic against an author-based perspective on literature, see the deeply anti-authoritarian essay by Roland Barthes: The Death of the Author, in: id.: Image-Music-Text, trans. by Stephen Heath, New York 1978, pp. 142–148. Further thoughts on the function of the author and the possibilities that exist after his 'death' can be found in Michel Foucault: What Is an Author?, in: id.: Language, Counter-Memory, Practice. Selected Essays and Interviews, ed. by Donald F. Bouchard, trans. by id./Sherry Simon, Ithaca/New York 1977, pp. 113–138. For a discussion of the authorial function in the context of film studies, see Jürgen Felix: Autorenkino, in: Moderne Film-Theorie, ed. by id., Mainz 2003, pp. 13–61.

If one ignores the question of who is correct – the witnesses or the fictional world of the film – and instead regards the use of witnesses from the perspective of temporal relations I develop in this book, the argument could be made that the witnesses constitute the aforementioned connection between the historical events of the 1910s, the historical cinema audience of the early 1980s, and contemporary viewers of the film. The witnesses demonstrate to the audience of the early 1980s and the New Hollywood generation that the counterculture of the 1960s and 1970s was by no means the first youth culture in the US. Rather, against all questioning of the film's political content – as expressed e.g., in the anecdote about Ronald Reagan told at the beginning of this chapter – one could argue that through the use of witnesses, the film produces a connection between different political struggles and movements.[38]

The film's closing credits support this argument. If the opening credits can be described as a "mediator between not-yet-film and film,"[39] the closing credits mediate between film and no-longer-film. The closing credits still belong to the film, yet not to the diegesis, and can be understood as a direct address to the spectator.[40] During the closing credits in REDS – after three hours spent following the life of John Reed and Louise Bryant – as the names of the crew appear on the screen and disappear again to the song 'Goodbye for Now,' composed by Stephen Sondheim for the film,[41] the voices of the witnesses again emerge on the soundtrack, speaking about the legacy and deeds of John Reed and Louise Bryant:[42] "He was just a man in the prime of life. I don't even know. Did they ever have any children? They probably didn't have any children, he and Louise. Again, you can't tell, when you have children, whether they will carry on your revolutionary tradition or not." And another voice: "He's well known amongst a few, but not everybody. They don't know who in heck he is. I look for myself to die any day. [chuckles]." And finally, closing out the film: "Of course, nobody goes with the

---

38 It would be a shortcut to equate the historical situation of the early twentieth century with the situation of the early 1980s. Instead, there is a genealogical relationship [*Traditionslinie*].
39 Karl Sierek: Aus der Bildhaft. Filmanalyse als Kinoästhetik, Vienna 1993, p. 197 [Translator's note: my translation].
40 The French terms for opening and closing credits encapsulate this notion more precisely: The French 'générique' for opening credits clearly implies the world-building function, the relationship to generating and genesis. This sense is not lost in the term 'générique du fin' for closing credits.
41 Stephen Sondheim, who composed the film's score, identifies this piece as a "love theme" and appropriately qualifies it with the description "romantic and slightly sad." See his remarks in the documentary included as bonus material on the DVD "Witness to REDS: Propaganda" (Timecode: 00:02:28 and 00:02:44).
42 Timecode: 01:24:18–01:27:20 (Disc 2).

idea of dying. Everybody wants to live. I don't remember his exact words, but the meaning was that grand things are ahead, worth living and worth dying for. He himself said that." Thus, not only at its opening, but also at its close, the film establishes a connection between the revolutionary judgments and ideas of its protagonists and the historical present of its viewers. Now the question arises of which strategies are used to realize and present the life of the characters as well as the motifs and themes that are already signaled in the opening credits.

The question of the relationship between historical events and their cinematic representation, which is raised by the use of witnesses and which has been extensively discussed in the literature on the film, is quickly taken up again shortly after the film's opening. It is paired with the question of the difference between film and photography as media, as the film uses photographs to introduce the inhabitants of early twentieth century Greenwich Village. The film works both with pictures of historical figures (when the figure does not appear later on as a character, as with Isadora Duncan and Walter Lippmann) and with pictures that show the actors in their roles (when this person also appears as a character in the film; for example, a photograph of Maureen Stapleton as Emma Goldman and Jack Nicholson as Eugene O'Neill, which closes out the series of photographs).[43] If one sees the relationship between photography and film from the perspective of Jean Epstein's essays, this use of (or return to) photography becomes useful for the questions discussed here. Unlike André Bazin or Roland Barthes, for example, who understand photography as a trace of the signified and thus see in photography a tool to protect against time, a tool of preservation or connection to the past, Epstein is skeptical of photography.[44] In photography, he first sees only "rigid comedy," "pitiful awkwardness," and "a sign of lost time."[45] Photography is not capable of arresting life: "Each moment possesses a quality that even the fastest shutter could not capture: it is the quality of being:

---

[43] See Grindon: Shadows on the Past, op. cit., p. 209. The timecode of the photographs runs from 00:22:17–00:23:07 (Disc 1).

[44] I am not interested in giving a full account of the much-discussed relationship between film and photography, or their respective relationships with death. I simply aim to provide context for Jean Epstein's contribution to the debate and its relevance for the use of photographs in Beatty's film. On Bazin see André Bazin: The Ontology of the Photographic Image, in: id.: What Is Cinema? Vol. 1, trans. by Hugh Gray, Berkeley/Los Angeles/London 2004, pp. 9–16; on Barthes, see Roland Barthes: Camera Lucida. Reflections on Photography, trans. by Richard Howard, New York 1980.

[45] Jean Epstein: Le cinématographe dans l'Archipel, in: id.: Écrits sur le cinéma. 1921–1953. Édition chronologique en deux volumes. Vol. I: 1921–1947, Paris 1974, pp. 196–200, here p. 198 [Translator's note: my translation].

the present."⁴⁶ If, however, the person pictured in the photo has died, the situation completely changes: Paradoxically, the photograph then "receives life," for the soul of the dead person becomes visible within it.⁴⁷ It is only death that allows the true essence of a person to come to light; only death reveals who somebody was. Before a person's death, according to Epstein, it is always possible for them to change, for new character traits to appear. Only death puts an end to this constant changeability, which is also why only death elevates photography from a random snapshot to an impression of someone's essence and personality: "The living person becomes himself only in death."⁴⁸

As already became clear in my summary of the concept *photogénie*, for Epstein there is another potential way for the essence, the soul, the personality to emerge: through cinematographic recordings. In the context of his comparison with photographic recordings, Epstein writes: "Like death, the cinematograph – which otherwise would hardly exist – is an instrument of justice."⁴⁹ When a static recording becomes a recording of movement, the latter shows the essence of what is depicted – and does so without requiring a detour through death, but through movement, which for Epstein means: through life.⁵⁰

Working from Epstein's premises, the use of photography in REDS paints this picture: both the photographs of real historical persons, as well as the photographs of fictional, 'represented' figures, are brought to life by the film. The most important distinction is this: For the real personalities, this enlivening comes from the fact that those people were already dead by the time the film came out, while for the 'represented' figures it happens through the fact that

---

46 Ibid., pp. 197 f. [Translator's note: my translation].
47 Ibid., p. 198 [Translator's note: my translation].
48 Ibid. [Translator's note: my translation].
49 Ibid., p. 199 [Translator's note: my translation – the following paragraphs are based on the German translation of Epstein's text where it reads: "Like death, the cinematograph – which otherwise would hardly exist – makes visible the true essence of things and humans" (Jean Epstein: Der Kinematograph auf dem Archipel, in: Bonjour Cinéma und andere Schriften zum Kino, ed. by Nicole Brenez/Ralph Eue, trans. by Ralf Eue, Vienna 2008, pp. 57–62, here p. 60). It is worth noting that this essay was written in 1928. As I thoroughly explained in the section "Film, Time, and Movement: Epstein's and Deleuze's Conception: Epstein," in his post-World War II essays, Epstein no longer grants the cinematograph the capacity to make visible a human being's true essence.
50 Just as the cinematograph and its movement are derived from the projection of individual photographic images (which are not recognized as such in the perception of film), for Epstein the relationship between life and death is not one of simple opposition. Instead, they are tightly interwoven: "One will see that life and death accompany each other, play with each other, tell each other everything, can never leave each other" (Epstein: Le cinématographe dans l'Archipel, op. cit., p. 200 [Translator's note: my translation]).

they later on become a part of the film, and their images move. With that, the depictions of real people are associated with death, and the fictional figures with life. The use of photographs should thus be understood as a case for the possible, and for fictionalization. In this way, the film adopts Aristotle's distinction between poetry and history. In showing the fictionalized figures first in photographs and later in motion, i.e., showing them enlivened, but confining the historical figures who are not fictionalized to still photographs, the film (like Aristotle) privileges the possible. Fictionalization – from an Epsteinian perspective – becomes associated with life. Through the way in which the film deals with photographs, it becomes clear that it is not primarily interested in showing "history;" instead, it seeks to envision a *possible* time, a *possible* history of the Revolution, and to bring it to life.

The other motifs and themes of the film are summarized in the first extensive encounter between Louise Bryant and John Reed, in a scene in which Bryant interviews Reed.

The Asynchronous Rendezvous

As previously noted, the film is divided into two halves; that is, there is a planned intermission in the middle. In the first half, the protagonists meet, fall in love, break up, yet still travel together to St. Petersburg, experience the Russian Revolution together, and then reconcile. The second half centers on the protagonists' attempt to bring the Revolution back to America, the failure of this attempt, and the protagonists' renewed life as outsiders, which leads to John Reed returning alone to the USSR and experiencing the failure of the Russian Revolution there as well. Because of Reed's declining health and the impossibility of remaining in contact from a distance, Louise Bryant ultimately follows him. Shortly after her arrival and the protagonists' reunion, Reed dies of kidney failure. The film ends there.

In their affective qualities, the two halves are clearly distinct. Broadly speaking, the first half tells a story of ascent, which culminates in the Bolsheviks' seizure of power, while the second half tells a story of downfall and decline. The first half is marked by acceleration, by scenes in which large periods of time are condensed by montage. In addition, a humorous note runs through the first half of the film: Again and again, there are ironic breaks and moments of comic relief. These are absent from the second half. Here, a dark mood predominates and is sustained (only once, at the beginning of the second part, is there a moment of humor, when the film shows Reed attempting to cook) until it finally ends with the failure of the Russian Revolution and the death of John Reed. In contrast to the scenes in the first half, there is hardly any compression of time; instead, time is stretched out and slowed down. The scenes analyzed in the following subchapters can each be understood as standing in for this macro-structure, that is for the general process of the half in which they are respectively situated.

The next scene to be analyzed comes relatively early in the film and shows the first long meeting of the two protagonists, John Reed and Louise Bryant.[51] Bryant had previously asked Reed for an interview on his political activities. This meeting was supposed to happen at her home. At the beginning of the scene, however, the characters do not speak about the topic at hand, but about the apartment in which they are located, which is not actually Bryant's home, and the question of whether each is married or believes in marriage. Thus, the dialogue leads both the characters and the spectators to expect a love scene more than a political discussion. The scene's brief exposition already contains much of what will be addressed throughout the film: the relationship between men and women, life, desire, language (whether writing or speech), work, – and how all of this relates to politics.

Through cinematography, image composition, and performance, the scene stages an image of a meeting between the two protagonists that shifts between insecurity, attraction, and confrontation, which transforms into an image of violence and overwhelm in the form of men and women's asynchronicity and tendency to miss each other. In the first EMU, the image composition and performance present an image of oscillation between attraction and separation, which is then transformed through editing (the dominant formal principle of the EMU) into an image of confrontation, violence, and overwhelm. The second EMU, which begins with shot 28, repeats the image of attraction through performance (the dominant formal principle) and image composition, but this time the attraction turns into an image of comedic surprise.

First EMU: 00:00:00:00–00:01:41:16
In the interplay between cinematography, image composition, and performance, the first EMU stages an image of insecurity and attraction as a hesitant approach of movements, which transforms into an image of confrontation and violence.

The first take of the first EMU begins in Louise Bryant's apartment. The dominant colors in the image are the beige of the walls and the bright, warm light that fills the room. In this setting, the image of attraction and uncertainty is produced through performance. Both actors build moments of uncertainty into their speech: Diane Keaton repeats certain words, which has the effect of a stutter. Warren

---

51 The timecode for this scene is 00:08:35–00:12:06 (Disc 1).

Beatty expresses himself in part with inarticulate, meaningless sounds, but no fully formed words or sentences. This image of attraction, however, is interrupted by a pan that follows John Reed's stride to the left and that brings with it a radical change in the lighting. After this move, Reed stands in front of a large window that lets in dark blue light,[52] and only his dark silhouette is visible; the entire visual space is immersed in dark blue light. Through this change in the lighting, the space in which Reed is located seems completely separate from the (same) space occupied by Bryant. Yet the performance and particularly the prosody of the voices counteract the staging of the space and continue to produce an image of attraction and erotic tension. The dialogue, whose content is equally fraught with sexual tension, about the value of marriage, is marked by clear shifts in prosody. Keaton's voice is sometimes clear, articulate, and brisk; then it will rise into a very high register, until she begins to whisper and her questions for Reed venture into the coquettish. Beatty's voice also oscillates between clear and direct statements and quiet, tentatively posed questions ("Are you married?"). Yet the protagonists are repeatedly separated by editing: Bryant in beige room with warm lighting, Reed backlit in dark blue, seemingly in a completely different space.

The transformation to the image of confrontation and violence occurs – content-wise – with the start of the interview. In formal terms, there is a shift in the elements of performance and editing, which dominate this EMU. First, the tonality of Keaton's speech changes completely; her subsequent statements can best be described as a tirade. Keaton speaks quite fast, very clearly, and articulately. Punctuation is still barely detectable, but not emphasized; even after a period, comma, or question mark, Keaton continues without pausing, and there are only a few variations in her tonality. The confrontational (almost aggressive) mood created by this speaking style is further intensified by the fact that she stares at Reed continuously. Reed lightly wrinkles his brow, raises his head a little, and inhales, creating the impression that he wants to answer. Yet he breaks off halfway through and looks down again, as Bryant, who seems like she is wound up, keeps reciting her questions uninterrupted, maintaining her speed. The decisive point is the end of her speech: She is cut off midsentence by the editing. For the spectator, this sudden interruption of speech comes as an experience of violence. This violent experience is then pushed further by editing and sound as the scene progresses.[53] The cut that interrupts Bryant's speech is further underscored by the fact that it is accompanied by a

---

52 Diegetically, this lighting is motivated by the fact that the scene takes place at night.
53 The spatial arrangement of the two figures during Reed's subsequent monologue also reveals a hierarchical relationship: While she sits on the sofa and looks up at him, he stands across from her and looks down at her.

hard and sudden change on the level of sound. Now we hear Beatty's voice, which does not 'fade in,' but immediately emerges at full volume. He begins with a question, "Alright Miss Bryant, you want an interview?," followed by a command that is delivered in a clear, articulate, and determined voice, which falls off toward the end and in which each individual word is emphasized: "Write this down!" Beatty delivers the half-sentence that follows in the next shot, "Are you naïve enough to think [...]," in a very high tone of voice, which lends it a mocking air. After that there is no halt to his speech. He speaks extremely quickly, without pausing, hammering at Bryant in a staccato delivery.

Reed's staccato declamations are associated with an elliptical montage. Strung together by rapid (some shots are barely even a second long) jump-cuts, the sequence shows Bryant writing down his words, turning the page of her notebook, looking quickly up at him; he appears standing in the room, talking and repeatedly pouring coffee into Bryant's cup. The association of continuous speech and discontinuous montage creates an asynchronicity between image and sound that the spectator experiences as violence. This impression is intensified by the use of hard cuts on the soundtrack. The image of confusion, overload, and overwhelm on the spectator's end culminates acoustically when two tracks of Reed's monologue are laid over each other and mixed together.[54] After this climax, the EMU fades out; the high editing speed, the elliptical montage, the asynchronicity of image and sound and the hard cuts on the soundtrack end. Tolling bells sound in the distance, Reed abruptly interrupts his monologue[55] and looks wide-eyed at Bryant.

Second EMU: 00:01:41:17–0:03:30:01
Through the interplay of performance and image composition, the second EMU stages an image of attraction that transforms into an image of surprise as the missing of men and women.

In the shift to this EMU, editing ceases to dominate; the brief shots of the previous EMU are replaced by notably longer shots (which last up to 49 seconds). At the beginning of the EMU, Bryant is shot at a slightly high angle, sitting on the sofa. Now, however, she is no longer sitting straight upright – as she was during the

---

54 This overwhelm, however, is not reflected in the characters' reactions: Diane Keaton's gestures – she rubs her cheeks, runs her hands through her hair (shot 21) – and her facial expression communicate a sense of exhaustion and boredom more than being overwhelmed.
55 In comparison with the scene a few shots earlier, this is a quite different form of interruption: In the former, it was the editing that brought Bryant's speech to an (unnatural) end; here it is the character who interrupts himself.

interview – but reclines casually, her right arm propped on the armrest of the sofa; she leans her head into her right hand. Her left arm lies extended between her legs (a little above the knee). She looks slowly up and to the right at Reed, and lightly shrugs her shoulders. She smiles in reaction to Reed's hesitation, even briefly laughs aloud. At the beginning of the second EMU, her speech is once again noticeably – and in contrast to the staccato of her interview questions – marked by pauses, repetitions, and filler words. Thus, her prosody once again – as at the beginning of the scene – stages an image of insecurity and uncertainty. The tone of Reed's speech changes as well: He speaks more slowly and less sonorously, aspirating his words and intensifying the scene's erotic mood.

The characters are also placed closer together in the image composition, now sitting next to each other on the sofa in a single frame. Bryant gives Reed a penetrating look; she stares at him, nods, pauses, and smiles mischievously, a look which gives way to a broad grin. After Reed sits next to her, she once again speaks clearly, directly, and briskly; there is no more uncertainty in her voice. Her advances also come at the level of dialogue, and Reed at first reacts hesitantly, occasionally emitting inarticulate, meaningless sounds. He stutters, speaks haltingly, repeats himself. After this brief moment of insecurity, however, Reed catches himself; he grins, and leans left toward Bryant to kiss her. The punchline of the shot – and of the whole scene – consists in Bryant moving at the same moment to the left to pick up a folder of papers that she wants to give Reed to read, thus foiling the kiss. The synchronous movements of the two characters reveal their asynchronous intentions, and the break with previously established expectations produces a comic effect.[56] Reed's grin abruptly vanishes, he gulps visibly, stutters again, and repeats himself. Bryant, on the contrary, again speaks quickly and clearly. She is also the first to stand up from the sofa (briefly touching Reed's knee as she does so), resolving the situation and putting an end to all erotic tension.

This constellation, which stages an image of surprise and missed connection, is further intensified as the EMU progresses. The image of missed connection is complete once Reed has left Bryant's apartment and stands in the building hallway. The background is now made up of dark beige and brown-to-black walls;

---

[56] The idea that comedy results from breaking expectations is foundational to the theory of incongruence. Although this is not the only theory of comedy, the *Historisches Wörterbuch der Philosophie* explains: "[...] the moment of incongruity continues to be an essential basis for definitions of the c[omical] across a wide variety of historical and hermeneutic standpoints and horizons" (Wolfgang Preisendanz: Komische (das), Lachen (das), in: Historisches Wörterbuch der Philosophie. Vol. 4: I–K, ed. by Joachim Ritter/Karlfried Gründer, Darmstadt 1976, pp. 889–893, here p. 890 [Translator's note: my translation]).

the image composition of the hallway is thus decidedly darker than the room in the previous shot. Man and woman have passed each other by.

The film thus stages the pre-revolutionary era as a state in which man and woman are unable to come together in either love or work. A seduction or even a conjunction of love and work do not come to fruition. After all, work and love are communicated through quite different, even opposed, methods of staging. There is no unification of the two realms and thus no unity of man and woman. While the private conversation in the first half of the first EMU that seemed to point towards an affair is realized using formal tools that evoke an image of insecurity and attraction, the professional conversation about politics in the second half of the first EMU is experienced as an act of violence. The EMU especially has clear sexual connotations. After Reed has taken command in the interview and speaks uninterruptedly, he repeatedly pours coffee from the coffeepot. The movement quality of pouring, a constant, quick stream, overlaps with the penetrating, hammerlike gesture of Reed's speech. Pot and cup become substitutes for Reed and Bryant: The pot 'pours' as Reed 'delivers' his speech, and the cup 'receives' the coffee as Bryant receives Reed's speech. In shots 24 and 25, the sexual connotation of this scene is further underscored when Reed speaks of "sexual freedom," as we see the pot pouring coffee. Under pre-revolutionary conditions, the unification of love, sex, and work is not possible, the metaphor implies.

The formal elements of the scene show clear traces of New Hollywood Cinema. In the asynchronicity of sound and image, and the staccato montages, the spectator experiences anew the shock and freedom of New Hollywood. The violence occurs not on the level of representation, but – in accordance with Sobchack's theory of phenomenological film experience – in embodied spectatorship. The discussion of the overpowering and splitting of the spectator can also be put into conversation with the scene analyzed above. The antagonism between attraction and repulsion, advance and retreat, eroticism and violence, occurs not only within the characters, but also in the staging and through it in the spectator's experience. In spite of its distance from New Hollywood cinema in terms of both time and the logic of production, the film still carries this movement's influence – and does not ignore it.[57]

---

[57] That New Hollywood was not 'forgotten' with the advent of the 1980s is also one of Lehmann's central assumptions: "Keeping in mind the radicalism of this upheaval [of New Hollywood], the present work opposes the hypothesis that New Hollywood represents an exception and, in particular, that there was a return to neo-classicism around 1980, which cashed in, as it were, on the achievements of the 1970s. The present work insists, to the contrary, that the 1967 rupture not only could never be undone, but also that the phase around

The Condensed Temporality of Utopia

Generally speaking, it is notable that post-revolutionary utopian conditions usually play no role in films about revolution. Most of them end with the transition from one society to the next. The apparent explanation for this phenomenon is that post-revolutionary conditions lack dramatic tension.[58] Most films avoid painting a picture of post-revolutionary conditions.[59] When films do address the post-revolutionary period and its development, they usually present a discrepancy between pre-revolutionary hopes, demands, and illusions, and post-revolutionary disappointment.[60] Nevertheless, revolution films have a close relationship with utopia. This relationship appears in how they stage the moment of transition between the old society and the new one, the *kairos* of revolution – the moment in which the revolution is decided:[61]

> *Kairos* is the moment on which everything depends, and in a quite particular way. Not as is suggested by the temporal model of *chronos* that has been exclusively taken up by the modern philosophy of history, which defines this point and its importance through narration as a sensibly suggested sequence of all moments in time. It is precisely the opposite: working with kairological premises, all *preceding* moments are defined by *it* [...].[62]

1980 has to be grasped as an additional transformation, which took this rupture as its starting point. From this perspective, however low its standing may be in cinephile circles, the cinema of the 1980s cannot be understood without the cinema of New Hollywood" (Lehmann: Affect Poetics of the New Hollywood, op. cit., p. 43).

58 On this point see Norbert M. Schmitz: Gibt es einen demokratischen Revolutionsfilm? Zum dialektischen Pathos in Jean Renoirs "La Marseillaise", in: Revolutionsmedien – Medienrevolutionen, ed. by Sven Grampp et al., Konstanz 2008, pp. 597–620, here pp. 605 f.

59 A notable exception to this rule are the films of Dziga Vertov. It remains an open question, however, on which level these films, which were certainly intended to be understood as utopian, actually realized their utopias; that is, whether they contain utopian features beyond the level of represented content, which today often seems alien.

60 A particularly clear and therefore interesting example of this phenomenon is the film LAND OF THE BLIND (Robert Edwards, GB/US 2006). The film follows the protagonist's shift from the freedom fighter that he was before the revolution to the dictator he becomes after the revolution, completely without motivation – as though it were the nature of things that freedom fighters become dictators.

61 Schmitz also writes of the "*kairos* of revolution" (Schmitz: Gibt es einen demokratischen Revolutionsfilm?, op. cit., p. 598), but does not connect it with utopia.

62 Ralf Konersmann: Nachwort. Walter Benjamins philosophische Kairologie, in: Walter Benjamin: Kairos. Schriften zur Philosophie, Frankfurt/Main 2007, pp. 327–348, here p. 332. Konersmann formulates these sentences with regard to Benjamin's philosophy; they are, however, valid as a definition of *kairos* even beyond this context [Translator's note: my translation].

Kairos refers to the moment introduced in my chapter on Arendt, into which a revolution is often condensed and which can thus stand paradigmatically for the entire revolution, like the storming of the Bastille or the Winter Palace. For Arendt, this moment has a negative connotation as a loss of control, which becomes a problem especially when its quality of movement comes to encompass the entire revolutionary process. A positive conceptualization of this moment within the theory of revolution can be found in the work of Slavoj Žižek.[63] On the question of possible legitimization of revolution, he writes the following:

> The only criterion is the absolutely inherent one: that of the enacted utopia. In a genuine revolutionary breakthrough, the utopian future is neither simply fully realized, present, nor simply evoked as a distant promise which justifies present violence – it is rather as if, in a unique suspension of temporality, in the short circuit between the present and the future, we are – as if by Grace – briefly allowed to act *as if* the utopian future is (not yet fully here, but) already at hand, there to be seized. Revolution is experienced not as a present hardship we have to endure for the sake of the happiness and freedom of future generations, but as the present hardship over which this future happiness and freedom already cast their shadow – in it, we are already free even as we fight for freedom; we are already happy even as we fight for happiness, no matter how difficult the circumstances.[64]

Especially in the staging of this moment, which Žižek describes elsewhere as the "magic moment of universal solidarity when 'everything seems possible',"[65] films provide a utopian perspective on what is to come.[66] In REDS, this moment comes at the end of the first half, through the staging of the storming of the Winter Palace. On the narrative context of the scene I will analyze next: The protagonists have traveled as journalists – and explicitly not as a romantic couple – to revolutionary Russia. There, they observe and experience the revolutionary events. The scene begins with a workers' meeting at which Reed and Bryant are present and

---

[63] In the following, when I expand on the theoretical background first of Žižek's position and then of several Marx quotes, I neither mean to imply that they can be unconditionally combined with Arendt's thoughts (on the contrary, Arendt's and Žižek's positions are directly opposed in many points), nor to indulge in theoretical eclecticism. I am much more interested in working from the film and doing justice to it. A quite brief and polemical attack by Žižek on Arendt can be found in Slavoj Žižek: On Belief, London/New York 2001, p. 113.

[64] Slavoj Žižek: Afterword. Lenin's Choice, in: Vladimir Ilyich Lenin: Revolution at the Gates. A Selection of Writings from February to October 1917, ed. by Slavoj Žižek, London/New York 2002, pp. 165–336, here pp. 260 f.

[65] Slavoj Žižek: Introduction. Between the Two Revolutions, in: Lenin: Revolution at the Gates, op. cit., pp. 3–12, here p. 7.

[66] I attempt to connect an analysis of revolutionary *kairos* in V FOR VENDETTA with Pascal's wager as a strategy for legitimizing revolution in Hanno Berger: Pascals Wette, die Revolution und "V for Vendetta", in: Periphere Visionen. Wissen an den Rändern von Fotografie und Film, ed. by Heide Barrenechea/Marcel Finke/Moritz Schumm, Paderborn 2016, pp. 223–236.

Reed is invited to get onstage and speak.[67] My analysis of the scene will show that the film attempts – as suggested by Deleuze in his theory of how films think – to capture and think the moment of *kairos* through metaphor.

One EMU: 00:00:00:00–00:04:56:15
In the interplay between sound design, cinematography, and image composition, the scene stages an image of euphoria as the crescendo and unification of visual and acoustic movements that show the synchronicity of love, work, sex, and revolution.

In the dramaturgical course of the film, the scene acts as conclusion and climax of the first part. The scene opens with the sounds of pattering feet and lightly murmuring voices, which ebb into silence after Reed begins speaking. His voice is uncertain at first; he repeats the beginning of his sentence, stutters a little. His voice then becomes firmer, clearer, sharper. At first, however, he speaks not to the working men and women standing beneath him; instead, his body and his gaze are directed at the Russian worker who also stands on the stage and translates his speech. Only gradually does Reed turn more directly to his audience, his voice becoming increasingly firm, clear, and loud. The staging of the audience reaction also follows a dynamic of crescendo: not only are the audience reactions shown in increasingly close shots, the noises they make also grow constantly louder. At first only scattered clapping is audible but it gets louder and louder. And Reed addresses the audience more directly by beginning to speak Russian. As he does so, his voice becomes not only firmer, but also relentlessly louder and higher, until it peaks in a euphoric fervor. This development is mirrored by his Russian interpreter and the audience, which also grows louder and louder.

This movement of increasing convergence between Reed and the workers reaches its climax when Reed steps off the stage. In this moment, the separation established by the stage between him and the audience disappears, and the image composition suggests that he is merging with the audience. A shot-countershot montage stages an exchange of glances between Bryant and Reed. While at first only Bryant is surrounded by other people in the audience, Reed is also increasingly surrounded and obscured by other people. Neither figure, however, disappears entirely into the masses.[68] They are and remain recognizable as individuals.

---

67 The timecode of the scene is 01:34:45–01:39:38 (Disc 1).
68 In this analysis, I am not focused on the question of staging the masses. I will thus use 'masses' and 'crowd' synonymously. In doing so, however, I do not intend to say that a closer analysis of the concept of the masses and their representation, which would have to distinguish between the two terms, is not possible or worth doing. One would have to consider how

This movement of increasing proximity between the protagonists and the masses is associated with the movement of the sound design: The cheering and bellowing of the crowd develops into a choral rendition of the "Internationale" in Russian. Indistinct at first and confined to the background, it becomes increasingly clear, and after the first verse, by the first round of the chorus it also appears as an extra-diegetic element on the soundtrack, much fuller and with instrumental accompaniment. The sound design travels a course that starts with silence, moves through Reed's increasingly clear and sharp speech and the cheering and bellowing that becomes diegetic singing in the background, then climaxes in the extra-diegetic use of the "Internationale." This climax is maintained for the rest of the scene. The music frames the rest of the scene and connects all the shots that follow. It thus anchors the euphoric mood that is visually staged, for the extradiegetic music dominates the sound design in the rest of the scene; diegetic sound effects can only be heard faintly in the background.

The approach between the protagonists and the masses is sustained over the rest of the scene and the expressive movement. Shots showing Bryant and Reed alone alternate with shots that show the revolutionary masses or the two protagonists surrounded by other people, becoming part of the revolutionary masses. Yet in these movement sequences, the film does not equate 'private couple' with 'political mass.' The bustling and chaotic image created by the cheering masses at the beginning of the scene is endowed with a unified vector of motion after the first change of scenery leaves the meeting room. All shots that show political events are characterized by movement to the left. Not only do masses of people move leftward, but also camera movements; a hat that flies through the air also follows this directional pattern. The images of the couple, by contrast, are characterized by longer shot duration, vertical movements, and most especially slower movements, forming a harmonic counterpoint to the movements with which the public events are staged.

The end of the expressive movement is marked by declining movement. In the last shot – at 16 seconds, the longest in the scene – the image composition exhibits an almost abstract quality, as both protagonists are backlit and can only be seen as embracing, kissing bodies. It becomes impossible to see where one body stops

---

this scene relates to Deleuze's thesis on the people's absence from modern cinema. An overview of the history of the term 'masses' can be found in Stephan Günzel: Der Begriff der 'Masse' in Philosophie und Kulturtheorie (I), in: Dialektik. Zeitschrift für Kulturphilosophie, 2004 (2), 2004, pp. 117–135, and id.: Der Begriff der 'Masse' in Philosophie und Kulturtheorie (II), in: Dialektik. Zeitschrift für Kulturphilosophie, 2005 (1), 2005, pp. 123–140. On the question of the "cinematic masses," see the chapter "Masse des Films" in Gertrud Koch: Die Wiederkehr der Illusion. Der Film und die Kunst der Gegenwart, Berlin 2016, pp. 172 ff.

and the other begins – meaning this last shot of the scene can to some extent be seen as a visualization and embodiment of Deleuzian affect theory. The image fades to black, and the "Internationale" also comes to an end. It is not only the melody that descends into its final chord; the volume also constantly decreases, and the song goes silent when the image is completely veiled in black.

Through formal strategies alone, quite independent of its represented content, the scene thus stages a euphoric atmosphere through the logic of crescendo that is present on multiple levels, the use of music as well as the motion sequences. Yet what content is anchored by this atmosphere? What is cut together and – as will be explored in more detail below – what is metaphorically dissolved? Alongside the scenes of the storming of the Winter Palace, the film shows the couple having sex, working together on articles, at demonstrations, distributing leaflets, listening to speeches by Trotsky and Lenin, in a flirtatious snowball fight, and celebrating Christmas. Formulated as a metaphor, the Revolution – or more precisely, the *kairos* of the revolution – is experienced as the interplay and synchronicity of love, work, politics, and sex. Yet what does this mean? What conclusions can be drawn from this scene?

Most academic writing on REDS is critical of this scene. Although some writers praise the film for its use of the "Internationale,"[69] the scene is generally taken as an example of the film's failure to deliver an adequate (whatever that means) representation of the Revolution. According to Grindon, the film does not present a convincing picture of historical St. Petersburg. Instead, he asserts, the city feels like a studio set, more like a shiny, polished postcard than a distinct image of the past. He blames this impression on backlit shots in this scene both in exterior and interior locations, as well as the presentation of Lenin and Trotsky, who make a stiff and wooden impression that is jarring next to the 'naturalistic' performances of the Hollywood stars.[70] As an analytical observation, there is nothing wrong with Grindon's impression that the setting and spaces seem artificial. His reference to the lighting used in the scene is also insightful. It is worth adding that this impression could also be traced back to the absence of any patina on the building facades.[71] His critique of the acting is plausible, even if it does not seem

---

69 See for example Rosenstone: Reds as History, op. cit., p. 299.
70 See Grindon: Shadows on the Past, op. cit., p. 209.
71 Siegfried Kracauer refers to the importance of the patina on buildings when creating atmosphere in films (for Kracauer, of course, the end goal of these atmospheres is realism). He writes: "Natural objects, then, are surrounded with a fringe of meaning liable to touch of various moods, emotions, runs of inarticulate thoughts; in other words, they have a theoretically unlimited number of psychological and mental correspondences. Some such correspondences may have a real foundation in the traces which the life of the mind often leaves in material

very convincing given that Lenin and Trotsky only appear for a few seconds, speak in Russian, and are largely drowned out by the cheering of the crowd – their roles are simply too insignificant to merit a serious analysis of the acting. The main problem with Grindon's observation, however, is its normative application: The artifice that emanates from the scene should not be seen as a weakness of the film. Instead, precisely because of its ostentatious artifice, it makes sense to look at the scene as a utopia.[72] This idea suggests itself from the sole fact that the scene – as shown in the above analysis – stages an image of euphoria regardless of its represented content.

Although Grindon does address aesthetic elements (which, however, are associated with the question of historical representation), content is the main focus of his critique of this scene. This criticism has been made most pointedly – and this is quite surprisingly in the context of his theory of revolution – by Slavoj Žižek, who describes the scene as follows:

> REDS integrates the October Revolution – for Hollywood the most traumatic historical event – into the Hollywood universe by staging it as the metaphorical background for the sexual act between the movie's main characters, John Reed (played by Beatty himself) and his lover (Diane Keaton). In the film, the October Revolution takes place immediately after a crisis in their relationship. By delivering a fierce revolutionary oration to the turbulent crowd, Beatty mesmerizes Keaton; the two exchange desirous glances, and the cries of the crowd serve as a metaphor for the rebirth of passion. The key mythical scenes of the revolution (street demonstrations, the storming of the Winter Palace) alternate with the depiction of the couple's lovemaking, against the background of the crowd singing the International. The mass scenes function as vulgar metaphors for the sexual act: when the black mass approaches and encircles the phallic tramway, is this not a metaphor for Keaton who, in the sexual act, plays the active role, on top of Beatty? Here we have the exact opposite of that Soviet socialist realism in which lovers would experience their love as a contribution to the struggle for socialism, making a vow to sacrifice all their private pleasures for the cause of the revolution and to drown themselves in the masses: in REDS, on the contrary, revolution itself appears as a metaphor for the successful sexual encounter.[73]

---

phenomena; human faces are molded by inner experiences, and the patina of old houses is a residue of what has happened in them" (Siegfried Kracauer: Theory of Film. The Redemption of Physical Reality, New York 1960, p. 68).

72 Carolyn Porter also describes this scene as a utopia in her review of the film. See Carolyn Porter: Reds, in: Film Quarterly, 35 (3), 1982, pp. 43–48, here p. 47.

73 Slavoj Žižek: From *Che vuoi?* to Fantasy. Lacan with *Eyes Wide Shut*, in: id.: How to Read Lacan, New York 2007, pp. 40–60, here pp. 50 f. Žižek also makes this critique in "A Pervert's Guide to Family" in which he describes the scene as a "ridiculous climax of this Hollywood-procedure of staging great historical events as the background of the formation of a couple." See Slavoj Žižek: A Pervert's Guide to Family, in: Lacan.com, 2007. http://www.lacan.com/zizfamily.htm [last accessed 23 May 2022].

The reproach is clear: The film uses the October revolution as a mere metaphorical background to show the couple coming together. Worse still: Even the Russian Revolution is acceptable to Hollywood if all it serves to do is create a couple, i.e., a bourgeois family.[74] In any case, the film treats the Revolution the same way it treats a purely private romantic relationship.

But what if one inverts the metaphor, swaps the source and target domains? What happens if one no longer regards the Revolution as a metaphor for sex or orgasm, but – as seems closer to what the scene suggests – sex as a metaphor for the *kairos* of the revolution? The connection between the two seems so close in this scene that it is hard to determine with clarity where the metaphor begins and where it ends. Without equating the two ideas, the scene allows us to see each one within the other. Seen in this way, the film loses its private tendencies and turns out to be surprisingly radical. The imbrication of revolution and sex becomes interesting when seen alongside the temporality that is foundational to each. The temporality at the heart of both *kairos* and sex can be described as 'right now,' or "on time!" – it forms their common denominator.[75] The temporalities of revolution and sex, however, differ with regard to frequency. Whereas revolution is understood as a unique event that lays the foundation for the politics of the future, sexual temporality is characterized by the opposite phenomenon: repetition.[76] Thus when the scene crossfades between sex and revolution, it demands nothing less radical than a constantly repeating revolution.

Another metaphorical crossfade that appears in this scene receives similar treatment: revolution and Christmas celebrations. At first, the superimposition of Bolshevik revolution and family Christmas festivities seems strange and absurd. This connection seems difficult to reconcile with the theory of revolution. After all, Christmas is a celebration of the birth of Christ – yet, as Arendt emphasizes, modern revolutions are not Christian in origin: She claims that "no revolution was ever made in the name of Christianity prior to the modern age."[77] Yet given the specific staging of time and temporalities in REDS, this metaphor makes sense:

---

74 This is Žižek's thesis in "A Pervert's Guide to Family".
75 According to Linda Williams in her essay on 'body genres,' this is the temporality of pornography. See Linda Williams: Film Bodies. Gender, Genre, and Excess, in: Film Genre Reader III, ed. by Barry Keith Grant, Austin 2003, pp. 141–159, here p. 152. The connection between revolutionary *kairos* and sex is also drawn in V FOR VENDETTA. See Berger: Pascals Wette, die Revolution und "V for Vendetta", op. cit., p. 236, footnote 34.
76 Thomas Morsch made this argument in his lecture *Rückkehr nach Strasbourg. Ein Wiederholungsversuch*. Held on 25 November 2014 at the FU Berlin as part of the lecture series *Wiederholung* at the Institut für Theaterwissenschaft, FU Berlin.
77 See Hannah Arendt: On Revolution, London 1990, p. 27.

In celebrating the birth of Christ, Christmas acknowledges the beginning of a new Western calendar that is still used today. And the fact that revolutions represent the beginning of a new calendar is a decisive (if neither necessary nor sufficient) criterion for modern revolutions, as demonstrated by the introduction of new calendars after the French and Russian Revolutions. Yet in the superimposition of these events as well, there is a difference in frequency: Christmas is celebrated every year – and thus at first seems opposed to the one-time, unique quality of a revolution. Precisely in the periodic return of Christmas, however, this superimposition suggests a radical revolutionary utopia: the constantly repeating revolution.

This adjusted perspective on the critique of the film opens it up to possible positive references on a theoretical level. Starting with the fact that the film shows a communist revolution suggests connections to Marxist positions in revolutionary theory. Ultimately, the staging of the scene as an image of euphoria recalls a contemporary position in the theory of revolution that is oriented toward both Marx and Deleuze: that of Antonio Negri and Michael Hardt. They answer the question of what it means to be communist as follows:

> [...] we find ourselves [...] posing against the misery of power the joy of being. This is a revolution that no power will control – because biopower and communism, cooperation and revolution remain together, in love, simplicity, and also innocence. This is the irrepressible lightness and joy of being communist.[78]

Love, simplicity, innocence: This revolutionary utopia occurs in the *kairos* of REDS, and not only in the scene's represented content. The joy invoked by Hardt and Negri also permeates the image of euphoria that is produced by the staging and that realizes itself in the spectator's perception.

Yet connections can also be found to the writings of Karl Marx, which bring to the fore the true power and significance of the scene. While Marx is very restrained when it comes to prospects for a postcapitalist society,[79] there are individual passages on this topic in his work, which – probably because they are so rare – have become quite well-known. These are not simply definitions *ex*

---

[78] Michael Hardt/Antonio Negri: Empire, Cambridge, MA 2000, p. 413. The authors have a different concept of power than Arendt. They distinguish their definition of a communist from "the sad, ascetic agent of the Third International whose soul was deeply permeated by Soviet state reason [...]" (ibid., p. 411). In REDS, this position is exemplified by the character Zinoviev.

[79] An overview of the reasons for this hesitancy with regard to the conceptualization of utopias, and the "gestures toward the economy of socialism and communism" that Marx nevertheless did make, can be found in Christian Iber: Grundzüge der Marx'schen Kapitalismustheorie, Berlin 2005, pp. 74–81. On Marx as a utopian thinker, see also the final chapter "Karl Marx and Humanity; Stuff of Hope," in: Bloch: The Principle of Hope, op. cit., pp. 1354 ff.

negativo – for example when Marx calls for the "[...] *overthrow* [of] *all relations* in which man is a debased, enslaved, forsaken, despicable being [...]."[80] Positive definitions can also be identified. In the first volume of *Capital*, Marx describes an "association of free men," in which there is no longer any private ownership of the means of production, and in which the commodity form has been overcome.[81] The freedom referenced here can be related particularly to the joy in working that is expressed in the scene from REDS. In the third volume of *Capital*, Marx writes:

> In fact, the realm of freedom actually begins only where labour which is determined by necessity and mundane considerations ceases; thus in the very nature of things it lies beyond the sphere of actual material production.[82]

In his "Critique of the Gotha Programme," Marx calls for an end to "the enslaving subordination of the individual to the division of labour," overcoming the opposition of intellectual and physical labor and a "common wealth;" this concept culminates in the slogan: "From each according to his abilities, to each according to his needs!"[83] Though the proximity to the *kairos* in REDS is apparent here, even stronger connections exist to early Marx. With Friedrich Engels, he writes in *The German Ideology*:

> For as soon as the distribution of labour comes into being, each man has a particular, exclusive sphere of activity, which is forced upon him and from which he cannot escape. He is a hunter, a fisherman, a shepherd, or a critical critic, and must remain so if he does

---

80 Karl Marx: Contribution to the Critique of Hegel's Philosophy of Law. Introduction, in: id./Friedrich Engels: MECW 3. Karl Marx March 1843 – August 1844, London 2010, pp. 175–187, here p. 182.
81 On the "association of free men," see Karl Marx: Capital. A Critique of Political Economy, Vol. 1, trans. by Ben Fowkes, London 1976, pp. 171 f. It is no coincidence that this paragraph appears in the chapter on commodity fetishism; for Marx, the commodity form concentrates the essence of capitalist production and falsely naturalizes it. On commodity fetishism, in which Marx's radical approach can be seen in its entirety, see ibid., pp. 163–177.
82 Karl Marx: Capital. A Critique of Political Economy, Vol. III, in: id./Friedrich Engels: MECW 37. Karl Marx – Capital Volume III, London 2010, pp. 5–982, here p. 807. The passage appears in the chapter "The Trinity Formula," in which Marx takes up the question of the commodity fetish and expands it to the "fetishism of capital" (ibid., p. 816).
83 Karl Marx: Critique of the Gotha Programme, in: id./Friedrich Engels: MECW 24. Marx and Engels 1974–83, London 2010, pp. 75–99, here p. 87. A summary of Marx's views on postcapitalist society and "The Economic Basis of the Withering Away of the State" can be found in the fifth chapter of Lenin's *State and Revolution*, which appears under this title. See Vladimir Ilyich Lenin: The State and Revolution. The Marxist Theory of the State and the Tasks of the Proletariat in the Revolution, in: id.: Lenin Collected Works. Volume 25, June–September 1917, Moscow 1974, pp. 385–497, here pp. 461 ff.

not want to lose his means of livelihood; whereas in communist society, where nobody has one exclusive sphere of activity but each can become accomplished in any branch he wishes, society regulates the general production and thus makes it possible for me to do one thing today and another tomorrow, to hunt in the morning, fish in the afternoon, rear cattle in the evening, criticise after dinner, just as I have a mind, without ever becoming hunter, fisherman, shepherd or critic.[84]

I do not intend to make a concrete comparison between the scene and the passage. What is important is the emphasis on movement, freedom, and variety that are expressed in both the passage and the scene. The scene develops a utopia insofar as it shows the protagonists as revolutionaries, lovers, listeners, players, working journalists, i.e., as people who write, create, and criticize, celebrate Christmas and sleep with each other, all at the same time. This utopia is realized in the *kairos* of the revolution. This scene thus condenses all the themes introduced at the beginning of the chapter, which define the film, and brings these themes to a euphorically grounded conclusion: gender relations, politics, private life, work, and writing in perfect harmony.

It would therefore be a mistake to see the scene under discussion as a mere illustration of the above-cited utopian concepts. While the film does this work, it does not stop there. Instead, through its staging of this scene, the film gives spectators a chance to understand what it means when – in Žižek's words – "in a unique suspension of temporality, in the short circuit between the present and the future, we are – as if by Grace briefly allowed to act *as if*" utopia is within reach. Only the "machine which thinks temporally," the time-condensation-machine of cinema makes it possible to understand and experience this connection between utopia and the condensation of time. For Epstein, the 'personality' of a family only becomes visible in the cinema through the temporal condensation of a long period; similarly, cinema makes this utopia of people flourishing on many levels comprehensible and tangible. However, this possibility is actualized not in the filmic medium per se, but in the concrete staging of REDS and its realization in the spectator's embodied experience.[85]

If one were to stop here, the potential of the scene would be far from exhausted. For it not only shows a communist revolution, but also maintains a

---

[84] Karl Marx/Friedrich Engels: The German Ideology. Critique of Modern German Philosophy According to Its Representatives Feuerbach, B. Bauer and Stirner, and of German Socialism According to Its Various Prophets, in: id.: MECW 5. Marx and Engels 1845–47, London 2010, pp. 19–539, here p. 47.
[85] Looking to the 'problem of authority' discussed in the section "The Authority of State Foundation," one could argue that in REDS the new foundation is legitimized by the euphoria of transition, the *kairos* – and tension is once again created by the metaphors that point toward repetition.

strong connection to the revolution of its country of production. This is the case, at least, if one shares Arendt's understanding of the American Revolution, which forms the basis (but not the sole basis) for a utopia of the council system.[86] She describes the council system as "the only new form of government born out of revolution."[87] And still in every revolution, she writes, councils have emerged spontaneously and in direct connection with the revolution. The problem, however, was that no one, not even Thomas Jefferson, theorized and analyzed the role of councils in a revolution – they lacked spectators, so to speak – making it impossible to develop a revolutionary tradition of the council system.[88] Instead, in every case the councils came into competition and conflict with the parties, which ultimately destroyed them. The downfall of the councils and the dominance of the parties then always led to the end of the revolutionary spirit.[89] In Arendt's eyes, only Jefferson, at the end of his life and after he had withdrawn from public political life, tried to keep the notion of councils alive for the future political life of the new nation. These gatherings were familiar from the townhall meetings that already existed during the colonial era. In the letters that he wrote to friends in his old age, Jefferson supported making the councils, which he also called 'small republics' or 'elementary republics,' into a cornerstone of the United States, since only with these could the goals of the revolution be attained:

> If the ultimate end of revolution was freedom and the constitution of a public space where freedom could appear, the *constitutio libertatis*, then the elementary republics of the wards, the only tangible place where everyone could be free, actually were the end of the great republic whose chief purpose in domestic affairs should have been to provide the people with such places of freedom and to protect them. The basic assumption of the ward system, whether Jefferson knew it or not, was that no one could be called happy without his share in public happiness, that no one could be called free without his experience in public

---

86 Once again, I am not interested in the historical accuracy of Arendt's characterization. The historian Sophia Rosenfeld casts doubt on it when she describes Arendt's reconstruction of the role of townhall meetings as follows: "Conjuring a fantasy past with echoes of the Anglo-Saxon mythology that urban radicals had exploited at the start of the American Revolution, Arendt paid tribute to the 'council' or 'ward' system of New England town governments [...]" (Sophia Rosenfeld: Common Sense. A Political History, Cambridge 2011, p. 249).
87 Arendt: On Revolution, op. cit., p. 258.
88 Arendt offers a brief history of the relationship between council systems and revolutions in ibid., pp. 261–266. She explains the 'sociétés populaires' as a form of council that represented a counterweight to the rule of the Jacobins, and their fate, in: ibid., pp. 240–244.
89 On the conflict between the council and party systems, see ibid., p. 273.

freedom, and that no one could be called either happy or free without participating, and having a share, in public power.[90]

In the scene from REDS analyzed above, it is a situation just like Arendt describes, a council of free and public speech, that sparks the euphoric mood of the rest of the scene.[91] Yet – and this is the second point of connection between the scene and Arendt's council utopia – the scene shows not only revolution and politics, but also the protagonists' private lives. The private and the political are linked in the scene, but not equated – which becomes clear not least through the differing qualities of movement with which each realm is staged. For Arendt, the council system is also characterized by the fact that it does not force politics on anyone. Unlike a vote, in which everybody – whether interested and competent or not – is called on to participate, in a council system only those who are interested in politics, that is in public freedom, would participate:

> [...] only those who [...] are concerned about the state of the world would have the right to be heard in the conduct of the business of the republic. [...] And such self-exclusion, far from being arbitrary discrimination, would in fact give substance and reality to one of the most important negative liberties we have enjoyed since the end of the ancient world, namely, freedom from politics [...].[92]

The most important element of the scene from REDS is then that politics and freedom from politics, positive, and negative freedom come to life in a single utopian moment, and show the compatibility of both notions.

With regard to compatibility, it is worth once again turning to staging strategies. Seen from the perspective on the sublime developed through analysis of NAPOLÉON, the scene from REDS exhibits a mixture of concordance and divergence. This scene certainly shows approaches to a sublime aesthetic, when it repeatedly shows unimaginably large crowds of people, or cuts together shots that do not directly follow each other chronologically, taking attention away from sensory experience, and allowing for the creation of ideas and metaphors. However, while in the conflicts of the faculties at NAPOLÉON the imagination is completely overpowered and no uniform image can be synthesized from the chaos, leaving recognition entirely on the side of reason, here things are different. In the scene from

---

90 Ibid., p. 255.
91 Within the diegesis, the film marks a difference between the Russian Revolution and the political situation in the United States in the early twentieth century: The scene parallels another moment in the film, in which Reed is forbidden from speaking at a meeting of the Socialist Party in the US, where he is in attendance as a journalist and not a delegate; he has no "credentials." This contrasting parallel scene can be found at 01:05:30–01:06:56 (Disc 1).
92 Arendt: On Revolution, op. cit., pp. 279 f.

REDS, the relationship between imagination and reason favors imagination, and although temporarily overwhelmed, the imagination largely manages to achieve a synthesis. In this way, however, the scene departs from the cinema of New Hollywood. While the latter was characterized by a segmentation of the spectator, in this scene the spectatorial experience is unified – which is expressed not least by the fact that the scene is staged as an undivided expressive movement. This decision should not be understood, however, as a simple regression to the cinema before New Hollywood. As demonstrated by my analysis of Bryant's interview with Reed, New Hollywood Cinema is also contained within REDS: in the *kairos* scene, the film returns to pre-New Hollywood cinema *in full awareness of the anachronism of this reference.* In this way, it showcases this scene even more clearly as a utopia, a non-space that has fallen not only out of space, but also out of time. And it is precisely as a utopia that the scene develops its power and significance, as I have tried to demonstrate by situating the scene in the theory of revolution.

In contrast to what one might expect from the reconstruction of the film's production history or the academic literature about it, concrete analysis of the film and its staging processes show that it is by no means an apolitical or conservative film. Rather, the film thinks revolution from various thematic and temporal perspectives, and in doing so decisively extends and specifies the theory of revolution.

5.3 The Decline of the Revolution

As previously mentioned, it is extremely unusual for films to engage with the post-revolutionary situation apart from condensing it into the *kairos* of the revolution. In REDS too, after the staging of the successful transition, there is no depiction of a utopia, but rather the decline of kairotic euphoria and the discrepancy with the ideals of the Revolution. In its second half, the film tells of John Reed's and Louise Bryant's attempts to bring the Revolution to America, and Reed's efforts to make the newly established Soviet Union conform to the ideals of the Revolution. Where the Revolution results in the perfect interplay between private and political, man and woman, work and free time, speech and understanding, the film handles the decline of the Revolution on the level of content in these same areas: Private and political life can no longer be united, man and woman separate, work and free time remain irreconcilable, and the connection between speech and understanding is also limited, whether through intentional or unintentional problems in translation, or through the failure of technologies that were supposed to enable Bryant and Reed to communicate from the US to the USSR.

Even a cursory glance at the film's content clearly reveals that its second half no longer engages in thinking the Revolution. In the following pages, I nevertheless examine the movement figurations in the film's last ninety minutes in two scene analyses. I do this for two reasons: First, it is important to do justice to the film in its complexity, and not to reduce it to its first part. Second, examining the staging of revolution's decline allows us to draw conclusions *ex negativo* about the revolutionary ideals postulated by the film. The two scenes analyzed below can be understood as contrasting and complementary scenes to the already analyzed excerpts from the film's first part. First is the analysis of another discussion between a man and a woman, in this case Louise Bryant and Eugene O'Neill, who in the narrative takes on the role of John Reed's competition and rival for Bryant's affections. The second scene, which will be analyzed in detail, is about Reed and Bryant's reunion after a long separation.

The Confrontational Rendezvous

The scene shows Louise Bryant's visit to her former lover Eugene O'Neill, after John Reed has returned to Russia.[93] *In the interplay between image composition, performance, and acoustics/sound design, the scene stages an image of tension in a confined visual space, which shifts and erupts into an image of anger and aggression in a confrontation between the two characters.*

Especially at the beginning of the scene, the image composition is characterized by a confined visual space, which the spectator also experiences as tight: Throughout, the images are framed by cut-off doorways, lamps, and furniture. Reflections and shadows further condense and enclose the visual space. This image of closeness is reinforced through sound; first, there is only diegetic music coming from a record player in the background, which falls silent as soon as the hallway door closes and background noises disappear almost entirely. The sound effect that anchors and dominates the characters' conversation is the creaking of an old wooden chair, which instantly generates a sense of unease. The EMU and the feeling it produces of confinement and tension climax in the longest shot of the scene, in which the two characters sit across from each other and come into conflict, which manifests on the level of sound. In the silence that follows this shot, the EMU also fades out. In the second EMU, the tension that remained implicit in the first EMU erupts into an image of anger and aggression. The second EMU begins with the shift to performance

---

[93] The timecode of the scene is 00:26:38–00:30:09 (Disc 2).

as the dominant formal element. The previously cool, restrained, and somewhat withdrawn performance of Diane Keaton and Jack Nicholson becomes increasingly irascible and aggravated. The image of aggression produced by this shift is reinforced by the cinematography; as their voices grow louder, the shots get closer. Louise Bryant's silence at the end of the scene is accompanied by distance between the camera and the characters, and the scene fades out ['klingt' aus]. The dark mood is emphasized by weak lighting and the dominance of dark, subtle colors, primarily brown and beige tones.

First EMU: 00:00:00:00–00:02:04:23
Through the interplay of image composition, performance, and acoustics/sound design, the EMU stages an image of tension in the increasingly cramped visual space.

The dark mood that anchors the entire scene is connected in the first EMU with an intensifying confinement in the image composition. While the first shot shows building walls in a long shot with an open composition (passersby enter and leave the frame; street noises can be heard as ambient sound), the second shot already counters this tendency. The shift to the building interior, i.e., O'Neill's apartment, creates a closed image composition. This image of closeness is intensified by the acting as another subdominant element in this image of tension. Both actors cast penetrating looks at each other, hardly blinking. They speak quickly and sharply, with only an occasional note of uncertainty sneaking into Diane Keaton's voice. The first EMU climaxes in shot 10 (by far the longest of the EMU and of the entire scene), when O'Neill and Bryant sit across from each other. He cuts her off and interrupts her irritated, quick torrent of words. His deep voice is quiet, clear, and decisive. When she in turn attempts to interrupt him, he raises his voice (without shouting), which quiets her again. Nicholson's particularly harsh and almost caustic emphasis on individual words further underscores the feeling of tension that permeates the scene. The tension reaches a climax when Nicholson underscores his speech with facial expressions: A light jut to his chin at the end of his tirade gives his face a cold and cruel expression.

After that, the tension fades; we see Keaton's face and her reaction to O'Neill's words, which is more of a non-reaction. She remains silent (there are also no audible background noises), blinks, and briefly looks down.

Second EMU: 00:02:04:24–00:03:36:12
The second EMU begins with Bryant rising from the armchair (shot 14); through the interplay of performance, cinematography, and acoustics/sound design, it stages an image of rage and aggression as confrontation erupts between the two characters.

Bryant's rise from the chair at the beginning of the second EMU introduces an element of imbalance into the scene: She stands in front of O'Neill with her arms crossed, while he sits. The dominant function in the staging of this EMU, however, is performance. Nicholson's prosody is emphasized by the lack of any ambient sound, and is defined by his deep, sonorous voice as well as his clear, precise, and penetrant pronunciation and emphasis. The forcefulness of his speech is intensified by the use of alliteration. Nicholson's "s" is sharp, almost hissing ("I'm *sorry* to *see* you and Jack *so serious* about your *sports*"), and further builds on the tense, confrontational atmosphere.

This eruption, which is cathartic for the spectator, begins with Keaton's response. Like the image composition, the characters' speech also loses its balance. Keaton speaks faster and faster, and most importantly her speech gets louder and louder, until by the end she is actually shouting. Her pointed emphasis on individual words ("duplicitous," "contemptible," "bottle") releases the tension in the scene's atmosphere. The constantly rising volume of her speech and increasingly exaggerated prosody are paired with a change in camera distance. Up to this point, the dialogue is shown in alternating American and medium close-up shots; here the shots and counter-shots switch to close-ups. This shift has the following effects: It further encloses the space, lifts both faces out of the room, makes the facial expressions of each actor more legible. In short, it creates affection-images. The powerful effect of these images climaxes when Keaton, her whole body trembling, breaks off in midsentence; no more sounds emerge from her throat, but her mouth keeps moving. The image of rage, aggression, and eruption is reinforced by O'Neill's response, which appears in a cut to another close-up, accompanied by a grin that grows wider and wider. His expression is linked to his clear and quiet voice; he lays particular emphasis on the word "wound" in the line "I seem to have touched a wound," and further underscores it by raising his eyebrows. The openly confrontational mood and cathartic release seem to have ended, and the noticeably tense and latently aggressive atmosphere from earlier in the scene returns once more. Yet another reversal comes in the following shot, when Bryant turns her back on O'Neill and heads for the door. Her movement away from the camera results in a slight opening of the space. Before she leaves the room, however, she turns back and speaks her last words. Once again she speaks quickly, loudly, and energetically. There is a renewed sense of cathartic release. The second EMU

5.3 The Decline of the Revolution

'fades out,' showing O'Neill once again left behind in his room, alone on the sofa and gazing after Bryant.

Compared with the central dialogue scene between Reed and Bryant in the first part of the film, the staging of this scene clearly has a darker mood. Whereas in the staging of the interview, the violence ultimately dissolves into a form of playful humor, here it generates tension and confrontation. The latter scene is far removed from the perfect synchronicity of the kairotic moment; rather than merge together, bodies collide in verbal attacks. The confrontational disintegration of gender relations functions as a substitute for the decline of the Revolution. The scene's somber atmosphere is related not only to private life, but also the political realm. On the level of content, O'Neill's lines ultimately present a reckoning with the role of intellectuals in the Revolution. He says: "Ah, yes, Russia. [...] Russia's been good for you and Jack. [...] Given you a way to meet people, given him a reason to leave home. Russia. Russia." Despite Bryant's repeated attempts to stop him, he continues:

> Louise, something in me tightens, when an American intellectual's eyes shine and they start to talk to me about the Russian people. [...] Something in me says, "Watch it. A new version of Irish Catholicism is being offered for your faith." [...] And I wonder why a lovely wife like Louise Reed who's just seen the brave new world is sitting around with a cynical bastard like me instead of trotting all over Russia with her idealistic husband. It's almost worth being converted.

His argument comes down to questioning the Bohemian intellectual's connection to the proletariat and the Revolution:

> You and Jack have a lot of middle-class dreams for two radicals. Jack dreams that he can hustle the American working man, whose one dream is to be rich enough not to have to work, into a revolution led by his party. And you dream that if you discuss the revolution with a man before you go to bed with him, it will be missionary work rather than sex. I'm sorry to see you and Jack so serious about your sports. It's particularly disappointing in you, Louise. You had a lighter touch when you were touting free love.

In connection with the affective foundation of the scene, these statements produce a dark image of the role of intellectuals in a revolution. Furthermore, O'Neill's argument here coincides with some of Arendt's observations on the "temporary alliance between the mob and the elite" in totalitarian movements after the First World War. Arendt writes:

> What appealed to the elite was radicalism as such. [...] the attraction which Soviet Russia exerted almost equally on Nazi and Communist intellectual fellow-travelers lay precisely

in the fact that in Russia "the revolution was a religion and a philosophy, not merely a conflict concerned with the social and political side of life."[94]

Regardless of whether O'Neill's accusations are true or not or what differences there might be between Jack Reed and Louis Bryant and the elites after World War One Arendt is talking about, the political topics do not disappear in the second half of the film. They only get debated less openly. With Louise Bryant's reply, the film offers a counter position to O'Neill. As has been described above, the movie combines Bryant's rebellious position with a cathartic experience. In contrast to the dark reality of the totalitarian movements which the movie refers to via O'Neill's talk, the movie keeps – through Bryant's cathartic backtalk – the possibility of a connection between the proletariat and intellectuals alive that is different from the alliance between the mob and the elite.

The Extended Temporality of the Couple

First, a brief note on the scene's narrative context: it is situated toward the end of the film.[95] After a long separation and a difficult journey, Bryant has come to Russia, where she hopes to find Reed. He, however, has traveled on a Party agit-train to Azerbaijan to initiate the Revolution there as well. The train has been attacked by enemy forces there. Bryant waits on a platform for the train to return. Neither she nor the spectator knows whether Reed has survived the attack.

Through constellation of character, cinematography, and sound, the scene stages an image of disquiet and chaos, which transforms into an image of successful reunion in the form of intermittent movement formations and temporal delay.

Dramaturgically, the scene marks the climax of the film's second half. After the attack on the agit-train, Bryant waits at the station for the train to return, so she can reunite with Reed on the platform after a long separation. In the first segment (EMU 1), the scene stages Bryant's search for Reed as intermittent movement and temporal elongation. This sequence awakens a sense of chaos and disquiet in the spectator, achieved through the three dominant formal elements of constellation of character, cinematography, and sound. Tracking shots transfer the character's increasing and then abating movements to the

---

94 Hannah Arendt: The Origins of Totalitarianism. New Edition with Added Prefaces, San Diego 1979, pp. 336 f.; Arendt cites Nikolai Berdyaev: The Origins of Russian Communism, London 1937, pp. 124 f. For the chapter "The Temporary Alliance Between the Mob and the Elite," see ibid., pp. 326–340.
95 The timecode is 01:13:01–01:16:41 (Disc 2).

entire visual space. The bustling mise-en-scène and the crowded image composition generate a sense of hectic unrest. The sound reinforces that sense; from the beginning, it is marked by the squealing sounds of the train and the murmur of voices from those waiting on the platform.

A change in axis signals the shift to the second EMU, which at first is also characterized by intermittent movement. Over the course of the EMU, however, this develops into an image of reunion and merging, when Bryant finds Reed. This development is staged through the introduction of extra-diegetic music into the scene (making the score the dominant formal element of the EMU) and its crescendoing formation. The musical shift is associated with a change in Bryant's movements from intermittent to linear, as well as the use of extreme closeups in the final embrace, which remove the previously staged tumult and confusion from the frame.

First EMU: 00:00:00:00–00:02:05:04
Through the interplay of cinematography, constellation of character, and sound design, the EMU stages an image of hectic unrest and disconcertion in the form of intermittent movement formations and temporal deceleration.

The very first shot shows three divergent movement formations, creating a sense of unease. A cut shows a black train slowly approaching the camera, white steam pouring from its smokestack. This vertical movement of the steam is noticeably faster than the hissing and pounding of the train. The feeling of inertia and exhaustion generated by the train's extremely slow movement is further reinforced by the image composition: Perforated flags mounted on the train hang limply from their poles, rather than flying heroically in the wind. An even greater contrast of movement speeds comes from the smoke that rushes from a vent to the left that is hidden by the front smokestack. These differing movement formations are associated with a droning ambient sound, which further bolsters the sense of unease. The train's whistle, the squealing of its brakes, and the rattle of its wheels become louder over the course of the shot. The train's signal blast blows again at the end of the first shot. This sonic tapestry is maintained in the following shots, which alternate between the approaching train and Bryant waiting on the platform with a crowd of other people. The images of the seated Bryant also feel crowded and disorganized, as she is surrounded by several other people whose bodies are cut off by the edge of the frame and who leap to their feet as soon as the train arrives.

The beginning of the EMU consists of a constant alternation between these two scenes (arrival of the train/people waiting on the platform). In the scene's sixth shot, by far the longest shot in the EMU (and the scene) at 21 seconds and 18 frames, Bryant also jumps up and walks along the side of the train. Once again, the image composition is quite confusing and restless, as many people are moving about the platform and headed toward the train. Bryant takes quick steps toward the train, following the crowd (or swept along by it). She then slows down, however, as too many people are in her way. She disappears from the spectator's view for a few seconds, obscured by other people. When she re-emerges from the crowd, the industrial ambient sound associated with the train becomes quieter: The rattling of the wheels slows and falls silent as Bryant briefly comes to a standstill in the image center and the spectator has a clear view of her again. As the shot progresses, her once again speedy forward movement is linked to a rightward tracking shot that dynamizes the entire visual space. Tellingly, however, the lateral tracking shot ends after a few seconds and the camera merely pans slightly right to keep Bryant, who is dashing forward, in frame.

In the following shots, there is a steady alternation between closeups of Bryant struggling along the platform through the crowd, which are associated with a reverse tracking motion, and her point-of-view shots on the train cars, which are represented by a forward tracking motion. Here too, there is no rigorous movement; instead, it is repeatedly interrupted and stalled. The movement into the depths of the image, which is undertaken by both the character and the camera, is repeatedly disrupted and stopped by people who stand on the platform, or by embracing couples who do not move along but turn in a circle. In addition, Bryant's trajectory is repeatedly thwarted by people hopping from cars or being hoisted into them, running across the frame or into her. (In the scene's tenth shot, there are four different vectors of motion. The camera, which shows Bryant's point-of-view in this shot, moves to the right. A man leaps diagonally towards it from the train. A couple stands in the center of the frame, embracing and turning in a circle. A few people walk toward the camera.) The anticipated reunion with Reed is thus delayed over and over again. Shot and countershot repeatedly alternate between the searching Bryant and her point-of-view, without any sighting of Reed. Bryant's tempo also varies, and comes in intermittent waves. While her push forward (and with it the tracking shots that correspond with her movements in both shot and countershot) is quite fast at first, it slows, then accelerates again – then eases up once more. The final slowing of her movement, which also marks the end of the EMU, is associated with a shift in the sound design. Over the course of the EMU, the hubbub of the crowd, with the occasional discernible Russian word, takes the place of the train noises as ambient sound. With the second slowing of Bryant's movement, however, applause emerges and becomes louder, at first on the soundtrack only. This is the movement when Zinoviev and another Party member descend from the train, but not Reed. The applause, which is neither euphoric nor sluggish, but simply constant, is associated with Bryant's gradually decelerating forward movement. All of this culminates in a shot in which the camera lingers for several seconds on the door from which the Party members have emerged, which is riddled with bullet holes. Bryant's movement (she shakes her head lightly) and the movement of the visual space come to a standstill. The end of the movement is further marked by a crossing of the axis, which shows Bryant looking to the left for the first time, disrupting the spatial organization. The EMU ends with this shot, in which the applause slowly fades and finally falls silent.

Second EMU: 00:02:05:05–00:03:26:21
Through sound, constellation of characters, and cinematography, the EMU stages an image of joyful reunion in the form of approach and merging of the characters' bodies coupled with separation from their immediate environment.

This EMU also begins with intermittent movement and a temporal delay. At first, Bryant and the camera start moving once again – yet in comparison to the earlier movements, their speed is greater. Yet this movement too quickly stops, when Bryant sees a body wrapped in a red flag being carried toward her on a stretcher. Yet this is the last retardation before the two protagonists meet. The shot that shows Bryant's reaction to the stretcher – a closeup on her face – ends when she turns around, and a rack focus reveals Reed in the background of the image in her line of sight. The next shot shows her face in closeup. Interestingly, in order to make the spectator experience the long-awaited end of her search, the film relies less on Keaton's facial expression (which reveals no reaction), and more on the texture of the image: The quality of the image differs clearly from earlier shots. It is much grainier and thus produces a minor perceptual shock for the spectator.[96]

Now the climax of the EMU begins. First, the characters exchange glances. A closeup of Reed reveals his unshaven face and messy hair; Bryant's face is shown in medium closeup. The alternation of shot and countershot repeats twice, further slowing down the action, before Bryant appears in a *plan américain*. She begins to walk toward Reed, staring at him steadily and never letting him out of her sight. She does not walk fast, but her movements are determined; in a decisive departure from the movement figurations of the first EMU, she does not allow anyone to get in her way. Only occasionally does she bump into people who move in the opposite direction. At the moment when she begins to walk, extradiegetic music begins, making sound the dominant formal element of the EMU. One of the film's central motifs plays on the soundtrack in a piano arrangement with strings in the background. The interplay of

---

[96] This effect was probably achieved through the use of a zoom lens.

constellation of character, music, and camera movement culminates when Bryant smiles lightly before she reaches Reed, lowers her eyes and sinks her head while the music steadily grows louder, completing a crescendo formation while the ambient sound (the murmur of voices) falls silent. The camera zooms out, bringing Reed into the visual field, and thereby situating the two characters in a shared visual space for the first time in this scene. Then comes the embrace. This is staged with a change to the shot size. In extreme closeup, the viewer sees the back of each character's head and the (mostly closed) eyes of the other person. Their tight embrace blurs the boundaries between the two bodies; it is not always easy to determine which body part belongs to which body. The intermittent movements and the repeated delays have led to a climax after all, the joyful merging of the characters' bodies. Through extreme closeups and the replacement of ambient sound through extradiegetic music (the romance motif), the characters are further highlighted and separated from their environment. They seem decoupled from it and at the same time sufficient unto themselves. The reunion has succeeded. The audiovisual form of this staging ends with a steady alternation between shot and countershot (extreme closeups of the embracing couple) as the piano plays the melody to its end, the strings hold the final chord, and Reed sighs and exhales deeply.

In fact, this scene is diametrically opposed to the *kairos* of the revolution from the first half of the film in both content and movement formations. Of the perfect interplay of love, work, sex, and politics, only private happiness, the private reunion of the couple remains. The woman is reduced to her role of 'waiting-for-a-man,' and the man's political ideals are as tattered as the red flags that hang limply from the train. The synchronicity of the kairotic moment, which united everything in a temporal condensation, gives way to the almost infinitely extended moment of reunion. In addition, there is – significantly for Arendt's understanding of politics as well as that of the film – the silence. Whereas speech was very present during the kairos scene through Reed's lecture, the couple's reunion occurs with almost no words spoken; only a murmured "Don't leave me … Please don't leave me" can be heard from Reed. Every form of politics is erased. As a negative foil, the scene refers once more to the importance of speech and language for politics. It is precisely the lack of language that marks this scene as the representation of a purely private situation. If, however, one wants to extract a positive aspect from the scene – and it would fail to do the scene justice to characterize it as merely a negative foil for the successful revolution – one could argue that the scene holds on to the ideal of love. Even when all other levels of perfection through revolution (politics, work, free time) fall away in this scene, in spite of everything the couple's reunion – though oft deferred – remains. Love is the last residuum of utopia.

6 JOHN ADAMS: Before the Birth Comes the Revolution

6.1 The Missing Afterlife of the American Revolution

As already demonstrated, for Arendt the historical insignificance into which the American Revolution has fallen, and its lack of theorization, are failures of revolutionary theory whose magnitude is difficult to comprehend. According to Arendt, the American Revolution played no role in the European revolutionary tradition as it developed over the course of the nineteenth century; hardly anyone thought of it or attempted to follow the lead of the American republic. Arendt expresses a clear judgment with regard to this phenomenon: Revolutionaries "speak and act as though they [...] had never heard of such a thing as the American Revolution."[1] Yet it was not only in Europe that no one took notice of the American Revolution; in the US too, it slipped into oblivion. Arendt argues:

> Less spectacular perhaps, but certainly no less real, are the consequences of the American counterpart to the world's ignorance, her own failure to remember that a revolution gave birth to the United States and that the republic was brought into existence by no 'historical necessity' and no organic development, but by a deliberate act: the foundation of freedom.[2]

According to Arendt, "all thought begins with remembrance" – with memory, the lingering (and *Nach-Denken*) of what once was.[3] And what was missing not only in Europe, but also in the United States, was any memory – or continued thinking – of the Revolution. This is why it was never theorized, preventing it from ever achieving the same level of significance as the French Revolution for the course of world history.[4] The American Revolution quite simply lacked the audience that, according to Kant and Arendt, is necessary for a revolution to become meaningful.

---

[1] Hannah Arendt: On Revolution, London 1990, p. 216.
[2] Ibid.
[3] On this idea, see ibid., p. 220.
[4] See Arendt's reasoning for the importance of the French Revolution: "By the same token, I am inclined to think that it was precisely the great amount of theoretical concern and conceptual thought lavished upon the French Revolution by Europe's thinkers and philosophers which contributed decisively to its world-wide success, despite its disastrous end" (ibid., pp. 219 f.).

Arendt's thesis on the failure to remember or theorize the American Revolution in nineteenth- and twentieth-century America noticeably corresponds to the scarcity of audiovisual restagings of this revolution. When it comes to the history of the US on television and in film, the Civil War dominates all other topics. This war seems to function as a myth of national origin more than the Revolution does. D.W. Griffith's titling of his Civil War film THE BIRTH OF A NATION (US 1915) is a paradigmatic example of this phenomenon. The birth metaphor, however, requires a preceding act of procreation, and one can rightly identify John Adams – the title character of the mini-series on which this chapter focuses – as one of the fathers of the American Revolution. On the other hand, it is important to take care not to over-extend Griffith's metaphor; to ontogenetically project onto the nation the developmental phases of childhood, adolescence, mid-life, old age, and death would be to naturalize historically contingent events in a way that is clearly problematic, in the case of the American Revolution especially. With regard to the Civil War, however, Griffith's birth metaphor holds true for audiovisual stagings of the history of the US. By contrast, film history contains only a few scattered examples that deal with the American Revolution.[5] A plot summary of the Western DRUMS ALONG THE MOHAWK (John Ford, US 1939) promises that at the beginning of the film, American settlers are threatened by the British and their Indian allies.[6] Yet the expectation that British, banded together with indigenous people, will in fact attack the settlers, is left unmet, as the former appear only marginally in the film. Unlike what one might guess from reading the summary, the film does not address the American Revolution or the conflict that gave rise to it. In THE HOWARDS OF VIRGINIA (Frank Lloyd, US 1940), Cary Grant plays a fictionalized Thomas Jefferson – yet the film does not engage with the American Revolution, no more than the musical comedy 1776 (Peter H. Hunt, US 1972).[7] More recent productions include the 1985 film REVOLUTION (Hugh Hudson, GB/NO) with Al Pacino, as well as Roland Emmerich's THE PATRIOT (US/DE 2000) with Mel Gibson. Beyond the cinema, besides JOHN ADAMS there is the children's TV series LIBERTY'S KIDS: EST. 1776 (Michael Maliani/Kevin

---

[5] See also Cotten Seiler's contribution to the *Columbia Companion to Film*: "The American Revolution," in: The Columbia Companion to American History on Film. How the Movies Have Portrayed the American Past, ed. by Peter C. Rollins, New York 2004, pp. 49–57.

[6] See http://www.imdb.com/title/tt0031252/plotsummary?ref_=tt_stry_pl [last accessed 25 May 2022].

[7] The film is based on a successful Broadway musical. Interestingly, the argument that there is a lack of interest in pop culture treatments of the American Revolution does not hold true for musicals. In 2015, the hip hop musical *Hamilton* about the American revolutionary and first Secretary of the Treasury (!) in the United States enjoyed extreme success. See Erik Piepenburg: Why "Hamilton" Has Heat, in: The New York Times, 12 June 2016.

O'Donnell/Andy Heyward, US 2002–2003) about the adventures of three young people during the American Revolution, as well as the series TURN: WASHINGTON'S SPIES (Craig Silverstein, US 2014–2017), which tells the story of the Revolutionary War in the mode of spy thriller. This brief, cursory overview of the audiovisual stagings of the American Revolution, which is by no means comprehensive, is simply meant to demonstrate that even the few films that address the American Revolution do not think it or thoughtfully illuminate it.[8] There are certain individual elements of the American Revolution and the Revolutionary War that do turn up in films or series. One example that also appears in JOHN ADAMS are the thousands of Hessian mercenaries who were rented out by Frederick II., Landgrave of Hesse-Kassel to King George III. to fight against the Americans. At least one of these Hessian mercenaries continues with his nefarious deeds as the headless horseman in the Legend of Sleepy Hollow.[9] Yet no intensive engagement with the American Revolution occurs in these audiovisual moving images.

In the first chapter of their book *American History and Contemporary Hollywood Film,* which focuses on the films REVOLUTION and THE PATRIOT, political scientist Trevor B. McCrisken and literary theorist Andrew Pepper also conclude that films about the American Revolution are rare. They offer a "speculative" reason for this phenomenon: The subversive and rebellious dimension of the American Revolution must not be shown, as it would draw attention to how far contemporary America has strayed from the ideals of the Revolution, and how few of these ideals have been realized. On the other hand, the American Revolution also cannot be portrayed as insignificant, since this would not serve American exceptionalism. In order to avoid this dilemma, many films have transposed the basic idea of the Revolution – rebels defeat a tyrannical power – into another setting, as is the case in the STAR WARS films, for instance.[10]

---

8 Seiler's overview is somewhat more detailed, yet he comes to the same conclusions: There are very few films about the American Revolution, and the ones there are have little to contribute theoretically. See Seiler: The American Revolution, op. cit.
9 On the practice of renting soldiers during the American Revolutionary war, it is worth looking into the research on Johann Gottfried Seume. Seume was not Hessian but was among the recruited soldiers. See Georg Meyer-Thurow: Über Dichtung und Wahrheit, in: Seumes Lebensbericht. An Beispielen aus Seumes hessischer Rekrutenzeit. Nebst einem Anhang, in: "Weimar ist ja unser Athen. Mit Seume in Weimar", ed. by Jörg Drews/Gabi Pahnke, Bielefeld 2010, pp. 13–36. On the headless horseman, see the film SLEEPY HOLLOW (Tim Burton, US/DE 1999) and the series SLEEPY HOLLOW (Alex Kurtzman/Roberto Orci, US 2013–2017).
10 See Trevor B. McCrisken/Andrew Pepper: American History and Contemporary Hollywood Film, Edinburgh 2005, pp. 16 f. The authors rely on Michael Ventura: A Revolution Worth Having, in: LA Weekly, 27 December 1985 – 2 January 1986, p. 21. The example they name from

Underlying these considerations, however, are a few assumptions that seem extreme even for a speculative argument. These include assumptions about both the lack of subversive potential in Hollywood films and the contemporary political situation in the United States that absolutely cannot be taken for granted. I would therefore like to introduce another explanation for the meager filmic interest – both in cinema and television series – in the American Revolution: What it lacks is the one moment, the singular event, into which one can condense the course of the entire revolution, and which can bring together all its dramatic incidents. Arendt gestures toward this conclusion when she writes, in a polemic against the historian's preference for dramatics:

> If, however, one keeps in mind that the end of rebellion is liberation, while the end of revolution is the foundation of freedom, the political scientist at least will know how to avoid the pitfall of the historian who tends to place his emphasis upon the first and violent stage of rebellion and liberation, on the uprising against tyranny, to the detriment of the quieter second stage of revolution and constitution, because all the dramatic aspects of this story seem to be contained in the first stage and, perhaps, also because the turmoil of liberation has so frequently defeated the revolution.[11]

This dynamic emerges from a failure to distinguish between liberation and freedom: To reduce revolution to mere liberation is to misunderstand it. Yet even if this should not present an obstacle to rigorous historical engagement with the American Revolution, it remains a real problem for audiovisual stagings thereof: The American Revolution had no dramaturgically useful *kairos*. There was the Boston Tea Party in 1773, but that was three years *before* the Declaration of Independence. There is nothing in the American Revolution like the storming of the Bastille or of the Winter Palace, or a moment like the one Benjamin describes during the French July Revolution in 1830, when suddenly, simultaneously, and yet completely independently, people began shooting at clock towers.[12] There are no comparable images that show the American Revolution as a dramatic uprising. This revolution is associated with men who are no longer young, but very wise, who debate and vote on the notion of independence from the British

---

the Star Wars series is Star Wars: Episode IV – A New Hope (George Lucas, US 1977). The argument for a lack of interest in the American Revolution on the part of producers is shored up by the fact that Revolution was such a huge flop that it bankrupted its (British) production company (see ibid., p. 16).

11 Arendt: On Revolution, op. cit., p. 142.

12 "On the first evening of fighting [of the July revolution 1830, H.B.], it so happened that the dials on clocktowers were being fired at simultaneously and independently from several locations in Paris" (Walter Benjamin: On the Concept of History, in: id.: Selected Writings. Vol. IV 1938–1940, ed. by Howard Eiland/Michael W. Jennings, trans. by Edmund Jephcott et al., Cambridge, MA et al. 2003, pp. 389–400, here p. 395).

Kingdom, or work on the Declaration of Independence. Proofreading a text is hardly a dramatic act. John Adams does attempt to crystallize the American Revolution into a single moment when he says that in the colonies, thirteen clocks struck at once.[13] What he means, however, is that there was a widespread constitution fever and that all the colonies created their constitutions at the same time – not a terribly cinematic subject. Even the image used by Adams to capture this unspectacular occurrence lacks the dramatic shot at the clock that is so central to Benjamin's otherwise similar parable.

In *Difference and Repetition*, Gilles Deleuze introduces another aspect: "[...] as Péguy says, it is not Federation Day which commemorates or represents the fall of the Bastille, but the fall of the Bastille which celebrates and repeats in advance all the Federation Days [...]."[14] The logical extension of this argument is that the fall of the Bastille already contains within it all films about the fall of the Bastille, just as the storming of the Winter Palace repeats and celebrates in advance all future reenactments and films thereof. It would be more difficult to imagine that the men proofreading a text are celebrating all commemorations and stagings of this event in advance. For the American Revolution is a revolution without an *event* in Žižek's sense: "[...] something shocking, out of joint that appears to happen all of a sudden and interrupts the usual flow of things; something that emerges seemingly out of nowhere, without discernible causes, an appearance without solid being as its foundation."[15] Žižek uses love to demonstrate how the event is an effect that exceeds its causes. One does not fall in love with somebody because that person is charming or pretty. Quite the opposite: The person appears charming or pretty because one is in love. He attempts to understand revolutions using the same concept of the event – here, his example is the protests at Tahrir Square in Cairo.[16] In the American Revolution, there is no similar form of eventfulness. Although something new did emerge that broke with previous traditions, it happened without a moment that could be defined as an effect which exceeds its causes; without a moment that – like love – follows a circular logic; and without a moment which possesses – as in Arendt – an

---

13 See Arendt: On Revolution, op. cit., p. 141.
14 Gilles Deleuze: Difference and Repetition, trans. by Paul Patton, London 2004, p. 2.
15 Slavoj Žižek: Event. A Philosophical Journey through a Concept, Brooklyn 2014, p. 4.
16 See ibid. Žižek acknowledges that he is attempting to use the same structure to explain both an individual psychological phenomenon like love and a political phenomenon like revolution. He legitimizes this approach with the notion that events undermine established frameworks and allow for the discovery of something new and unexpected. This is why it is impossible to create a taxonomy of events; instead, they must be approached on their own terms, i.e., without any attempt at strict classification (see ibid., p. 7).

unstoppable quality of movement. Precisely this sort of event is lacking in the American Revolution. The question arises, with what audiovisual format can one not only do justice to the American Revolution, but also make it productive and think it? With what format can one approach the American Revolution when it lacks the decisive kairotic moment that exists in so many other revolutions and in memorializations thereof?

In JOHN ADAMS, the format is a mini-series. What defines a mini-series? It is difficult, if not impossible, to answer this question, as there is no general agreement on what constitutes a mini-series. Instead, they resemble a notion in genre theory developed by the philosopher Daniel Martin Feige: Only in retrospect does it become clear that something has been a mini-series, and each new mini-series contributes to the broader definition of the term.[17] In order to construct a *heuristic* framework, I will offer a tentative definition for the genre "mini-series," which might lend some sense of direction. In her book *Komplexe Welten. Narrative Strategien in US-amerikanischen Fernsehserien*, Kathrin Rothemund comments briefly on the mini-series: "In a mini-series […] a story is told through a clearly limited number of episodes, meaning that from the beginning, the narrative's end is already written into the story."[18] A mini-series consists of individual episodes – in the following section I will focus on the second episode of JOHN ADAMS, which is about the drafting, revision, and publication of the Declaration of Independence. These events are the closest the American Revolution gets to a moment of crystallization. Building on Rothemund's observations, it is worth noting that in the case of JOHN ADAMS, the length of each episode – ranging from 67 to 88 minutes – makes the spectatorial experience feel more like a stand-alone film than an episode of a series of which one might watch two or three episodes in a row. Second, a mini-series tells a story over the course of multiple episodes – in my second section on the series, therefore, I will go into more depth on the other episodes. In the third section, I address Rothemund's remark that "from the beginning" of a mini-series, "the narrative's end is already written into the story." This third point seems to me a possible specification of a mini-series that allows it to be distinguished from both *serials* and the other common series format, the *episodic series*, whose structure

---

[17] See Daniel Martin Feige: Alle Genres sind prekär und kein Genre ist prekär, oder: Die Logik des Genres im Genre der (hegelschen) Logik, in: Prekäre Genres. Zur Äesthetik peripherer, apokrypher und liminaler Gattungen, ed. by Hanno Berger/Frédéric Döhl/Thomas Morsch, Bielefeld 2015, pp. 17–29.
[18] Kathrin Rothemund: Komplexe Welten. Narrative Strategien in US-amerikanischen Fernsehserien, Berlin 2013, p. 18.

can be found in sitcoms, for instance.[19] The Australian film and media scholar Angela Ndalianis understands *serials* that do not already contain their ending from the beginning through the concept of the neo-baroque. She thereby directs attention to the open, labyrinthine, potentially infinite nature of narrative threads in a sequential series.[20] Yet Rothemund's criteria allow the mini-series to be differentiated from the episodic series as well. Based on the sitcom, Bert Rebhandl characterizes the episodic structure as follows:

> At the end of a sitcom episode, nothing has really changed; on the contrary, this return to the beginning has often been described as the sitcom's actual dramatic movement. The sitcom's primary objective is to perpetuate itself, a task which is mutually exclusive with dramatic transformation.[21]

Of course, this concept rarely appears in such pure form in the series themselves, but Rebhandl's argument demonstrates why there is a potential infinitude inherent to episodic series as well.

But now the question arises: What points of connection exist between the structure of the mini-series and the American Revolution? As a first approach to this question, which will remain in view through the following subchapters, it is clear that in both the historical American Revolution as understood by Arendt, and in a mini-series about this revolution – through the fact that it consists of multiple episodes – there is a turn away from the idea that a revolution must be crystallized in a kairotic moment. In direct contradiction to the concept of a revolution as a singular event, both the American Revolution and the process of watching a mini-series center on continually renewing re-entry, the incompleteness of the individual episode and of the political understanding that Arendt

---

19 This is a pointed and heuristic statement that is supposed to make my argumentation on JOHN ADAMS plausible: It opens up a perspective on JOHN ADAMS that can make this mini-series productive. I am not seeking to make a broader claim or to establish a rigid generic definition of the mini-series. It is not difficult to find counter-examples to the thesis that only mini-series have their end written in from the beginning. For example, the end to the series BABYLON 5 (Joseph Michael Straczynski, US 1994–1998), which stretches over five seasons and 110 episodes, was written in from the beginning. I thank Tobias Haupts for the reference to this series. On the (always gradual) difference between series with self-contained episodes (episodic series) and shows that have a narrative arc spanning multiple episodes (sequential series), see Rothemund: Komplexe Welten, op. cit., pp. 16 ff.
20 See Angela Ndalianis: Television and the Neo-Baroque, in: The Contemporary Television Series, ed. by Michael Hammond/Lucy Mazdon, Edinburgh 2005, pp. 83–101.
21 Bert Rebhandl: Exzess des Ausdrucks. Endliche und unendliche Serialisierung: Was ist episch an der Sitcom "Frasier?", in: Autorenserien. Die Neuerfindung des Fernsehens. Auteur Series. The Re-invention of Television, ed. by Christoph Dreher, Stuttgart 2010, pp. 287–311, here p. 293.

develops with regard to the American Revolution. Through the division into individual episodes, moreover, the overwhelming duration of historical epics that is so important in NAPOLÉON and REDS falls away, and along with it the connection to the sublime and to the overpowering movement of the revolutions thematized by these films. In this way, too, the format of the mini-series is appropriate to the course of the American Revolution. There is, however, a difference between the preceding description of the mini-series and openness in political and historical thought: Although its episodes are not self-contained, the mini-series itself forms a self-contained whole. It is thus important not to push the analogy too far, but instead to examine how in the concrete case of JOHN ADAMS, this intrinsic completeness can be used to think the American Revolution in a productive way. In my third section on the series, therefore, I will go into more depth on the consequences that result in the mini-series JOHN ADAMS from the end that is inscribed in it from the beginning. First, I attend more closely to the episode that is most significant to the question of staging the American Revolution, the second episode, titled INDEPENDENCE (Tom Hooper, US 2008).

6.2 The American Revolution as Mini-Series

The Episode INDEPENDENCE

At the center of JOHN ADAMS is the character John Adams, one of the founding fathers of the American Revolution. He was the first Vice President and second President of the United States. He was thus the first *second* man of the state and only the *second* first man of the state. This is likely one reason why he always stood in the shadow of George Washington, the first President, but also of Thomas Jefferson, who became the third President of the US, or of Benjamin Franklin, who has a much greater presence than John Adams does in American popular culture. The series is thus doubly important as an act of remembrance, for the 'forgetting' of John Adams is part of the broader 'forgetting' of the American Revolution identified by Arendt.[22] The idea of being forgotten seemed to worry already the historical John Adams, who wrote to his friend Benjamin Rush on 4 April 1790:

---

22 The subordinate role played by John Adams in the historical memory of the United States is expressed partially in the fact that – in contrast to other presidents or leaders of the Revolution – he is not depicted on any dollar bills or regular coins.

> The History of our Revolution will be one continued Lye from one end to the other. The essence of the whole will be *that Dr Franklins electrical Rod smote the Earth and out Sprang General Washington. That Franklin electrified him with his Rod – and thence forward these two conducted all the Policy Negotiations Legislation and War.*[23]

This passage reveals not only Adams' fear of being forgotten, but is thoroughly illuminating for the series, its mode of staging and its concept of revolution, insofar as its protagonist is not one of the great and renowned historical personalities, but rather a figure whose fate was to receive little regard even before the American Revolution was over. John Adams started as a lawyer, and in the first episode of the series we see him in this profession: how he defends British soldiers who are accused of shooting at unarmed demonstrators, and how against all expectations, Adams brings their innocence to light.[24]

The second episode, as indicated by its title, is about the colonies' journey to independence from the English monarchy. It centers on John Adams' endeavor to build consensus in Congress over the schism. A second narrative thread tells of Abigail Adams' efforts to protect her family from the encroaching violence of the British and the raging smallpox virus. The episode's macro-structure reveals an emotional dramaturgy with a clear logic of crescendo in both subplots. This choice is particularly true of the scenes that play out in Congress. The scene's first episode, a cold open, shows a session to debate the question of how to react to increasing violence from the British. John Adams' distance from the speakers who urge appeasement – he responds to them with sarcastic commentary – is associated with calm and restrained staging. Yet with each of the seven additional scenes set in Congress, the atmosphere becomes thicker, more charged, intense, and sometimes hectic, which in large part is due to the increasingly energetic performances by the actors. Yet the debates never seem out of control. Furthermore, the episode ends neither with a triumphant climax nor with its opposite, collapse and decline of the previously staged tension and intensity. Instead, the tension transforms into uncertainty and openness, as I will show at the end of this section. And it is quite indicative that the scenes of debate form the basis for the emotional dramaturgy of the episode. Speech, discussion, and

---

23 John Adams: From John Adams to Benjamin Rush, 4 April 1790, in: Founders Online, National Archives. https://founders.archives.gov/documents/adams/99-02-02-0903 [last accessed 25 May 2022].
24 See JOHN ADAMS. PART I: JOIN OR DIE (Tom Hooper, US 2008).

persuasion are the central elements of the American Revolution, according to the series. Therefore, a discussion, namely about the American Declaration of Independence, occupies the center of the first scene, which I wish to examine more closely.[25]

John Adams, Benjamin Franklin, and Thomas Jefferson discuss Jefferson's draft of the Declaration of Independence. While Adams and Franklin each sit on a chair and read the draft, Jefferson stands and paces a bit nervously at first, before he also sits down on a chair. Two points are discussed in this scene: First, there is a brief discussion about slavery. Franklin remarks that Jefferson holds the British monarchy responsible for the evil of slavery in his draft, yet does not address slavery itself. He thus condemns the slave trade and characterizes it as unjust, but reserves judgment on slave ownership. This would have the result that already enslaved workers would become an even more desirable commodity. Jefferson responds that this was not his intention, and adds that slavery is an abomination and must be identified as such. He adds the caveat, however, that neither he nor anyone else has a quick solution for this problem. After a brief silence, Franklin answers: "Oh, it ... Well, 'tis no matter. The issue before us is independence and not emancipation." And after another remark by Franklin that Congress would never endorse an attack on slavery, slavery does not come up again. In Arendt's writing on the American Revolution too, slavery does not play a large role. Her thesis is that "the institution of slavery carries an obscurity even blacker than the obscurity of poverty; the slave, not the poor man, was 'wholly overlooked'."[26] Although she immediately adds that Jefferson, "and others to a lesser degree," occasionally referred to the crime of slavery, her remarks suggest that the question of slavery simply played no role for the men of the American Revolution. When JOHN ADAMS gives such prominent place to a brief discussion of the problem of slavery – without presenting Jefferson, Adams, or Franklin as heroes of abolition – it can be understood as an attempt to refer to this 'blind spot' of the American Revolution.[27]

The second salient point shows us how the famed opening of the Declaration of Independence, "We hold these truths to be self-evident," could have come to be written. The three men agree that Jefferson's proposed language,

---

25 Its timecode is 00:58:03–01:01:51 (episode: INDEPENDENCE).
26 Arendt: On Revolution, op. cit., p. 71.
27 The series goes further with this attempt to reference this lacuna of the American Revolution in a later episode: In a sinister atmosphere – with desaturated, greyish coloration, and ominous scoring – it shows how the White House is built by "half-fed slaves" (a line from the series character Abigail Adams). See JOHN ADAMS. PART VI: UNNECESSARY WAR (Tom Hooper, US 2008), timecode 00:47:51–00:52:02.

"sacred and undeniable," should be changed to "self-evident." In comparison to Arendt's remarks on the first sentence of the Declaration of Independence, the discussion of language in the mini-series shows that the contradiction Arendt identifies between 'we hold' and 'self-evident' was even more stark in the original version by Jefferson that is discussed here. Where Arendt sees 'self-evident' (a phrase that the series primarily attributes to Franklin in this scene) as referring to an apolitical realm, the phrase suggested by Jefferson, 'sacred and undeniable,' does so even more clearly – Franklin complains that it is too religious: "Smacks of the pulpit," he says in this scene. The contradiction between the initial phrase 'we hold' was even clearer (here, however, it does not receive any attention). After they have agreed on the edits to the text, the topic of conversation changes; Franklin turns a bit in his chair and the three men discuss the advantages of Jefferson's invention of the swivel chair. In this way, the series closely links political and technological progress.[28] Of greater significance for my work than this connection and the debates shown by the scene are the calm and composure with which Jefferson, played by Stephen Dillane, reacts to suggested edits to his draft. This is not aimed at the question of the character's psychology; rather, Dillane's performance strikes me as symptomatic of the series' staging of the Revolution.

Early in the scene, Jefferson is still standing, his arms crossed over his chest, turning in a semi-circle. Although his movements are gentle, he seems a bit nervous. This slight disquiet leaves him completely when he sits down after John Adams's first compliment. He is mostly shown in medium shots or medium close-ups; the camera thus maintains a certain distance from him (only toward the end of the scene are there two closeups). He sits sideways on a chair, turned toward Franklin and Adams, his right arm propped on the armrest and his chin in his hand. Occasionally he stares into the distance, then looks down, moves his fingers back and forth. His body is somewhat limp and leaned slightly forward. His only reactions to Franklin's suggested edits are a slight raise of the eyebrows, a wrinkle of his brow – a movement that is paired with a slight straightening of his

---

28 The fact that the series creates a direct transition between the discussion of the Declaration of Independence and a discussion about the swivel chair and the technological progress it represents suggests that *the series* wants to understand the Declaration of Independence as political progress. I, however, by no means want to argue that historical development should be understood as a narrative of progress. For a critique of teleological narratives of progress, see Benjamin: On the Concept of History, op. cit.; cf. especially Benjamin's analysis of Klee's drawing "Angelus Novus" (ibid., p. 392) as well as the passage in the preceding section: "The current amazement that the things we are experiencing are 'still' possible in the twentieth century is *not* philosophical. This amazement is not the beginning of knowledge – unless it is the knowledge that the view of history which gives rise to it is untenable" (ibid.).

torso – as well as a brief defense that he has chosen each word in the draft carefully. After he is overruled by Franklin and the phrase is changed to 'self-evident,' there is no emotional outburst. He remains calm and composed on his chair: The emotional impression in the scene is quite restrained. Composure, distance, and – one might say – self-control also characterize the series' staging of the revolution. And for Arendt, precisely this self-control on the part of the actors was the decisive element of the American Revolution – in contrast to the French Revolution, the revolution in America was not experienced as an unstoppable, tempestuous movement. In order to further pursue this avenue of inquiry, I will delve deeper into Adams' final speech before the vote on the Declaration of Independence, his final plea before Congress, before I undertake an EMU analysis of the staging of the definitive break with the British monarchy.

The scene with Adams' final speech is divided into two parts. After the first half, when John Dickinson, Congressman from Pennsylvania and Adams' antagonist, has given his speech against breaking with England and argued for a chance at peace, the scene's second half consists of Adams' appearance: He speaks in favor of independence, thereby accepting a war with England.[29] Adams' presentation is a plea for the independence of the colonies. It is familiar from countless American legal dramas: Before a jury, lawyers make their closing arguments for guilty or not-guilty, once again deploying all their arguments and rhetorical capacities in an effort to influence the result in their favor. In other words, through the content of their speech, as well as through prosody and rhetoric, they use their power in an Arendtian sense and seek to persuade a group of people. This is precisely the mode in which the Revolution is staged. The scene shows that revolutions are not always nor exclusively won (say nothing of started) through violence, but that the power of revolutionaries can be just as central, if not an even more meaningful factor. The scene refrains from musical accompaniment; John Adams' plea is underscored by occasional rumbling thunder, splashing raindrops, and lightning that momentarily illuminates the room and plunges it into cold, blue light. The storm – a central metaphor for the French Revolution – here remains outside as a meteorological phenomenon, spatially removed from the revolution that is taking place inside the building, where arguments are exchanged and visions of the future debated. Compared with the earlier scene about the drafting of the Declaration of Independence, this scene has heightened emotion, which manifests in Paul Giamatti's more expressive performance as John Adams. At the beginning of his speech, which is shot mostly in closeup, he looks down toward the floor; then he lifts his gaze and looks around

---

29 The timecode of Adams' speech is 01:09:08–01:13:37 (Episode: INDEPENDENCE).

at the audience. He speaks clearly and articulately, beginning quietly and becoming steadily louder, without losing control, shouting, or wildly gesticulating. His facial expressions and gestures are restrained: a raise of the eyebrows, a pointed finger, balled fist, calm smile. His voice and the skillful dramaturgical use of pauses, as well as the particular emphasis on certain words and the resulting melody of his sentences, suffice to lend rhetorical force to the historical significance of the decision at hand. In short, with his plea, Adams realizes in advance what the American Revolution will go on to constitute: the freedom of public speech, action, formation. And instead of staging the revolution as an unstoppable storm, here the series paints a picture with static closeups of thoughtful faces in the audience, slow and even tracking shots, zooms, and pans, as well as Adams' considered arguments. This image is the exact opposite of the excessive movement found in NAPOLÉON. After the end of his speech, Adams takes a seat and gazes straight ahead into the distance in almost complete silence – only the sounds of weather are audible in the background. Only gradually do the other congressmen around him begin to clap. The increasingly loud applause is associated with a tracking shot away from John Adams, which opens the space as more and more congressmen rise to congratulate Adams. The audiovisual gestalt of the scene ultimately ends with a climax that relieves tension, yet without coming anywhere close to the unfettered movement figurations of NAPOLÉON.

The most important scene of the episode for the question of staging the American Revolution, however, is the vote on seeking independence from Great Britain, and the declaration of independence that follows it. It forms the conclusion and dramaturgical climax of the series' second episode. I will now examine this scene by analyzing its EMUs.[30]

Through the interplay of sound design, image composition, and cinematography, the scene stages an image of oscillation between awakening and hesitation by alternating between decisive, forceful, rising movements and shaky, stagnating, falling movements. Both EMUs have a clear preparation, hold, and retraction. The alternation that dominates the scene, between awakening and hesitation, plays out in the first EMU as it takes shape over time. The EMU begins with decreasing volume in the sound design, increasing clarity in the image composition, and cinematography that is already calm. Particularly the sound design, the dominant element of the first EMU and of the entire scene, undergoes an upward movement over the course of the EMU, through the increasing emotion in characters' voices and the rising crescendo of extradiegetic music, creating an image of awakening. The climax, however, is quite brief and quickly resolved. The extradiegetic music fades

---

[30] The timecode is 01:20:25–01:27:06 (Episode: INDEPENDENCE).

out, the spoken words and phrases become calmer, and at the end of the EMU the sound design is completely silent save for the sound of the congressmen's breath. The image thereby created of hesitation and reluctance is underscored by calm, slow, and unexcited camera movement.

The shift to the second EMU comes with an opening of the space and a clear change in color composition. Whereas desaturated and somewhat dark colors dominate the enclosed space of the first EMU, here a more vibrant, bright color palette enters the scene, with the foreground outdoors under the clear blue sky. This EMU also has a very clear preparation, hold, and retraction. This time, however, the oscillation between awakening on the one hand, and hesitation and uncertainty on the other, is already inscribed from the beginning in the rising movement (the preparation), and also in the downward motion that comes after the climax (the retraction). This dynamic is exemplified by the voices that read the Declaration of Independence during the rising movement: on the one hand the firm, clear, and sonorous voice of the parliamentarian, and on the other the uncertain, shaky, and somewhat mumbling voice of the convalescent Nabby Adams. Yet this alternation also moves toward a climax, peaking with the collective cry of "God save our American States," the high point extended by the use of drums through several more shots. The descending movement that follows is clearly expressed through the ever quieter soundtrack. The alternation between awakening and hesitation is particularly evident during the retraction in the different lighting and color composition of the shots that are cut together in this sequence. While the shots of Abigail Adams in her garden are dominated by warm light and bright, vibrant colors, the shots of John Adams in his study are characterized by cold, pale lighting and a desaturated, dark color palette.

First EMU: 00:00:00:00–00:03:01:17
Through the interplay of sound design, image composition, and cinematography, the EMU stages an image of awakening that transforms into an image of hesitation in the form of a shift from rising, increasing movements to falling, decreasing movements.

The EMU is dominated by its sound design. At the beginning of the scene's first shot, strings are still holding the high note from the extradiegetic music of the previous scene. This sound is suddenly interrupted by the closing of doors, the pounding of a gavel, and a loud, brisk statement by John Hancock, the Senate President. Alongside Hancock's voice is a murmur of voices that cannot be precisely identified. A door creaks briefly as it is being closed. A few footsteps and canes striking the wood floor complement the somewhat restless ambient sound. This sound continues for the next few shots, yet recedes and gradually fades out, so that only Hancock's voice remains. Thus, at the beginning of the EMU the soundtrack almost goes quiet. This process is accompanied by increasingly clear and organized image composition (with many frames within the frame), which is dominated by desaturated, restrained, and somewhat dark colors: the all-encompassing grey wall of the room, the pale green cloths on the tables, Franklin's grey costume, his grey hair, the mostly light brown wigs of the congressmen, Adams' light brown jacket, the slightly brighter but still quite pale jackets of Hancock and Jefferson. The vote that follows is staged with a calm but not static camera. It begins with a gentle track to the right, filming the congressmen who sit facing the camera in a medium closeup. As the EMU progresses, the camera movement is largely limited to minimal pans or tracking shots. In the sound design, however, after the opening quiet comes crescendoing movement. Extradiegetic music comes in when the congressmen from New York cast their votes. The score is comprised of a few strings supported by a piano and, later, panpipes. This creates an aspirational, buoyant atmosphere that is reinforced by the congressmen's increasingly emotional voices. Whereas the parliamentarian calls the representatives of individual states in a sober tone at first – in a clear, brisk voice – over the course of the vote his voice becomes more agitated, less firm, and a bit shaky, which charges it with more emotion. In addition, he calls each state as though asking a question, his voice rising at the end of the state name. This upward movement is then repeated by the congressmen as they rise to their feet.

The upward reaching form of the audiovisual staging, however, descends again once the vote comes to an end. This falling movement begins in shot 49: In a closeup, the face of the congressman from South Carolina appears in the right half of the frame. In the left half, out of focus, the congressman from Georgia rises to his feet. As he stands, the congressman from South Carolina looks up; once the congressman from Georgia sits back down in the background, the congressman from South Carolina lets his head sink as well, only to raise it again in an almost continuous motion (after a very brief rest). The dual downward motion of the body in the background and the face in the foreground are underscored by the decrescendo of the extradiegetic music. Most instruments fall silent; only a high string tone remains, which is sustained over several shots. The voice of the parliamentarian has once again lost its emotion, and even the small spark of euphoria that was previously there has been extinguished. It seems more austere, impersonal, restrained. Once he has read the results in this voice, the high string sound also falls silent. The only remaining sound is the congressmen's breath, and the occasional quiet squeak or creak of a chair. In static shots or calm, gliding tracking shots, the silent congressmen appear in closeup. Their faces are largely expressionless. They look around, swallow visibly, and breathe heavily. No other movements are to be seen. The beginning of independence is characterized not by euphoria or sublimity, but largely expressionless, somewhat baffled faces and heavily breathing bodies. With regard to Deleuze's suggestion that films should restore our belief in the body, one might argue that also in the American Revolution of JOHN ADAMS, where speech, debate, and public action play such a large role, the body participates in the beginning of this revolution.

Second EMU: 00:03:01:18–00:06:38:20
Through the interplay of sound design, image composition, and cinematography, the EMU stages an image of oscillating between uncertain and decisive awakening as a shift from clear, forceful, unified, and open movements toward uncertain, shaky, and restrained movements.

The shift to this EMU is marked by a clear change in the image composition. While the previous EMU displayed dark, desaturated, and crowded image compositions in an interior space, the first shot of this EMU creates an entirely different image. Now the viewer is confronted with a very open image composition. In the upper half of the frame, the blue sky appears with a few scattered clouds; in the lower part of the image, a crowd of people extends beyond the edges of the frame. In the middle of the image is a building with a tower at its center that stretches to the upper edge of the image. The crowd is denser closer to the building, lending it a strong central perspective in spite of the wide angle shot. Behind the building are a few green trees. The vibrant blue, white, and green produce a much stronger color contrast than was in the preceding shots. Yet the EMU is once again dominated by its sound design, especially audible voices and extradiegetic music. At the beginning of the EMU, the parliamentarian reads the Declaration of Independence. Alongside his sonorous voice, deep string notes also begin to sound. His voice is very clear; he speaks quite loudly; every word is distinctly emphasized, lending his voice a very official and ceremonious air. After five shots, however, the voice reading the Declaration of Independence changes. Now the viewer hears Nabby, the ailing daughter of John Adams. Her voice presents a sharp contrast to that of the parliamentarian. It is much higher, and Nabby speaks less clearly and officially: She mumbles a little. Furthermore, she reads very quickly and does not emphasize individual words as distinctly. In spite of the speed with which she reads, her voice sounds somewhat frail, uncertain, sickly, and fragile. In addition, after a few shots she falters and, due to a word she does not recognize, must interrupt her speech to ask her mother for help. In the return to the voice of the parliamentarian, the upward movement is clearly noticeable. His deep, sonorous voice is now reinforced by elegiac, ceremonious strings. Another switch of the reader's voice to that of Abigail Adams presents less of a contrast, since her voice, while noticeably higher than the parliamentarian's, is firmer and clearer than Nabby's.

After another switch back to the parliamentarian's sonorous and solemn voice comes the climax of the EMU, when he reads the words "God save our American States," and the crowd as well as all the congressmen repeat the phrase in chorus. With that, drums – both visible in the diegesis and extradiegetically as part of the score – and horns begin to play. And the crowd begins to cheer audibly. The celebration leads to intensified movement in the image composition. Whereas the previous shots showed little movement, the image composition now becomes much more dynamic, with the exuberant crowd, the marching drummers and soldiers, a rearing horse, and smoke rising from cannons.

The retraction movement of the EMU begins in shot 102 with a closeup of John Adams' face, which appears in the right half of the frame. He is shown in quarter-profile looking to the left. In the left half of the image are a white doorframe and part of a red brick wall. Adams looks slightly down, his face revealing no emotion. On the soundtrack, the musical climax and drums come to an end; in their place comes a deep string tone. In the background, at first, the celebrating crowd – much quieter – remains. For the first time in the scene, we hear John Adams' voice. His deep voice is quiet, clear, and articulate. He speaks – and this is important for the EMU's descending motion – quite matter-of-factly, without notable fluctuation in his intonation. The image of oscillation between uncertain and decisive awakening that was staged in the beginning of the EMU is now emphasized primarily through the different image composition in the two locations that are cut together in the shots that follow. First comes a sparely furnished and weakly lit room. The walls are greenish white, the wood floor light brown. At the center of the back wall is a pale pink sofa with an empty glass in front of it. To the left, part of a brown mirror frame is visible. On each side wall hangs a small picture in a black frame. Adams stands at a window in the left half of the frame. He has neither wig nor hair. He is wearing a white shirt with a brown vest, dark pants, and somewhat lighter, long stockings and dark shoes. His entire body faces left; he appears in profile. He looks out the window, his arms crossed behind his back. Besides lightly rubbing the fingers of his right hand and a slight rightward movement of his head (both at the end of the shot), he does not move. During the rest of the EMU, Adams appears in this somewhat dark and austere room in dim lighting. There, he writes a letter to his wife. The shots showing Abigail Adams, the addressee, in her garden form a sharp contrast. The first of these shots shows a barn against a radiant blue sky. The barn casts a shadow to the left. In the background are green trees, to the left of the barn a few cows and a covered feeding trough. To the right of the building is a cart full of hay, in front of the barn a pile of wood and a bench. The barn is surrounded by green grass. Abigail cuts wood in front of it. She is wearing a pale blue dress. On the left edge of the frame, part of another cart is visible. The image composition is open, the color palette bright and generally quite warm. The bright but warm light and the vibrant green and blue also dominate in the subsequent shots, filmed with a dynamic camera, when Abigail walks across the grass and picks a peach. This idyllic image of awakening is underscored by birdsong and chirping crickets.

Yet this scene is cut together with shots showing John Adams, which conclude the EMU. The penultimate shot is a *plan américain* in which Adams, shown from a slightly left angle, stands at a window through which wan light shines. Otherwise, the only objects in view are the bare wall and part of the mirror frame. His hands are clasped behind his back, his head lowered; he looks down. His body is oriented to the left. He is situated slightly to the right of the image center. He sways a bit in his torso, then quite suddenly looks up, appearing in profile. The viewer hears John Adams' voice and extradiegetic music. The piano sounds that previously intensified the extradiegetic music have fallen away; now there is only a high, sustained string tone. The chirping of birds and crickets has also disappeared. Adams speaks with falling intonation, marking the end of his speech and signaling the end of the EMU. This comes with the scene's final shot, which is also the last shot of the episode – a closeup of Adams' face, which occupies the center of the image. He looks directly into the camera. He holds his head high and upright; it is slightly cut off at the top of the frame. To the left and right only the bare wall is visible. He is frontally lit, and does not throw a visible shadow (though the left half of his face is somewhat better lit than the right). The light, however, is once again pale, cold, and weak. The brown vest and white shirt, both of which are partially visible, suit the restrained, undersaturated color palette of the shot. As the shot begins, Adams raises his head very slightly and blinks once. Then he remains completely motionless, rigid. His mouth is closed, his face expressionless. On the soundtrack, the high string tone continues at first, then fades out. There are no other sounds to be heard. In the end, the shot fades to black. Ultimately, the beginning of independence consists not only in the idyll associated with the character of Abigail, but also the image of uncertain awakening: a face that is not euphoric but doubtful, if also calm and open.

With regard to Arendt's theory of revolution, three connections emerge in this scene: novelty, violence and freedom. First and foremost, the way the scene expresses foundation and newness seems important: through calm and bafflement. After the passage of the declaration, the first thing we see is quiet, speechless, and perhaps even somewhat bewildered faces. And not only that: Neither the score nor the cinematography imparts any sense of euphoria or ecstasy. To summarize the above analysis of the first EMU in a few words: While the vote is still accompanied by an elegiac and somewhat emotional score, whose volume increases slowly but continuously, this music fades after the result is announced, and silence reigns on the soundtrack, while the camera films the congressmen's faces with calm, gliding, and even tracking shots. The faces and the way in which they are staged here, however, seem not only to express a certain bewilderment, but rather an openness and indeterminacy that make it possible to experience what it means to break with the English king, found a nation, and create something entirely new.[31]

The series is much less open and indeterminate when it comes to its position on violence in a revolution. Here it is worth attending more closely to the relationship between image and sound in the scene. While the second EMU begins with the voice of the parliamentarian reading out the Declaration of Independence, after five shots – during a closeup of Jefferson that still shows the official reading of the Declaration – the voice on the soundtrack changes, and the Declaration is read by Nabby Adams. This shift creates an overlap between the two settings. It is not the first time that a connection is drawn between political events and the fate of Adams' daughter. At the very beginning of the vote, the final note from the extradiegetic music of the previous scene, which shows Nabby sick in bed, is still audible. And the repeated switch of the reader's voice in the second EMU only occurs once the image track has shown the official announcement. Thus, there are multiple superimpositions between the sequences showing Adams' family, including the convalescent Nabby Adams, and the sequences showing the official announcement of secession from the British monarchy. This structure expresses on the one hand the idea that the Revolution and the Declaration of Independence are oriented toward children, i.e., the future. On the other, John Adams' family, who read a reproduction – that is, a mediated form – of the Declaration of Independence and offer commentary through their facial expressions (Abigail smiles and reads the text with great enthusiasm), show not only the private

---

[31] With that, the scene expands Arendt's argument that in the American Revolution, the "problem of authority" is solved through the act of collective foundation, to include another element: Here it is not only the collective decision – over the course of the episode, John Adams emphasizes how important it is that independence be declared with no votes against (timecode: 01:13:37–01:14:55) – but also the shared sense of openness and indeterminacy that is realized in the congressmen's faces, and which stands at the beginning of the new state's foundation.

realm, but also the judging public that is so important for both Kant and Arendt in a revolution. In this way, however, the series also shifts gender relations. While Arendt always writes about the men of the American (and French) Revolution, here the readers and commentators of the Declaration of Independence are two women.[32] With regard to the role of violence in a revolution, however, another aspect of this scene is central: Nabby Adams had previously been vaccinated against smallpox, nearly died from side effects of this early form of vaccination, and is now protected from the disease. Thus, when the series has Nabby read the Declaration of Independence and alternates these shots with shots of the official announcement, it creates an association and metaphorical superimposition between inoculation and independence, medical advances, and political 'progress;'[33] and the two mechanisms overlap as well.[34] Just as in a vaccination, the body is injected with a small dose of the pathogen in order to develop immunity against it, the series suggests that the best protection against British violence is to take up arms. Although the series does not stage revolution as a collective ecstasy of violence, and thus displays the significance of power in an Arendtian sense, it in no way represents a pacifist understanding of revolution. In order to protect against violence or liberate oneself from violence, it seems to say, one must become violent oneself – thus the image-sound overlay suggests inoculation as a metaphor for revolutionary violence.

With regard to freedom, two aspects seem important. On one hand, the series stages freedom as private when it shows Abigail Adams picking peaches in her idyllic garden.[35] It is not just the vibrant colors, warm light, and chirping birds that create an idyllic impression. Dynamic camera movements through

---

[32] In fact, the role of Abigail Adams could be the starting point for a deeper analysis of how gender is staged in the series.
[33] See my earlier footnote on this point.
[34] The metaphor, however, is closer to Eisenstein's intellectual montage, rather than a metaphor that is realized through qualities of movement.
[35] Whereas staging strategies that create a pleasant atmosphere are associated with the private realm (Abigail Adams in her garden) at the end of the second EMU, at the beginning they were connected with the political realm (the official announcement of the Declaration of Independence). Similarly, the negatively-tinged staging strategies also switch realms: While at the beginning of the EMU, Nabby's sickly, uncertain voice characterized the private realm, by its end, dark, undersaturated colors dominate the image of the politician John Adams. By not clearly assigning positive and negative atmospheres in this way, the series resists staging either the familial *or* the political realm as positive or utopian. In doing so, it departs from the formal approach of the *kairos* scene in REDS, which focuses on staging both the private and the public/political in perfect harmony and unity with each other.

the grass also contribute.³⁶ Furthermore, these shots recall Arendt's freedom *from* politics, which is quite central to her idea of a functioning polity. On the other hand, the end of the second episode is about the *positive* freedom of politics, about public freedom. The series highlights the freedom of formation when Adams writes in a letter to his wife that the task is now to organize the country independently of Great Britain. We hear the content of the letter in a voiceover narration by Adams:

> My dearest friend, the break is made. Now our work begins. You will think me transported with enthusiasm but I am not. It is the will of heaven that Britain and America should be sundered forever. It may be the will of heaven that America shall suffer calamities still more wasting and distresses yet more dreadful. I am well aware of the toil and blood and treasure that it will cost us to maintain this declaration and support and defend these states. Yet through all the gloom, I can see the rays of ravishing light and glory. I can see that posterity will triumph ... in that day's transaction.³⁷

One hears of course that he describes himself as free of any enthusiasm. From the perspective of film historical context, one might argue that this utterance contrasts the American Revolution with the Russian Revolution and its audiovisual staging. After all, ENTHUSIASM: THE SYMPHONY OF DONBAS (SU 1930) is the title of Dziga Vertov's film about the completion of the first Five-Year Plan. One can also refer to the etymology of the word "enthusiasm." It comes from the Greek *enthousiasmós* = 'divine inspiration,' an abstraction of the Greek word *éntheos* = 'in God.' In Greek it means – drawing on Kluge's *Etymologisches Wörterbuch der deutschen Sprache* – first the permeation of human life with divinity; later, in a Christian context, the ecstatic worship of God, then also (pejoratively) religious rhapsody. Starting in the eighteenth century, its meaning became secularized and generalized as the original motives for its significance

---

36 From a distance, these shots recall the films of Terrence Malick. This association of freedom with Malick's style is also present – even more markedly than in JOHN ADAMS – in Sofia Coppola's MARIE ANTOINETTE (US/FR/JP 2006), when in some of the film's most significant shots, the protagonist runs through the grass and experiences a moment of freedom (the timecode of these shots is 01:19:42–01:22:33).

37 Most of the voiceover is the closing paragraph of a letter written by the real John Adams to his wife on 3 July 1776 – supplemented by a few sentences from a letter he sent her earlier on the same day. See Abigail Adams/John Adams: My Dearest Friend. Letters of Abigail and John Adams, Cambridge, MA 2007, p. 123 and p. 125. In the historical letter, there is a small skeptical addition that does not appear in the mini-series: "And that Posterity will tryumph in that Days transaction, even altho We should rue it, which I trust in God We shall not" (ibid., p. 125).

faded away.[38] I want to establish that enthusiasm speaks to a form of ecstasy, or of being beside oneself. But John Adams is not beside himself: He is not influenced by an overpowering momentum, does not act like a lover. Instead, he remains master of his senses, thoughts, and actions. With that, the character expresses something toward which the entire episode and its staging strategies are oriented: a departure from the concept of revolution that understands revolution as an event beyond the influence of individuals. Instead, the series presents the American Revolution as a struggle for freedom through debate, speeches, written work, strategic violence, bafflement and speechlessness, calm, slow movements, serenity, and sovereignty. Adams' lack of enthusiasm is relevant in another way as well: For Kant, it was precisely the *enthusiastic* spectators and commentators of the French Revolution who endowed the event with significance. Here, in JOHN ADAMS, there is no enthusiasm even in one of the central protagonists and actors of the revolution: The contrast between the French Revolution and the way in which the series thinks the American Revolution could hardly be clearer.

Mini-*Series*

The freedom that is referenced at the end of the second episode is the freedom of formation, acting, and continuing on. The fact that the series continues after the second episode is as banal as it is unusual among audiovisual stagings of revolutions. As already mentioned, revolution *films* tend to end with the revolutionaries' seizure of power and the transformation of society. Or they concentrate on showing how the new social order departs from the ideals of the revolution, and are divided – like REDS – into two parts. The series JOHN ADAMS is different. In the episodes that follow, it takes seriously the task of showing the consequences of the Revolution, and exploring the question of how the achievements of the revolution can be permanently established.[39] In the third episode, we first see John Adams attempting to secure a loan for the young nation, first in France and

---

[38] See the entry "Enthusiasmus", in: Etymologisches Wörterbuch der deutschen Sprache. 25. Auflage, ed. By Friedrich Kluge/Elmar Seebold, Berlin/Boston 2011, p. 248.
[39] The question of permanent establishment is discussed in the section "The Authority of State Foundation" with the problem of authority. Of course, this question is related not only with 'authority,' but also with 'power' and 'violence,' which are addressed over the course of the mini-series.

then in Holland.⁴⁰ In the fourth episode, the series turns to the period of John Adams' life when he served in London as the first ambassador from the United States of America to the court of King George III., representing the interests of the young nation; the series does not squander the opportunity to have the two characters meet and to savor the explosiveness of the situation.⁴¹ The fifth episode is about Adams' time as Vice President,⁴² the following and penultimate episode takes up his own presidency and his attempts to keep the United States out of the conflict between England and France.⁴³ This quite brief overview of the rest of the series makes clear that the series places great value on the question of formation and action *after* the Revolution.

One way to understand the post-revolutionary era in theoretical terms is the difference between *politics* on the one hand, and the *political* on the other. The term *political* speaks to the great and fundamental questions of collective life: Under what political or economic order do we wish to live? With regard to the revolutions examined by Arendt, this inquiry points to the question of the state and the difference between monarchy, democracy, or republic; for Arendt herself, however, this term also encompasses the difference between council and party democracy. From a Marxist perspective, the concept of the political asks who receives the surplus profit from production, as well as whether we assign an exchange value to products produced in a society, i.e., bestow upon them the commodity form. In summary, questions of the political center precisely on the fundamental topics of political life that are also at the core of revolutions.

As for *politics*, it can be distinguished from the concept of the political insofar as it deals with – to put it a bit pejoratively – *problems on the ground*, or everyday politics. It is about the *administration* of an established order and changes *within* that order.⁴⁴ The series JOHN ADAMS deals much more with the

---

40 See JOHN ADAMS. PART III: DON'T TREAD ON ME (Tom Hooper, US 2008).
41 See JOHN ADAMS. PART IV: REUNION (Tom Hooper, US 2008). The timecode of the scene is 00:33:34–00:40:26.
42 See JOHN ADAMS. PART V: UNITE OR DIE (Tom Hooper, US 2008).
43 See JOHN ADAMS. PART VI: UNNECESSARY WAR. For a more precise examination of a scene from the final episode PEACEFIELD (Tom Hooper, US 2008), see the next section.
44 On the difference between the two terms, see Uwe Hebekus/Jan Völker: Neue Philosophien des Politischen zur Einführung, Hamburg 2012, pp. 9 ff. I use the terms on a quite general level, which suffices for this context. The two authors, however, rightly point out that each term is used differently by different authors (see ibid., pp. 25 ff.). For an overview of the relationship between the two terms, see Thomas Bedorf: Das Politische und die Politik – Konturen einer Differenz, in: Das Politische und die Politik, ed. by id./Kurt Röttgers, Berlin 2010, pp. 13–37.

questions of politics than those of the political, not only quantitatively with regard to filmophanic time,[45] but also qualitatively insofar as politics is not staged as something subordinate to the political. In this way, the series works to reduce the distinction between these two realms and the discrepancy between their value that often accompanies it – the interesting questions of the political versus the tiresome and boring questions of politics. If one follows Arendt's conceptualization of the American Revolution, this revolution distinguishes itself precisely through the fact that the questions of politics and the political are not fixed in a strict dichotomy, but rather are closely interconnected and mutually determine one another. In the mini-series, which does not show the American Revolution as ending with the Declaration of Independence, the Arendtian conceptualization of the American Revolution has found its ideal, tailor-made audiovisual form. For Arendt, the lack of a dramatic and dramatizable kairotic moment to which the new political order can be traced back is also the lack of a moment in which movement becomes uncontrollable. Precisely this kind of moment is missing from the American Revolution; it cannot be reduced to such a moment.

In its dramatic form as well, the miniseries does not try to crystallize the American Revolution in such a moment, but rather uses the fact that it consists of multiple episodes to complicate the opposition between politics and the political. This phenomenon can be understood positively on a theoretical level as well. The series thereby inserts itself into debates on this relationship. The concept of a strict dichotomy and disjuncture between politics and the political has been criticized, e.g., by Maria Muhle in her article "Medienwissenschaft als theoretisch-politisches Milieu." She calls for a more precise determination of how these two realms are connected and the ways in which they are mutually dependent.[46] In not reducing the political to a foundational moment, but rather using its form as a series to realize the political through continuous action over

---

[45] Souriau uses the term 'filmophanic time' to describe the duration of a film, Étienne Souriau: Die Struktur des filmischen Universums und das Vokabular der Filmologie, in: montage AV, 6 (2), 1997, pp. 140–157, here p. 144.

[46] See Maria Muhle: Medienwissenschaft als theoretisch-politisches Milieu, in: zfm – Zeitschrift für Medienwissenschaft, 10 (1), 2014, pp. 137–142, here pp. 138 f. Muhle takes a strong position against drawing a connection between her ideas and Arendt's understanding of revolution. In an implicit shift of the terminology, Muhle identifies the political with revolution and politics not only with everyday politics, but also – this is where the shift begins – with the social and private realms. Her critique of Arendt consists in the separation of the private and social realms from the realm of politics. However legitimate one sees this critique to be: One cannot conclude from it that Arendt assumes a strict dichotomy between politics and the political; the opposition between society and politics or the political is not the same as the opposition between politics and the political.

multiple episodes, JOHN ADAMS exemplifies the fundamental relationship between politics and the political that, according to Thomas Bedorf, is also found in Arendt's work. He offers the following commentary on Arendt's position:

> Actual politics, i.e. the political, cannot be understood as work on the realization of a goal, but rather as an open "space of appearance," in which the collective actions of the many first become possible without their plurality being limited in advance in service of a unifying goal.[47]

Yet the series uses its own format not only to question the dichotomy between politics and the political; it also connects this question with that of the staging of history and memorializing the American Revolution. In order to draw out this connection and make it concrete, in the last subchapter on JOHN ADAMS I will examine the series finale more closely and then relate it back to the series opening.

Mini-Series

"The end is in the beginning and yet you go on."[48] With these grim words, the character Hamm in Samuel Beckett's *Endgame* expresses what Kathrin Rothemund observes in her concept of mini-series. One does not have to adhere to a problematic form-content determinism to argue that it would be obvious for a mini-series dedicated to a person's biography to deal with that person's old age, death, and the question of that person's legacy. In order to examine more closely how this happens in JOHN ADAMS, I will connect a scene from PEACEFIELD, the series finale, with the series opening, its very first shots. Both scenes are about the search for an appropriate and productive way to represent or stage – and to think – the American Revolution.

First one of the series' final scenes: Here we see an aged John Adams.[49] His hair has grown thin and gone grey; he has become obese, his face rounder and wrinkled, his teeth black, his gait halting; he walks with a cane. If one wished to find more eloquent descriptions of aged people than these, one might turn to the end of Marcel Proust's *In Search of Lost Time*, when the first-person narrator attends a soirée and imagines himself to be at a masquerade ball where all the guests have dressed up as elderly people. Only gradually does he realize that it was time and its passage that have led to the changed appearance of his fellow

---

47 Bedorf: Das Politische und die Politik, op. cit., p. 18.
48 Samuel Beckett: Endgame. A Play in One Act, in: id.: Endgame. A Play in One Act, followed by Act without words, a Mime for One Player, New York 1970, pp. 1–84, here p. 69.
49 The timecode of the scene is 00:44:01–00:47:53 (Episode: PEACEFIELD).

people.⁵⁰ In referencing Marcel Proust's book, I do not intend to claim that much time spent narrating necessarily implies the passage of much narrative time; even less do I wish to indicate agreement with the common but debatable argument that in order to be good, a series must function like a novel. Instead, I refer to Proust because his *Search* is associated perhaps more than any other work with the question of memory. Proust's remarks on involuntary memory, which he elaborates based on the effect of a madeleine dipped in tea, are well known. A bit less renowned is the reappearance of this theme at the end of the work in the form of two uneven cobblestones on which the protagonist steps while evading a carriage, and which remind him of his trip to Venice.⁵¹ In any case, the scene from the final episode of JOHN ADAMS also addresses memory. Unlike in Proust, however, it is about a form of voluntary memory: more specifically, the politics of memory. Alongside his son John Quincy Adams, the sixth President of the US, and the painter John Trumbull, John Adams looks at Trumbull's painting "Declaration of Independence" (Fig. 1). The painter explains that Congress commissioned him to create this painting for the fiftieth anniversary of the foundation of the republic – as a remembrance of this event. The painting shows – this is how it is discussed in this scene – the signing of the Declaration. In formal dress, in a grand room festooned with flags and heavy drapery, Congressmen gather around the Declaration.

In the center of the image, directly beside the table holding the document, stand John Adams, Thomas Jefferson, Benjamin Franklin, and two other members of Congress.⁵² Other members of Congress, seated and standing, surround the group. With the character John Adams's first glance at the painting, a slow, melancholy piano motif begins. Yet the attempt to create a sentimental remembrance of the Declaration of Independence through the painting fails. Adams'

---

50 Cf. Marcel Proust: In Search of Lost Time. Volume VI. Time Regained, trans. by Andreas Mayor/Terence Kilmartin, revised by D.J. Enright, and: A Guide to Proust, compiled by Terence Kilmartin, revised by Joanna Kilmartin, New York 1993, pp. 335 ff.
51 For the madeleine episode, see Marcel Proust: In Search of Lost Time. Volume I. Swann's Way, trans. by C.K. Scott Moncrieff/Terence Kilmartin, revised by D.J. Enright, New York 2003, pp. 60–64; on the uneven cobblestones, see Proust: Time Regained, op. cit., pp. 255 ff. In associating Proust's work with the question of memory, I follow a conventional reading of the *Search*. Deleuze's argument on the text is much more provocative: "What constitutes the unity of *In Search of Lost Time*? We know, at least, what does not. It is not recollection, memory, or even involuntary memory. What is essential to the Search is not in the madeleine or the cobblestones. [...] Proust's work is based not on the exposition of memory, but on the apprenticeship to signs" (Deleuze: Proust and Signs, op. cit., pp. 3 f.).
52 For a list of names of all the people depicted in the painting, see https://www.aoc.gov/sites/default/files/painting_key_declaration-of-independence_aoc.png [last accessed 25 May 2022].

Fig. 1: "Declaration of Independence" by John Trumbull.

first comment is dry: "All dead [...] All dead. The whole lot of them, except for me and Jefferson." The painting cannot bring back the dead. Adams destabilizes even the painting's remembrance of the American Revolution: The painting itself and its form receive no praise from him. Not only does the painting pale in comparison with the masterpieces of Rubens; even worse, there never was such a scene – it would have been impossible during such turbulent times. Adams' judgment is harsh: "It is very bad history." At the moment represented in the painting, war had already broken out against Great Britain, and such a calm and relaxed gathering of all members of Congress would have been unimaginable. The painting does not correspond to historical reality. In this way, it is the copy of a scene whose original never existed: a simulacrum, an illusion. Thus, the character John Adams turns out to be a steadfast proponent of what Jacques Rancière calls the ethical regime of images, which is closely associated with Plato. In this regime, art is reduced to an ethical (the danger of illusions) and a didactic function for the education of citizens in a polity. Any potential for fiction or artistic freedom is out of the question.[53]

---

[53] Jacques Rancière: The Politics of Aesthetics. The Distribution of the Sensible, ed. and trans. by Gabriel Rockhill, London et al. 2013, pp. 20 f. A productive and positive analysis of

And by these standards, the painting certainly fails. But it does not do justice to John Trumbull or his painting to hold his work exclusively to the standards of the ethical regime. The character Trumbull situates himself in a different context anyway: the representational regime of art. In the representational or poetic regime of art, which Rancière conceptualizes by drawing on Aristotle, art is liberated from this reduction to an ethical and didactic function. The fictions of art are no longer identified as lies.[54] The arts now follow a much more pragmatic principle of mimesis – in Trumbull's words: "You would not deny the artist a certain ... licence?" This principle of imitation, however, is ruled by a strict hierarchy, which determines who or what is worthy of imitation in which art form (thereby also determining who or what is not worthy of art and thus excluded from the realm of artistic representation). Furthermore, there are norms that establish the way in which something can be represented, i.e., to what genre it belongs and when it can be accepted as similar, appropriate, and corresponding.[55]

This brief recourse to the representative regime of art aims to show that the painter in this scene is of course attempting to create a situation that is *representative* of the American Revolution, in which the Revolution and its participants are memorialized, their historical significance put on display. In the series JOHN ADAMS, this becomes clear when the characters are repeatedly shown in long shots standing before the painting, staging the painting's larger-than-life dimensions in contrast with its seemingly small viewers. Yet Trumbull is seeking not only a situation that is representative of the American Revolution, but also to grant it a moment that can be described as celebrating and repeating all its anniversaries in advance. With that, he imposes a concept on the American Revolution that – if one accepts Arendt's conceptualization – it lacks. Adams' final judgment at the end of the scene refers not only to Trumbull's painting alone: "I consider the true history of the American Revolution ... as lost. ... Forever."

Of course, the scene is inherently self- and meta-reflexive. Yet paradoxically, it is the character of John Adams who denies that there is or will be a memorial to the American Revolution, thereby also denying the possibility that

---

simulacra can be found in Gilles Deleuze: Plato and the Simulacrum, trans. by Rosalind Krauss, in: October, 27, 1983, pp. 45–56: "Hence, to overthrow Platonism means: to raise up simulacra, to assert their rights over icons or copies. [...] The simulacrum is not degraded copy, rather it contains a positive power which negates *both original and copy, both model and reproduction*" (ibid., pp. 52 f.). Because of this, according to Deleuze, the simulacrum is particularly central to modernity; see ibid., pp. 55 f.

54 See Rancière: The Politics of Aesthetics, op. cit., p. 35.
55 See ibid., pp. 21 f.

there could ever have been a series character John Adams. When the series' protagonist criticizes Trumbull's painting and denies its fitness to memorialize the American Revolution, the show refers implicitly to itself and its own form of remembering the Revolution. The question that now arises is whether the series offers yet another position on the theme of historical representation beyond those of Trumbull and Adams.[56] It seems to me no accident that the series answers this question by engaging with a painting about the American Revolution and not by engaging with another film. Right at the outset of the series there is a reflection on another painting about the American Revolution.[57] These are the first shots in the diegetic world. They follow the opening credits of the first episode. In them, we see John Adams, hunched forward, riding a horse past a tree in a snowy winter landscape. He wears dark clothing and a hat. The sky takes up considerable space in the image composition and is covered in grey clouds; the tree is dark and leafless (Fig. 2).

Among visual representations of the American Revolution, a painting by the Mormon Arnold Friberg stands out.[58] Although Friberg's œuvre as a whole became famous particularly through his religious works, his best-known painting is "The Prayer at Valley Forge."[59] It shows General George Washington kneeling in prayer beside a white horse in a wintery forest at dusk. After losing the Battle of Long Island, he had retreated to southern Pennsylvania, beyond British-controlled territory, to allow his troops to recuperate at the Valley Forge

---

56 Here it might seem obvious to stay with Rancière's perspective and examine which connections can be found in the series to the aesthetic regime of art. Yet in my opinion, it is difficult to draw a connection between the series and Rancière's aesthetic regime without unduly diluting the latter. However, it is inarguable that simply in terms of media form, the series is closer to the aesthetic regime than the painting is (on film as a fulfillment of the aesthetic regime of art, see Jacques Rancière: L'historicité du cinéma, in: De l'histoire au cinéma, ed. by Antoine de Baecque/Christian Delage, Brussels 1998, pp. 45–60; on complicating this relationship, see the introduction "A Thwarted Fable," in: Jacques Rancière: Film Fables, trans. by Emiliano Battista, Oxford/New York 2006, pp. 1–20). More important at this point, however, is to point out that the filmic medium is also closer to the strain of historico-philosophical thought propagated by the American Revolution.
57 The timecode of these shots is 00:02:08–00:03:20 (Episode: JOIN OR DIE).
58 In the context of cinema, Friberg is probably only familiar to fans of Bible films: For Cecil B. DeMille's THE TEN COMMANDMENTS (US 1956), he painted 15 images that served as guides for the set design and décor and were then used as promotional material for the film (see Paul C. Gutjahr: The "Book of Mormon". A Biography, Princeton/Oxford 2012, p. 169 and Douglas Martin: Arnold Friberg, Painter of Historical Scenes, Is Dead At 96, in: The New York Times, 3 July 2010. With its reference to this painter, this miniseries thus also makes a claim to the tradition of Hollywood historical epics theorized by Sobchack.
59 See ibid.

Fig. 2: John Adams rides through the snow.

Fig. 3: "Winter at Valley Forge" by Arnold Friberg.

camp. Yet the image that the series references in its opening is not "The Prayer at Valley Forge," but – importantly – the subsequent and associated image "Winter at Valley Forge" (Fig. 3).

In this image too, we see a hunched rider on horse in a wintry landscape dotted with leafless trees. Here too, much of the image surface is filled by a grey sky. The rider also wears dark clothing and a hat. In comparison with the opening sequence of JOHN ADAMS, however, a few differences can be identified: The horse is white, and it moves to the right. Yet the main difference is: In Friberg's painting, we see George Washington.[60] In basing itself on this image, the series draws on another *representation* of the Revolution, rather than an unmediated 'history per se;' and it translates not only a still image into an image that can definitionally only be thought as movement, and that opens itself toward duration and the whole; it not only replaces the frame with the matte,[61] but it also replaces George Washington with John Adams. In doing so, it swaps out central figures in representations of the history of the American Revolution: the general for the lawyer; the war hero to whom godlike power is still attributed in one of the unofficial national anthems of the US for the author of *Thoughts on Government*, which praises and calls for the rule of law over the rule of men.[62]

With that, the series not only offers an advance commentary on the scene from the last episode with Trumbull's painting, and the question of the American Revolution and its actors' continued life. Here, in a condensed form, it does something that it will go on to pursue through seven episodes stretching over 502 minutes: It helps to extend our idea of what a revolution was, is, and will have been.

---

60 I do not seek to clarify whether the series' production team intentionally created this association. What is important to me are the points of association to be found in the visual design.
61 On the difference between the enclosing, centripetal frame of a painting and the open, centrifugal edges of the film image, see André Bazin: Painting and Cinema, in: id.: What Is Cinema? Vol. 1, trans. by Hugh Gray, Berkeley/Los Angeles/London 2004, pp. 164–169. Deleuze comments on this distinction in Gilles Deleuze: Cinema 1. The Movement-Image, trans. by Hugh Tomlinson/Barbara Habberjam, Minneapolis 1986, pp. 12 f.
62 "With equal skill, and godlike power/He governs in the fearful hour," according to the song "Hail Columbia" in reference to George Washington (see C.A. Browne: The Story of Our National Ballads, New York 1919, p. 30). In this way JOHN ADAMS differs also on this point from NAPOLÉON, which embraces this kind of religious exaltation. On the rule of law over the rule of men, see John Adams: Thoughts on Government, Applicable to the Present State of the American Colonies, in a Letter from a Gentleman to his Friend, in: The Works of John Adams, Second President of the United States. Vol. 4, Boston 1851, pp. 189–200, here p. 194: "[...] because the very definition of a republic is 'an empire of laws, and not of men.' That, as a republic is the best of governments, so that particular arrangements of the powers of society, or, in other words, that form of government which is best contrived to secure an impartial and exact execution of the laws, is the best of republics".

7 Conclusion

"Mourning a Metaphor: The Revolution is Over" – this was the title of a 2003 essay by the historian Martin Jay.[1] In this piece, he first sketches the history of the term 'revolution:' from a description of the movement of the stars through its metaphorical use in the political realm to mean a restoration of former relations, to a term for radical change and new beginnings that goes hand-in-hand with the loss of its original astronomical meaning of return. Jay argues that the contemporary context reveals a new form of metaphoric usage. According to him, the term in most cases no longer refers to political transformation, instead serving primarily as a metaphorical background in discussions of 'scientific' or 'industrial revolution;' a process that meanwhile had been extended to all kinds of areas. Any radical or even seemingly radical development in culture, technology, the economy, or even fashion is deemed a 'revolution.' For Jay, this expansion is associated with a loss of the term's former significance:

> 1989 and the collapse of the Soviet Empire betokened a rapid erosion of belief in it [i.e. revolution in a political sense, H.B.] as a mechanism of redemptive politics. [...] it is hard not to acknowledge a widespread deflation of enthusiasm for what they [revolutions] might ultimately do for human emancipation. And with that deflation has come a growing deliteralization of the term.[2]

Ultimately, Jay's argument boils down to drawing a connection between language use and the way in which political change is conceived. Because revolution has been reduced to just a (source) metaphor, it has become clear that with regard to politics it was only ever a (target) metaphor that is no longer adequate today:

> At times, as in the case at hand, we come to realize that we have forgotten that lesson [that while a metaphor serves to enrich our understanding, it is ultimately just a metaphor, H.B.] and mistaken a trope for the real thing. But perhaps in that very realization lies a more adequate basis for political involvement, which is no longer beholden to maximalist fantasies of redemption and epochal transformation, fantasies whose defeat leaves us feeling impotent and lost.[3]

---

[1] Martin Jay: Mourning a Metaphor: The Revolution is Over, in: parallax, 9 (2), 2003, pp. 17–20.
[2] Ibid., pp. 18 f.
[3] Ibid., pp. 19 f. The fact that Jay distances himself from the term 'revolution' yet still speaks of "irreversible ruptures in history that have occurred in the past and those that may still await us in the future," and "real, perhaps even ambitiously drastic, solutions to exigent problems," distinguishes him from the idea that the end of the USSR meant the end of history, a thesis famously proposed by Francis Fukuyama. See Francis Fukuyama: The End of History and the Last Man, New York 1992. For a critique of Fukuyama, see Jacques Derrida: Specters of

According to Jay, the problem was that people understood the metaphor of 'revolution' too literally, and applied the inexorability of astral movement to the political realm with fatal consequences. Jay does not intend this as a case against the use of metaphors – he observes correctly that it would be impossible to do without them entirely. Yet the revolution metaphor is no longer suited to describing political transformation.

I understand my study as challenging Jay's thesis that the term 'revolution' has become obsolete. I have shown that fictional films in particular are capable of casting doubt on his argument, insofar as they help to differentiate and extend the concepts of revolution's temporal processes. In doing so, they not only create consciousness of the contingency of political acts, but also demonstrate the pertinence of the term 'revolution.' To this end, I first explained why the American and French Revolutions have a quite fundamental significance for theorizing history and collective human life. After all, these Revolutions gave expression to the awareness that human life is not necessarily eschatologically organized or trapped in cycles, but that something totally new can come into being. Thus, when Jay calls for a turn away from the idea of revolution, he also turns his back on this tradition and unduly obfuscates the contingency of political life. I have demonstrated the fact that films can combat just such an obfuscation by connecting the thinking of history as an open process that is realized in the revolutions of modernity with film as understood by Jean Epstein and Gilles Deleuze. Through this work, I was able to establish why film in particular, as a medium for staging forms of time and movement, is well suited to thinking revolution. After all, Hannah Arendt's perspective on revolution was developed as a perspective on the spatial and temporal relations of revolution. Whereas Jay problematizes the fact that the term 'revolution' began with an "inexorable"[4] movement, I determined that the term began with *movement* – a movement that was worth differentiating.

What were the results of my film analyses? How do they contribute to contradicting Jay and showing how films and series about revolution can help to conceptualize political transformation? In NAPOLÉON, the medium of film is first used to stage an experience in the spectator of being overpowered, which can be more precisely described and understood through the Kantian sublime. The film thinks the Revolution as a tempest that cannot be controlled or understood either by the Revolution's actors or the film's spectators. In this way, the film accords not only

---

Marx. The State of the Debt, the Work of Mourning, and the New International, trans. by Peggy Kamuf, New York/London 2006, pp. 69–95.
4 Jay: Mourning a Metaphor, op. cit., p. 17.

with the original metaphoric meaning of revolution, but also Arendt's critique of the French Revolution, that it developed into an uncontrollable movement for both participants and spectators, leading to the end of freedom and ultimately the end of the revolution. Abel Gance's film stages the character of Napoleon as the master of overwhelming movement. The fact that he does not slip into an homage to fascism in the process has two explanations: First, the spectator's sense of chaos, of being overwhelmed and overpowered, as is the case in NAPOLÉON, is quite far removed from a fascist, militaristic aesthetic, which usually works with clear and organized formations. In this way, however, fascist aesthetics miss the point of the Kantian sublime, whose primary principle is the fact that the subject is overwhelmed by sensory phenomena and can only master it through the intervention of reason and moving beyond the sensory realm. Second, by the end of the film the figure of Napoleon remains only as a creature in the clouds, with no connection to his diegetic, spatial environment: It is a mythically inflated point of reference, without which new foundations achieved through revolutions *paradoxically* hardly ever come to pass.

My exploration of the filmic thinking of revolution continues with an examination of REDS. In contrast to Arendt, who understands the revolutionary moment of uprising as a loss of control, whose quality of movement was fatally imposed on the entire process of the French Revolution, the film understands this moment as a utopian *kairos*, of which one might say – with an eye to Faust's cunning line at the end of Goethe's drama – let it linger.[5] The film connects and interweaves the Revolution with the relationship between private and political that reaches its utopian climax in the kairotic moment of the Revolution. Whereas before the Revolution, the couples' meeting manifested as asynchronous missing of one another, and after it in an infinitely extended deferral, it is realized in the *kairos* as perfect interplay and condensed synchronicity. Here too, the staging of time is clearly specific to the filmic medium, which enables the spectator to think and experience revolution productively.

Finally – and here it becomes particularly clear how Jay fails to examine the concept of revolution closely enough and thus gives up on it too readily – with JOHN ADAMS I focus on an audiovisual staging of the American Revolution. Arendt's theorization of this revolution not only demonstrates that it was precisely the lack of spectators that led to the Revolution's lesser import in the course of history, but

---

5 "[...] to the moment, I could say: tarry awhile – you are so fair." In the original German, the line runs: "Zum Augenblicke dürft ich sagen: Verweile [translated above as *linger*] doch, du bist so schön!" The irrealis mood of the subjunctive *könnte*, "could," saves Faust from his deal with the devil by functioning as a fictional form. See Johann Wolfgang von Goethe: Faust I & II, trans. by Stuart Atkins, Princeton 2014, p. 292.

also that the American Revolution lacks a moment of uprising as either loss of control or utopia. This kind of moment played no role, or only a very small and unimportant one as in the case of the 'Boston Tea Party.' This characteristic can also explain the limited number of films about this revolution. It also clarifies why a mini-series is particularly appropriate for the topic of the American Revolution. Both Arendt and the mini-series format support the notion that a revolution is not and cannot be reduced to a one-time surge. This understanding destabilizes the rigid dichotomy between politics and the political: Politics, too, can be understood as work in service of the revolution, as revolutionary. When Jay understands revolution simply as "maximalist fantasies of redemption," at the same time denigrating it with this phrase, he fails to account for the American Revolution and thus espouses an overly narrow understanding of the term. With regard to the staging of revolution in JOHN ADAMS I attempted to show that it is thought here without enthusiasm – not only for the series' characters, but also the composition of the series itself. When Jay claims a "widespread deflation of enthusiasm" with reference to revolutions and their relevance, he fails to consider that revolutions do not necessarily require enthusiasm, and once again reveals that his understanding of the notion is too limited, and – as so often happens – leaves out the American Revolution. All three of the audiovisual stagings I have examined can be understood as expanding and diversifying concepts of revolution, helping to keep these concepts relevant and showing that revolution and its theorization are by no means obsolete.

I examined one filmic adaptation of the French Revolution, centered one look at the Russian Revolution, and focused on one audiovisual staging of the American Revolution. Two of the productions are American and one French, meaning in all cases – both on the level of production as well as the staged content – I dealt exclusively with theorizing revolution in a Western context. And of course, other films could be approached with the questions posed by this book – for example, Eric Rohmer's L'ANGLAISE ET LE DUC (FR 2001).[6] Expanding the analysis to include other films would also be an opportunity to expand the cultural context of the revolutions represented therein. This book is missing African, Latin American, Arabic, and Asian works on revolution like those

---

6 Of course, one could also take a different approach to the historical contextualization of the films and more closely examine their relationship to *individual* films. In the case of NAPOLÉON, for example, one might draw on the director's other films from the same period, J'ACCUSE! (FR 1919) and LA ROUE, as points of comparison; with regard to REDS, one could engage with thematically similar films of the same era, like for example JOE HILL (Bo Widerberg, SE/US 1971), SACCO E VANZETTI (Giuliano Montaldo, IT/FR 1971), BOUND FOR GLORY (Hal Ashby, US 1976) or HEAVEN'S GATE (Michael Cimino, US 1980).

found in the so-called 'Third Cinema.'[7] None of the films examined in this book are about – to use Frantz Fanon's phrase – the "wretched of the Earth."[8] This omission should not be misunderstood as a claim to Western cultural hegemony, but was a result first and foremost of my theoretical jumping-off points. I was interested first in how the films examined here, in analogy to Hollywood historical epics, enable an experience of historicity. In addition, working with Kant and Arendt meant centering the spectators and not the actors in my theorization of revolution. Films from the 'Third Cinema' movement like Fernando Solanas's and Octavio Getino's LA HORA DE LOS HORNOS: NOTAS Y TESTIMONIOS SOBRE EL NEOCOLONIALISMO, LA VIOLENCIA Y LA LIBERACIÓN (AR 1968), however – like Eisenstein's films – are characterized by an agitational approach.[9] These films, therefore, would at first glance not seem to fit into the theoretical framework I have constructed based on Kant and Arendt's work. It is worth exploring, however, whether agitational films can be understood as a thinking perspective on revolution. This would allow for examination not only of Eisenstein and the fictional films of the 'Third Cinema,' but also documentary formats that belong to this movement, like the aforementioned film by Solanas and Getino. It would be important to take the films seriously in terms of aesthetics, and not to limit them to their agitational and interventionist impetus. To do this would not rob the film of their political content, but rather – a provocation that could be placed at the beginning of this examination – allow their political value to emerge properly for the first time. And as in the film analyses in the preceding pages, these examinations could focus on the body and the corporeal effects produced by the films. In combination with the expanded corpus, this approach would clarify the outline of another perspective on political theory: It would open a perspective on political theory that, in a critique of Arendt and Kant, would center the body.

---

[7] For an overview of this topic, see Anthony R. Guneratne: Introduction. Rethinking Third Cinema, in: Rethinking Third Cinema, ed. by id./Wimal Dissanayake, London/New York 2003, pp. 1–28 and Teshome Habte Gabriel: Towards a Critical Theory of Third World Films, in: Questions of Third Cinema, ed. by Jim Pines/Paul Willemen, London 1989, pp. 30–52. Fundamental to engaging with this topic would of course be an interrogation of Eurocentrism; on this subject, see Ella Shohat/Robert Stam: Unthinking Eurocentrism. Multiculturalism and the Media, London/New York 1994.
[8] See Frantz Fanon: The Wretched of the Earth, trans. by Richard Philcox, New York 2007.
[9] Along with the film, see also the two directors' manifesto, Fernando Solanas/Octavio Getino: Towards a Third Cinema. Notes and Experiences of the Development of a Cinema of Liberation in the Third World, in: New Latin American Cinema. Vol. 1. Theory: Practices and Transnational Articulation, ed. by Michael T. Martin, Detroit 1997, pp. 33–58.

Bibliography

Abel, Richard: French Cinema. The First Wave, 1915–1929, Princeton 1987.
Adams, Abigail / John Adams: My Dearest Friend. Letters of Abigail and John Adams, Cambridge, MA 2007.
Adams, John: Thoughts on Government, Applicable to the Present State of the American Colonies, in a Letter from a Gentleman to his Friend, in: The Works of John Adams, Second President of the United States. Vol. 4, Boston 1851, pp. 189–200.
Adams, John: From John Adams to Benjamin Rush, 4 April 1790, in: Founders Online, National Archives. https://founders.archives.gov/documents/adams/99-02-02-0903 [last accessed 25 May 2022].
Adorno, Theodor W. / Max Horkheimer: Dialectic of Enlightenment, trans. by John Cumming, London / New York 1997.
Adorno, Theodor W.: Negative Dialectics, trans. by E. B. Ashton, London 1996.
Adorno, Theodor W.: Cultural Criticism and Society, in: id.: Prisms, trans. by Samuel and Shierry Weber, Cambridge, MA 1986, pp. 17–34.
Arendt, Hannah / Adelbert Reif: Interview mit Hannah Arendt. Von Adelbert Reif, in: Arendt: Macht und Gewalt, Munich / Zurich 2013, pp. 105–133.
Arendt, Hannah: On Violence, San Diego / New York / London 1970.
Arendt, Hannah: The Life of the Mind, San Diego 1971.
Arendt, Hannah: Thoughts on Politics and Revolution. A Commentary, in: id.: Crises of the Republic, San Diego / New York / London 1972, pp. 199–233.
Arendt, Hannah: The Origins of Totalitarianism. New Edition with Added Prefaces, San Diego 1979.
Arendt, Hannah: On Revolution, London 1990.
Arendt, Hannah: Lectures on Kant's Political Philosophy, ed. by Ronald Beiner, Chicago 1992.
Arendt, Hannah: The Human Condition, Chicago 1998.
Arendt, Hannah: Denktagebuch 1950 bis 1973. Vol. 2, Munich / Zurich 2002.
Arendt, Hannah: Introduction into Politics, in: id.: The Promise of Politics, ed. by Jerome Kohn, New York 2005, pp. 93–200.
Arendt, Hannah: Das Urteilen. Texte zu Kants Politischer Philosophie. Dritter Teil zu 'Vom Leben des Geistes', ed. by Ronald Beiner, Munich / Zurich 2012.
Arendt, Hannah: Macht und Gewalt, Munich / Zurich 2013.
Arendt, Hannah: Über die Revolution, Munich / Zurich 2014.
Aristotle: The Poetics of Aristotle, trans. by S.H. Butcher, Hazleton 2000.
Artaud, Antonin: Sorcery and the Cinema, in: The Avant-Garde Film. A Reader of Theory and Criticism, ed. by P. Adams Sitney, New York 1978, pp. 49 f.
Augustine: Confessions of St. Augustine. Book XI, trans. by F. J. Sheed, New York 1943.
Aumont, Jacques (ed.): Jean Epstein. Cinéaste, poète, philosophe, Paris 1998.
Balázs, Béla: Béla Balázs. Early Film Theory. Visible Man and the Spirit of Film, ed. by Erica Carter, trans. by Rodney Livingstone. New York / Oxford 2010.
Barra, Allen: The Incredible Shrinking Epic, in: American Film, 14 (5), 1989, pp. 40–45, 60.
Barthes, Roland: The Death of the Author, in: id.: Image-Music-Text, trans. by Stephen Heath, New York 1978, pp. 142–148.
Barthes, Roland: Camera Lucida. Reflections on Photography, trans. by Richard Howard, New York 1980.

Bazin, André: In Defense of Mixed Cinema, in: id.: What Is Cinema? Vol. 1, ed. and trans. by Hugh Gray, Berkeley / Los Angeles / London 2004, pp. 53–75.
Bazin, André: Painting and Cinema, in: id.: What Is Cinema? Vol. 1, trans. by Hugh Gray, Berkeley / Los Angeles / London 2004, pp. 164–169.
Bazin, André: Theater and Cinema, in: id.: What Is Cinema? Vol. 1, trans. by Hugh Gray, Berkeley / Los Angeles / London 2004, pp. 76–124.
Bazin, André: The Evolution of the Language of Cinema, in: id.: What Is Cinema? Vol. 1, ed. and trans. by Hugh Gray, Berkeley / Los Angeles / London 2004, pp. 23–40.
Bazin, André: The Ontology of the Photographic Image, in: id.: What Is Cinema? Vol. 1, trans. by Hugh Gray, Berkeley / Los Angeles / London 2004, pp. 9–16.
Beaver, Jim: Reds, in: Films in Review, 33 (2), 1982, pp. 112 f.
Beckett, Samuel: Endgame. A Play in One Act, in: id.: Endgame. A Play in One Act, followed by Act without words, a Mime for One Player, New York 1970, pp. 1–84.
Bedorf, Thomas: Das Politische und die Politik – Konturen einer Differenz, in: Das Politische und die Politik, ed. by id. / Kurt Röttgers, Berlin 2010, pp. 13–37.
Bellour, Raymond: Le dépli des émotions, in: Trafic, 43, 2002, pp. 93–128.
Benhabib, Seyla: The Reluctant Modernism of Hannah Arendt, Thousand Oaks 1996.
Benjamin, Walter: On the Concept of History, in: id.: Selected Writings. Vol. IV 1938–1940, ed. by Howard Eiland / Michael W. Jennings, trans. by Edmund Jephcott et al., Cambridge, MA et al. 2003, pp. 389–400.
Benjamin, Walter: Paralipomena to "On the Concept of History", in: id.: Selected Writings. Vol. IV 1938–1940, ed. by Howard Eiland / Michael W. Jennings, trans. by Edmund Jephcott et al., Cambridge, MA et al. 2003, p. 402.
Benjamin, Walter: The Work of Art in the Age of its Technological Reproducibility. Third Version, in: id.: Selected Writings. Vol. IV 1938–1940, ed. by Howard Eiland / Michael W. Jennings, trans. by Edmund Jephcott et al., Cambridge, MA et al. 2003, pp. 251–283.
Berdyaev, Nikolai: The Origins of Russian Communism, London 1937.
Berger, Hanno: Das Minoritäre als Genre der Revolution, in: Prekäre Genres. Zur Ästhetik peripherer, apokrypher und liminaler Gattungen, ed. by id. / Frédéric Döhl / Thomas Morsch, Bielefeld 2015, pp. 51–64.
Berger, Hanno: Revolution, Metapher und 'Napoléon', in: Überschreitungen. Beiträge zur Theoretisierung von Inszenierungs- und Aufführungspraxis [e-book], ed. by Nicole Haitzinger / Franziska Kollinger, Munich 2016, pp. 22–29.
Berger, Hanno: Pascals Wette, die Revolution und "V for Vendetta", in: Periphere Visionen. Wissen an den Rändern von Fotografie und Film, ed. by Heide Barrenechea / Marcel Finke / Moritz Schumm, Paderborn 2016, pp. 223–236.
Berger, Hanno: Rezension – Margrit Tröhler/Jörg Schweinitz (Hg.): Die Zeit des Bildes ist angebrochen! Französische Intellektuelle, Künstler und Filmkritiker über das Kino. Eine historische Anthologie 1906-1929, in: [rezens.tfm], 1, 2017, https://rezenstfm.univie.ac.at/index.php/tfm/article/view/r359 [last accessed 6 May 2022].
Bergson, Henri: The Possible and the Real, in: Henri Bergson. Key Writings, ed. by Keith Ansell Pearson / John Mullarkey, New York / London 2002, pp. 223–232.
Bergson, Henri: Matter and Memory, trans. by Nancy Margaret Paul and W. Scott Palmer, Mineola, NY 2004.
Bloch, Ernst: The Principle of Hope. Vol. 1, trans. by Neville Plaice / Stephen Plaice / Paul Knight, Cambridge, MA 1986.

Bloch, Ernst: The Principle of Hope. Vol. 3, trans. by Neville Plaice / Stephen Plaice / Paul Knight, Cambridge, MA 1995.
Bordwell, David: Narration in the Fiction Film, London 1988.
Bordwell, David: Historical Poetics of Cinema, in: The Cinematic Text. Methods and Approaches, ed. by R. Barton Palmer, New York 1989, pp. 369–398.
Branigan, Edward: Point of View in the Cinema. A Theory of Narration and Subjectivity in Classical Film, Berlin / Boston 2012.
Browne, C.A.: The Story of Our National Ballads, New York 1919.
Brownlow, Kevin: Napoleon. Abel Gance's Classic Film, London 1983.
Brunkhorst, Hauke: Kommentar, in: Karl Marx: Der achtzehnte Brumaire des Louis Bonaparte. Kommentar von Hauke Brunkhorst, Frankfurt/Main 2007, pp. 133–328.
Bulst, Neithard / Jörg Fisch / Reinhart Koselleck / Christian Meier: Revolution, Rebellion, Aufruhr, Bürgerkrieg, in: Geschichtliche Grundbegriffe. Historisches Lexikon zur politisch-sozialen Sprache in Deutschland, Vol. 5, ed. by Otto Brunner / Werner Conze / Reinhart Koselleck, Stuttgart 1984, pp. 653–788.
Buscombe, Edward: Making Love and Revolution. Edward Buscombe Reviews the Reviews of "Reds", in: Screen, 23 (2), 1982, pp. 71–75.
Canby, Vincent: Beatty's "Reds," with Diane Keaton, in: The New York Times, 4 December 1981.
Cantor, Milton: Review, in: The American Historical Review, 87 (5), 1982, pp. 1482–1484.
Cavell, Stanley: The World Viewed. Reflections on the Ontology of Film – Enlarged Edition, Cambridge, MA / London 1979.
Cavell, Stanley: Pursuits of Happiness. The Hollywood Comedy of Remarriage, Cambridge, MA / London 1981.
Chion, Michel: The Voice in Cinema, ed. and trans. by Claudia Gorbman, New York 1999.
Chung, Jihae: Das Erhabene im Kinofilm. Ästhetik eines gemischten Gefühls, Marburg 2016.
Combs, Richard: Reds, in: Monthly Film Bulletin, 49 (3), 1982, pp. 47 f.
Cuff, Paul: A Revolution for the Screen. Abel Gance's Napoleon, Amsterdam 2015.
Daney, Serge: La rampe. Cahier critique 1970–1982, Paris 1983.
Deleuze, Gilles / Félix Guattari: Kafka. Toward a Minor Literature, trans. by Dana Polan, Minneapolis 1986.
Deleuze, Gilles / Félix Guattari: A Thousand Plateaus. Capitalism and Schizophrenia, trans. by Brian Massumi, Minneapolis 1987.
Deleuze, Gilles / Félix Guattari: What is Philosophy?, trans. by Hugh Tomlinson / Graham Burchell, New York 1994.
Deleuze, Gilles: Cinema 1. The Movement-Image, trans. by Hugh Tomlinson / Barbara Habberjam, Minneapolis 1986.
Deleuze, Gilles: Cinema 2. The Time-Image, trans. by Hugh Tomlinson / Robert Galeta, London / New York 1989.
Deleuze, Gilles: Control and Becoming, in: Negotiations, 1972–1990, trans. by Martin Joughin, New York 1995, pp. 169–176.
Deleuze, Gilles: Bartleby; or, The Formula, in: id.: Essays Critical and Clinical, trans. by Daniel W. Smith / Michael A. Greco, Minneapolis 1997, pp. 68–90.
Deleuze, Gilles: Proust and Signs. The Complete Text, trans. by Richard Howard, Minneapolis 2000.
Deleuze, Gilles: Difference and Repetition, trans. by Paul Patton, London 2004.
Deleuze, Gilles: Kant's Critical Philosophy. The Doctrine of the Faculties, trans. by Hugh Tomlinson / Barbara Habberjam, London / New York 2008.

Gilles Deleuze: Plato and the Simulacrum, trans. by Rosalind Krauss, in: October, 27, 1983, pp. 45–56.
Delluc, Louis: Écrits cinématographiques I. Le Cinéma et les cinéastes, Paris 1985, pp. 31–77.
Demandt, Alexander: Metaphern für Geschichte. Sprachbilder und Gleichnisse im historisch-politischen Denken, Munich 1978.
Derrida, Jacques: Specters of Marx. The State of the Debt, the Work of Mourning, and the New International, trans. by Peggy Kamuf, New York / London 2006.
Descartes, René: Meditations on First Philosophy. With Selections from the Objections and Replies, trans. by Michael Moriarty, Oxford 2008.
Düttmann, Alexander García: Das Urteil in der Kunst, in: Affekt und Urteil, ed. by Thomas Hilgers et al., Paderborn 2015, pp. 63–73.
Eaton, Mick / Trevor Griffiths: History to Hollywood. Mick Eaton Talks to Trevor Griffiths, in: Screen, 23 (2), 1982, pp. 61–70.
Eisenstein, Sergei: Methods of Montage, in: id.: Film Form. Essays in Film Theory, trans. by Jay Leyda, San Diego / New York 1977.
Elsaesser, Thomas: Filmgeschichte und frühes Kino. Archäologie eines Medienwandels, Munich 2002.
Elsaesser, Thomas: Cinephilia or the Uses of Disenchantment, in: Cinephilia. Movies, Love and Memory, ed. by Marijke de Valck / Malte Hagener, Amsterdam 2005, pp. 27–43.
Elsaesser, Thomas: Ein halbes Jahrhundert im Zeichen Bazins, in: montage AV, 18 (1), 2009, pp. 11–31.
Engell, Lorenz / Oliver Fahle: Film-Philosophie, in: Moderne Film Theorie, ed. by Jürgen Felix, Mainz 2003, pp. 222–245.
Engels, Friedrich: Herr Eugen Dühring's Revolution in Science, in: Karl Marx / id.: MECW 25. Engels, London 2010, pp. 5–309.
Engels, Friedrich: Ludwig Feuerbach and the End of Classical German Philosophy, in: Karl Marx / id.: MECW 26. Engels 1882–89, London 2010, pp. 353–398.
Epstein, Jean: Bonjour Cinéma. Collection des tracts, Paris 1921.
Epstein, Jean: Abel Gance, in: id.: Écrits sur le cinéma. 1921–1953. Édition chronologique en deux volumes. Vol. I: 1921–1947, Paris 1974, pp. 173–177.
Epstein, Jean: Bilan de fin de muet, in: id.: Écrits sur le cinéma. 1921–1953. Édition chronologique en deux volumes. Vol. I: 1921–1947, Paris 1974, pp. 229–237.
Epstein, Jean: Guerre à l'absolu, in: id.: Écrits sur le cinéma. 1921–1953. Édition chronologique en deux volumes. Vol. I: 1921–1947, Paris 1974, pp. 361–363.
Epstein, Jean: La Langue de la grande révolte, in: id.: Écrits sur le cinéma. 1921–1953. Édition chronologique en deux volumes. Vol. I: 1921–1947, Paris 1974, pp. 359–361.
Epstein, Jean: Le cinématographe dans l'Archipel, in: id.: Écrits sur le cinéma. 1921–1953. Édition chronologique en deux volumes. Vol. I: 1921–1947, Paris 1974, pp. 196–200.
Epstein, Jean: Le Cinématographe vu de l'Étna, in: id.: Écrits sur le cinéma. 1921–1953. Édition chronologique en deux volumes. Vol. I: 1921–1947, Paris 1974, pp. 131–152.
Epstein, Jean: Le doute sur la personne, in: id.: Écrits sur le cinéma. 1921–1953. Édition chronologique en deux volumes. Vol. I: 1921–1947, Paris 1974, pp. 392–397.
Epstein, Jean: Mémoires inachevées, in: id.: Écrits sur le cinéma. 1921–1953. Édition chronologique en deux volumes. Vol. I: 1921–1947, Paris 1974, pp. 27–57.
Epstein, Jean: Photogénie de l'impondérable, in: id.: Écrits sur le cinéma. 1921–1953. Édition chronologique en deux volumes. Vol. I: 1921–1947, Paris 1974, pp. 249–253.

Epstein, Jean: Alcool et cinéma, in: id.: Écrits sur le cinéma. 1921–1953. Edition chronologiques en deux volumes. Vol. II: 1946–1953, Paris 1975, pp. 240–246.
Epstein, Jean: Cinéma, hysterie, culture, in: id.: Écrits sur le cinéma. 1921–1953. Edition chronologiques en deux volumes. Vol. II: 1946–1953, Paris 1975, pp. 253–259.
Epstein, Jean: Le grand œuvre de l'avant-garde, in: id.: Écrits sur le cinéma. 1921–1953. Edition chronologiques en deux volumes. Vol. II: 1946–1953, Paris 1975, pp. 72 f.
Epstein, Jean: Naissance d'une académie, in: id.: Écrits sur le cinéma. 1921–1953. Edition chronologiques en deux volumes. Vol. II: 1946–1953, Paris 1975, pp. 73–75.
Epstein, Jean: Magnification and Other Writings, trans. by Stuart E. Liebman, in: October, 3, 1977, pp. 9–25.
Epstein, Jean: Timeless Time, in: id.: Magnification and Other Writings, trans. by Stuart E. Liebman, in: October, 3, 1977, pp. 9–25, here pp. 16–20.
Epstein, Jean: Bonjour Cinéma und andere Schriften zum Kino, ed. by Nicole Brenez / Ralf Eue, trans. by Ralf Eue, Vienna 2008.
Epstein, Jean: Der Kinematograph auf dem Archipel, in: Bonjour Cinéma und andere Schriften zum Kino, ed. by Nicole Brenez / Ralph Eue, trans. by Ralf Eue, Vienna 2008, pp. 57–62.
Epstein, Jean: Cinema and Modern Literature, trans. by Audrey Brunetaux / Sarah Keller, in: Jean Epstein. Critical Essays and New Translations, ed. by Sarah Keller / Jason N. Paul, Amsterdam 2012, pp. 271–276.
Epstein, Jean: On Certain Characteristics of *Photogénie*, trans. by Tom Milne, in: Jean Epstein. Critical Essays and New Translations, ed. by Sarah Keller / Jason N. Paul, Amsterdam 2012, pp. 292–296.
Epstein, Jean: The Cinema Seen from Etna, trans. by Stuart E. Liebman, in: Jean Epstein. Critical Essays and New Translations, ed. by Sarah Keller / Jason N. Paul, Amsterdam 2012, pp. 287–292.
Epstein, Jean: Return to Pythagorean and Platonic Poetry, in: id.: The Intelligence of a Machine, trans. by Christophe Wall-Romana, Minneapolis 2014, pp. 103–105.
Epstein, Jean: The Law of Laws, in: id.: The Intelligence of a Machine, trans. by Christophe Wall-Romana, Minneapolis 2014, pp. 87–92.
Etymologisches Wörterbuch der deutschen Sprache: "Enthusiasmus", in: id., 25. Auflage, ed. by Friedrich Kluge / Elmar Seebold, Berlin / Boston 2011, p. 248.
Eyquem, Olivier: Reds, in: Positif, 256 (6), 1982, pp. 59 f.
Fahle, Oliver: Jenseits des Bildes. Poetik des französischen Films der zwanziger Jahre, Mainz 2000.
Fahle, Oliver: Zeitspaltungen. Gedächtnis und Erinnerung bei Gilles Deleuze, in: montage AV, 11 (1), 2002, pp. 97–112.
Fanon, Frantz: The Wretched of the Earth, trans. by Richard Philcox, New York 2007.
Favonius Eulogius: Disputatio de Somnio Scipionis, ed. by Alfred Holder, Leipzig 1901.
Feige, Daniel Martin: Alle Genres sind prekär und kein Genre ist prekär, oder: Die Logik des Genres im Genre der (hegelschen) Logik, in: Prekäre Genres. Zur Äesthetik peripherer, apokrypher und liminaler Gattungen, ed. by Hanno Berger / Frédéric Döhl / Thomas Morsch, Bielefeld 2015, pp. 17–29.
Felix, Jürgen: Autorenkino, in: Moderne Film-Theorie, ed. by id., Mainz 2003, pp. 13–61.
Förster, Lukas: John Adams, in: Cargo, 4 (12), 2011, pp. 61 f.
Fœssel, Michaël: Analytik des Erhabenen (§§ 23–29), in: Immanuel Kant. Kritik der Urteilskraft, ed. by Otfried Höffe, Berlin 2008, pp. 99–119.

Foucault, Michel: What Is an Author?, in: id.: Language, Counter-Memory, Practice. Selected Essays and Interviews, ed. by Donald F. Bouchard, trans. by id. / Sherry Simon, Ithaca / New York 1977, pp. 113–138.
Früchtl, Josef: Vertrauen in die Welt. Eine Philosophie des Films, Munich 2013.
Fukuyama, Francis: The End of History and the Last Man, New York 1992.
Gance, Abel: Qu'est-ce que le cinématographe? Un sixième art!, in: Ciné-journal, 185 (9) 1912, p. 10.
Gance, Abel: Le temps de l'image est venu!, in: L'art cinématographique, Vol. II, ed. by Léon-Pierre Quint et al., Paris 1927, pp. 83–102.
Gabriel, Teshome Habte: Towards a Critical Theory of Third World Films, in: Questions of Third Cinema, ed. by Jim Pines / Paul Willemen, London 1989, pp. 30–52.
Germann, Lukas: Die Wirklichkeit als Möglichkeit. Das revolutionäre Potential filmischer Ästhetik, Zurich / Berlin 2016.
Geulen, Eva: Gründung und Gesetzgebung bei Badiou, Agamben und Arendt, in: Hannah Arendt und Giorgio Agamben. Parallelen, Perspektiven, Kontroversen, ed. by id. / Kai Kauffmann / Georg Mein, Munich 2008, pp. 59–74.
Girshausen, Theo: Ursprungszeiten des Theaters. Das Theater der Antike, Berlin 1999
Goethe, Johann Wolfgang von: Goethe's letter to Jacobi from March 3, 1730, in: id.: Goethes Werke, Weimarer Ausgabe, Briefe, Vol. 9, Sec. 4, ed. by Eduard von der Hellen, Weimar 1891, p. 184.
Goethe, Johann Wolfgang von: Faust I & II, trans. by Stuart Atkins, Princeton 2014.
Griewank, Karl: Der neuzeitliche Revolutionsbegriff. Entstehung und Geschichte, Frankfurt/Main 1973.
Grindon, Leger: Shadows on the Past. Studies in the Historical Fiction Film, Philadelphia 1994.
Grosser, Florian: Theorien der Revolution zur Einführung, Hamburg 2013.
Guneratne, Anthony R.: Introduction. Rethinking Third Cinema, in: Rethinking Third Cinema, ed. by id. / Wimal Dissanayake, London / New York 2003, pp. 1–28.
Gunning, Tom: Preface, in: Jean Epstein. Critical Essays and New Translations, ed. by Sarah Keller / Jason N. Paul, Amsterdam 2012, pp. 13–21.
Günzel, Stephan: Der Begriff der 'Masse' in Philosophie und Kulturtheorie (I), in: Dialektik. Zeitschrift für Kulturphilosophie, 2004 (2), 2004, pp. 117–135.
Günzel, Stephan: Der Begriff der 'Masse' in Philosophie und Kulturtheorie (II), in: Dialektik. Zeitschrift für Kulturphilosophie, 2005 (1), 2005, pp. 123–140.
Gutjahr, Paul C.: The "Book of Mormon". A Biography, Princeton / Oxford 2012.
Hahn, Barbara / Marie L. Knott (eds.): Von den Dichtern erwarten wir Wahrheit. Hannah Arendts Literatur (Texte aus dem Literaturhaus Berlin), Berlin 2007.
Hall, Sheldon / Steve Neale: Epics, Spectacles, and Blockbusters. A Hollywood History, Detroit 2010.
Hansen, Miriam: Dinosaurier sehen und nicht gefressen werden. Kino als Ort der Gewalt-Wahrnehmung bei Benjamin, Kracauer und Spielberg, in: Auge und Affekt. Wahrnehmung und Interaktion, ed. by Gertrud Koch, Frankfurt/Main 1995, pp. 249–271.
Hardt, Michael / Antonio Negri: Empire, Cambridge, MA 2000.
Harer, Ingeborg: Ragtime. Versuch einer Typologie, Tutzing 1989.
Hebekus, Uwe / Jan Völker: Neue Philosophien des Politischen zur Einführung, Hamburg 2012.
Hegel, Georg Wilhelm Friedrich: Werke in zwanzig Bänden. Vol. 12. Vorlesungen über die Philosophie der Geschichte, Frankfurt/Main 1970.

Heinrich, Michael: An Introduction to the Three Volumes of Karl Marx's Capital, trans. by Alexander Locascio, New York 2012.
Heuer, Wolfgang / Irmela von der Lühe (eds.): Dichterisch denken. Hannah Arendt und die Künste, Göttingen 2007.
Hilgers, Thomas: Was ist ein ästhetisches Urteil?, in: Affekt und Urteil, ed. by id. et al., Paderborn 2015, pp. 23–48.
Hofmann, Hasso: Dezision, Dezisionismus, in: Historisches Wörterbuch der Philosophie. Vol. 2: D–F, ed. by Joachim Ritter, Darmstadt 1972, pp. 159–161.
Horwath, Alexander / Brigitte Mayr / Michael Omasta: Vorwort, in: Jean Epstein: Bonjour Cinéma und andere Schriften zum Kino, ed. by Nicole Brenez / Ralf Eue and trans. by Ralf Eue, Vienna 2008, pp. 5–7.
Hunkemöller, Jürgen: Was ist Ragtime?, in: Archiv für Musikwissenschaft, 42 (2), 1985, pp. 69–86.
Hunkemöller, Jürgen: Ragtime, in: Die Musik in Geschichte und Gegenwart. Allgemeine Enzyklopädie der Musik. Sachteil 8 Quer–Swi, ed. by Friedrich Blume / Ludwig Finscher, Kassel et al. 1998, pp. 57–68.
Iber, Christian: Grundzüge der Marx'schen Kapitalismustheorie, Berlin 2005.
James, Caryn: They're Movies, Not Schoolbooks, in: The New York Times, 21 May 1995.
Jameson, Fredric: The Political Unconscious. Narrative as a Socially Symbolic Act, London 1981.
Jameson, Fredric: 'End of Art' or 'End of History'?, in: id.: The Cultural Turn. Selected Writings on the Postmodern, 1983–1998, London / New York 1998, pp. 73–92.
Jay, Martin: Mourning a Metaphor: The Revolution is Over, in: parallax, 9 (2), 2003, pp. 17–20.
Jeancolas, Jean-Pierre: Abel Gance entre Napoléon et Philippe Pétain, in: Positif, 256 (6), 1982, pp. 17–21.
Kanfer, Stefan: Hollywood. The Shock of Freedom in Films, in: Time Magazine, 8 December 1967.
Kant, Immanuel: Critique of Judgement, trans. by J.H. Bernard, New York 1951.
Kant, Immanuel: The Conflict of the Faculties, trans. by Mary J. Gregor, Lincoln 1992.
Kant, Immanuel: Observations on the Feeling of the Beautiful and Sublime, in: Observations on the Feeling of the Beautiful and Sublime and Other Writings, ed. and trans. by Patrick Frierson / Paul Guyer, Cambridge 2011, pp. 9–62.
Kaplan, Nelly: Napoléon, London 1994.
Kappelhoff, Hermann / Cornelia Müller: Embodied Meaning Construction. Multimodal Metaphor and Expressive Movement in Speech, Gesture, and in Feature Film, in: Metaphor and the Social World, 2 (1), 2011, pp. 121–153.
Kappelhoff, Hermann / Jan-Hendrik Bakels: Das Zuschauergefühl. Möglichkeiten qualitativer Medienanalyse, in: zfm – Zeitschrift für Medienwissenschaft, 5 (2), 2011, pp. 78–95.
Kappelhoff, Hermann: Matrix der Gefühle. Das Kino, das Melodrama und das Theater der Empfindsamkeit, Berlin 2004.
Kappelhoff, Hermann: The Politics and Poetics of Cinematic Realism, trans. by Daniel Hendrickson, New York 2015.
Kappelhoff, Hermann: Front Lines of Community. Hollywood Between War and Democracy, trans. by Daniel Hendrickson, Berlin / Boston 2018.
Keller, Sarah: Introduction. Jean Epstein and the Revolt of Cinema, in: Jean Epstein. Critical Essays and New Translations, ed. by Sarah Keller / Jason N. Paul, Amsterdam 2012, pp. 23–47.
Keller, Sarah / Jason N. Paul (eds.): Jean Epstein. Critical Essays and New Translations, Amsterdam 2012.

Kessler, Frank: Photogénie und Physiognomie, in: Geschichten der Physiognomik. Text, Bild, Wissen, ed. by Rüdiger Campe / Manfred Schneider, Freiburg 1996, pp. 515–534.

Kessler, Frank: Etienne Souriau und das Vokabular der filmologischen Schule, in: montage AV, 6 (2), 1997, pp. 132–139.

King, Geoff: New Hollywood Cinema. An Introduction, New York 2002.

Koch, Gertrud: Filmische Welten – Zur Welthaltigkeit filmischer Projektionen, in: Dimensionen ästhetischer Erfahrung, ed. by Joachim Küpper / Christoph Menke, Frankfurt/Main 2003, pp. 162–175.

Koch, Gertrud / Christiane Voss: Einleitung, in: "Es ist, als ob". Fiktionalität in Philosophie, Film- und Medienwissenschaft, ed. by Gertrud Koch / Christiane Voss, Paderborn 2009, pp. 7–11.

Koch, Gertrud: Die Wiederkehr der Illusion. Der Film und die Kunst der Gegenwart, Berlin 2016.

Koller, Wolfgang: Historienkino im Zeitalter der Weltkriege. Die Revolutions- und Napoleonischen Kriege in der europäischen Erinnerung, Paderborn 2013.

Konersmann, Ralf: Nachwort. Walter Benjamins philosophische Kairologie, in: Walter Benjamin: Kairos. Schriften zur Philosophie, Frankfurt/Main 2007, pp. 327–348.

Koselleck, Reinhart: Über die Theoriebedürftigkeit der Geschichtswissenschaft, in: Werner Conze (ed.): Theorie der Geschichtswissenschaft und Praxis des Geschichtsunterrichts, Stuttgart 1972, pp. 10–28.

Koselleck, Reinhart: Historical Criteria of the Modern Concept of Revolution, in: id.: Futures Past: On the Semantics of Historical Time, trans. by Keith Tribe, New York 2004, pp. 43–57.

Kracauer, Siegfried: Theory of Film. The Redemption of Physical Reality, New York 1960.

Kurz, Gerhard: Metapher, Allegorie, Symbol, Göttingen 2004.

Lakoff, George / Mark Johnson: Metaphors We Live By, Chicago / London 1980.

Lefèvre, Raymond: Cinéma et Révolution, Paris 1988.

Lehmann, Hauke: Affect Poetics of the New Hollywood. Suspense, Paranoia, and Melancholy, trans. by James Lattimer, Berlin / Boston 2020.

Lenin, Vladimir Ilyich: The State and Revolution. The Marxist Theory of the State and the Tasks of the Proletariat in the Revolution, in: id.: Lenin Collected Works. Volume 25, June – September 1917, Moscow 1974, pp. 385–497.

Lenin, Vladimir Ilyich: What Is To Be Done? Burning Questions of Our Movement, in: id.: Lenin Collected Works. Volume 5, May 1901 – February 1902, Moscow 1977, pp. 347–529.

Lenin, Vladimir Ilyich: Where to Begin?, in: id.: Lenin Collected Works. Volume 5, May 1901 – February 1902, Moscow 1977, pp. 13–24.

Lexikon der Kunst. Architektur, bildende Kunst, angewandte Kunst, Industrieformgestaltung, Kunsttheorie: "Christuskind", in: id., Vol. I: A–F, ed. by Ludger Alscher et al., Leipzig 1973, pp. 449 f.

Liebman, Stewart E.: Jean Epstein's early Film Theory, 1920–22, Ann Arbor / New York 1980.

Lowry, Brian: HBO's Radical Chic, in: Variety, 410 (5), 2008, p. 28 and p. 35.

Lück, Michael: Poetiken der Demokratie?, in: Rabbit Eye – Zeitschrift für Filmforschung, 4, 2012, pp. 35–47.

Lyotard, Jean-François: Lessons on the Analytic of the Sublime, trans. by Elizabeth Rottenberg, Stanford 1994.

Marcuse, Herbert: Ethics and Revolution, in: Richard T. de George (ed.): Ethics and Society. Original Essays on Contemporary Moral Problems, Garden City, NY 1966, pp. 133–147.

Marinetti, Filippo Tommaso: The Manifesto of Futurism, in: Paths to the Present. Aspects of European Thought from Romanticism to Existentialism, ed. by Eugene Weber, New York 1960, pp. 242–246.

Martin, Douglas: Arnold Friberg, Painter of Historical Scenes, Is Dead At 96, in: The New York Times, 3 July 2010.

Marx, Karl / Friedrich Engels: Manifesto of the Communist Party, in: id.: MECW 6. Marx and Engels 1845–48, London 2010, pp. 477–519.

Marx, Karl / Friedrich Engels: The German Ideology. Critique of Modern German Philosophy According to Its Representatives Feuerbach, B. Bauer and Stirner, and of German Socialism According to Its Various Prophets, in: id.: MECW 5. Marx and Engels 1845–47, London 2010, pp. 19–539.

Marx, Karl: Capital. A Critique of Political Economy. Vol. 1, trans. by Ben Fowkes, London 1976.

Marx, Karl: A Contribution to the Critique of Political Economy. Part One, in: id. / Friedrich Engels: MECW 29. Marx 1857–61, London 2010, pp. 257–417.

Marx, Karl: Capital. A Critique of Political Economy, Vol. III, in: id. / Friedrich Engels: MECW 37. Karl Marx – Capital Volume III, London 2010, pp. 5–982.

Marx, Karl: Contribution to the Critique of Hegel's Philosophy of Law. Introduction, in: id. / Friedrich Engels: MECW 3. Karl Marx March 1843 – August 1844, London 2010, pp. 175–187.

Marx, Karl: Critique of the Gotha Programme, in: id. / Friedrich Engels: MECW 24. Marx and Engels 1974–83, London 2010, pp. 75–99.

Marx, Karl: The Class Struggles in France, 1848 to 1850, in: id. / Friedrich Engels: MECW 10. Marx and Engels 1849–51, London 2010, pp. 45–145.

Marx, Karl: The Eighteenth Brumaire of Louis Bonaparte, in: id. / Friedrich Engels: MECW 11. Marx and Engels 1851–53, London 2010, pp. 99–197.

Marx, Karl: Theses on Feuerbach, in: id. / Friedrich Engels: MECW 5. Marx and Engels 1845–47, London 2010, pp. 6–8.

McCrisken, Trevor B. / Andrew Pepper: American History and Contemporary Hollywood Film, Edinburgh 2005.

Merle, Jean-Christophe: Affekt, in: Kant-Lexikon, ed. by Marcus Willaschek et al., Berlin / Boston 2015.

Merleau-Ponty, Maurice: The Visible and the Invisible, ed. by Claude Lefort, trans. by Alphonso Lingis, Evanston, IL 1968.

Metz, Christian: On the Impression of Reality in the Cinema, in: Film Language. A Semiotics of the Cinema, trans. by Michael Taylor, Chicago 1974, pp. 3–15.

Metz, Christian: The Imaginary Signifier. Psychoanalysis and Cinema, trans. by Celia Britton et al., Bloomington / Indianapolis 1982.

Meyer-Thurow, Georg: Über Dichtung und Wahrheit in Seumes Lebensbericht. An Beispielen aus Seumes hessischer Rekrutenzeit. Nebst einem Anhang, in: "Weimar ist ja unser Athen. Mit Seume in Weimar", ed. by Jörg Drews / Gabi Pahnke, Bielefeld 2010, pp. 13–36.

Michotte van den Berck, Albert: Le caractère de 'réalité' des projections cinématographiques, in: Revue internationale de filmologie, 3/4, 1948, pp. 249–261.

Mohrmann, Judith: Affekt und Revolution. Politisches Handeln nach Arendt und Kant, Frankfurt/Main / New York 2015.

Morsch, Thomas: Filmische Erfahrung im Spannungsfeld zwischen Körper, Sinnlichkeit und Ästhetik, in: montage AV, 19 (1), 2010, pp. 55–77.

Morsch, Thomas: Medienästhetik des Films. Verkörperte Wahrnehmung und ästhetische Erfahrung im Kino, Paderborn 2011.

Muhle, Maria: Medienwissenschaft als theoretisch-politisches Milieu, in: zfm – Zeitschrift für Medienwissenschaft, 10 (1), 2014, pp. 137–142.

Mulvey, Laura: Visual Pleasure and Narrative Cinema, in: Screen, 16 (3), 1975, pp. 6–18.

Ndalianis, Angela: Television and the Neo-Baroque, in: The Contemporary Television Series, ed. by Michael Hammond / Lucy Mazdon, Edinburgh 2005, pp. 83–101.

Nessel, Sabine: Kino und Ereignis. Das Kinematografische zwischen Text und Körper, Berlin 2008.

Pappas, Peter: The Superimposition of Vision. 'Napoleon' and the Meaning of Fascist Art, in: Cinéaste, 11 (2), 1981, pp. 4–13.

Peirce, Charles Sanders: New Elements, in: id.: The Essential Peirce. Selected Philosophical Writings. Vol. 2, 1893–1913, ed. by Nathan Houser et al., Bloomington 1998, pp. 300–324.

Piepenburg, Erik: Why "Hamilton" Has Heat, in: The New York Times, 12 June 2016.

Pilz, Wolfgang: Das Triptychon als Kompositions- und Erzählform in der deutschen Tafelmalerei von den Anfängen bis zur Dürerzeit, Munich 1970.

Porter, Carolyn: Reds, in: Film Quarterly, 35 (3), 1982, pp. 43–48.

Preisendanz, Wolfgang: Komische (das), Lachen (das), in: Historisches Wörterbuch der Philosophie. Vol. 4: I–K, ed. by Joachim Ritter / Karlfried Gründer, Darmstadt 1976, pp. 889–893.

Preußer, Heinz-Peter: Massen im Monumentalfilm – Überwältigungsstrategien des Genrekinos. Versuch einer Typologie aus der Theorie des Erhabenen, in: Masse Mensch. Das ‚Wir' – sprachlich behauptet, ästhetisch inszeniert, ed. by Andrea Jäger / Gerd Antos / Malcolm H. Dunn, Halle 2006, pp. 308–325.

Proust, Marcel: In Search of Lost Time. Volume VI, Time Regained, trans. by Andreas Mayor / Terence Kilmartin, revised by D.J. Enright, and A Guide to Proust, compiled by Terence Kilmartin, revised by Joanna Kilmartin, New York 1993.

Proust, Marcel: In Search of Lost Time. Volume I. Swann's Way, trans. by C. K. Scott Moncrieff / Terence Kilmartin, revised by D.J. Enright, New York 2003.

Rancière, Jacques: L'historicité du cinéma, in: De l'histoire au cinéma, ed. by Antoine de Baecque / Christian Delage, Brussels 1998, pp. 45–60.

Rancière, Jacques: Film Fables, trans. by Emiliano Battista, Oxford / New York 2006.

Rancière, Jacques: Aesthetics as Politics, in: id.: Aesthetics and Its Discontents, trans. by Steve Corcoran, Cambridge, MA / Malden 2009, pp. 19–44.

Rancière, Jacques: The Politics of Aesthetics. The Distribution of the Sensible, ed. and trans. by Gabriel Rockhill, London et al. 2013.

Raunig, Gerald: Kunst und Revolution. Künstlerischer Aktivismus im langen 20. Jahrhundert, Vienna 2005.

Rebhandl, Bert: Exzess des Ausdrucks. Endliche und unendliche Serialisierung: Was ist episch an der Sitcom "Frasier?", in: Autorenserien. Die Neuerfindung des Fernsehens. Auteur Series. The Re-invention of Television, ed. by Christoph Dreher, Stuttgart 2010, pp. 287–311.

Rosenbaum, Jonathan: Jack Reed's Christmas Puppy. Reflections on REDS, in: Sight and Sound, 51 (2), 1982, pp. 110–113.

Rosenfeld, Sophia: Common Sense. A Political History, Cambridge 2011.

Rosenstone, Robert A.: Reds as History, in: Reviews in American History, 10 (3), 1982, pp. 297–310.

Rosenstone, Robert A.: Romantic Revolutionary. A Biography of John Reed, Cambridge, MA 1990.

Rosenstone, Robert A.: History on Film / Film on History, Harlow 2006.
Rothemund, Kathrin: Komplexe Welten. Narrative Strategien in US-amerikanischen Fernsehserien, Berlin 2013.
Rothöhler, Simon: Amateur der Weltgeschichte. Historiographische Praktiken im Kino der Gegenwart, Zurich 2011.
Saussure, Ferdinand de: Course in General Linguistics, ed. by Perry Meisel / Haun Saussy, trans. by Wade Baskin, New York 2011.
Schlegel, Hans-Joachim: Die Verfilmung der Revolution und die Revolutionierung des Films. Panzerkreuzer Potemkin (1925), in: Fischer Filmgeschichte, Vol 2. Der Film als gesellschaftliche Kraft. 1925–1944, ed. by Helmut Korte / Werner Faulstich, Frankfurt/Main 1991, pp. 42–57.
Schlesinger Jr., Arthur: History and the Imagination. Ragtime and Reds, in: American Heritage, 33 (3), 1982, pp. 42 f.
Schmitz, Norbert M.: Gibt es einen demokratischen Revolutionsfilm? Zum dialektischen Pathos in Jean Renoirs "La Marseillaise", in: Revolutionsmedien – Medienrevolutionen, ed. by Sven Grampp et al., Konstanz 2008, pp. 597–620.
Schweinitz, Jörg: "Genre" und lebendiges Genrebewußtsein. Geschichte eines Begriffs und Probleme seiner Konzeptualisierung in der Filmwissenschaft, in: montage AV, 3 (2), 1994, pp. 99–118.
Seiler, Cotten: "The American Revolution", in: The Columbia Companion to American History on Film. How the Movies Have Portrayed the American Past, ed. by Peter C. Rollins, New York 2004, pp. 49–57.
Shaviro, Steven: The Cinematic Body, Minneapolis 1993.
Shohat, Ella / Robert Stam: Unthinking Eurocentrism. Multiculturalism and the Media, London / New York 1994.
Sierek, Karl: Aus der Bildhaft. Filmanalyse als Kinoästhetik, Vienna 1993.
Silberg, Jon: Reds, in: American Cinematographer, 88 (5), 2007, p. 10 and p. 12.
Silverman, Kaja: Male Subjectivity at the Margins, New York / London 1992.
Solanas, Fernando / Octavio Getino: Towards a Third Cinema. Notes and Experiences of the Development of a Cinema of Liberation in the Third World, in: New Latin American Cinema. Vol. 1. Theory: Practices and Transnational Articulation, ed. by Michael T. Martin, Detroit 1997, pp. 33–58.
Sobchack, Vivian: "Surge and Splendor": A Phenomenology of the Hollywood Historical Epic, in: Representations 29, 1990, pp. 24–49.
Sobchack, Vivian: The Address of the Eye. A Phenomenology of Film Experience, Princeton 1992.
Sobchack, Vivian: What My Fingers Knew. The Cinesthetic Subject, or Vision in the Flesh, in: id.: Carnal Thoughts. Embodiment and Moving Image Culture, Berkeley / Los Angeles / London 2004, pp. 53–84.
Souriau, Étienne: Die Struktur des filmischen Universums und das Vokabular der Filmologie, in: montage AV, 6 (2), 1997, pp. 140–157.
Storaro, Vittorio: Photographic Aims – Reds, in: American Cinematographer, 63 (5), 1982, p. 487 and p. 490.
Studlar, Gaylyn: In the Realm of Pleasure. Von Sternberg, Dietrich, and the Masochistic Aesthetic, Urbana et al. 1988.
Tedjasukmana, Chris: Mechanische Verlebendigung. Ästhetische Erfahrung im Kino, Paderborn 2014.

Thomas Aquinas: In libros physicorum 2, 7, 6, in: id.: Opera omnia, Vol. 4, ed. by Roberto Busa, Stuttgart 1980, p. 72.

Thomson, David: Redtime, in: Film Comment, 18 (1), 1982, pp. 11–16.

Tröhler, Margrit / Jörg Schweinitz (eds.): Die Zeit des Bildes ist angebrochen! Französische Intellektuelle, Künstler und Filmkritiker über das Kino. Eine historische Anthologie 1906–1929, Berlin 2016.

Truffaut, François: Napoléon, in: id.: The Films in My Life, trans. by Leonard Mayhew, New York 1985, pp. 29–32.

Ventura, Michael: A Revolution Worth Having, in: LA Weekly, 27 December 1985 – 2 January 1986, p. 21.

Vertov, Dziga: Kinoks: A Revolution, in: id.: Kino-Eye. The Writings of Dziga Vertov, ed. and with an introd. by Annette Michelson, trans. by Kevin O'Brien, Berkeley / Los Angeles 1984, pp. 11–21.

White, Hayden: Metahistory. The Historical Imagination in Nineteenth-century Europe, Baltimore 1987.

Wihstutz, Benjamin: Urteilende Zuschauer. Über Geschmack und Öffentlichkeit um 1800, in: Geschmack und Offentlichkeit, ed. by Matthias Grotkopp / Hermann Kappelhoff / Benjamin Wihstutz, Zurich 2019, pp. 103–120.

Williams, Linda: Film Bodies. Gender, Genre, and Excess, in: Film Genre Reader III, ed. by Barry Keith Grant, Austin 2003, pp. 141–159.

Wimsatt Jr., William Kurtz / Monroe Curtis Beardsley: The Intentional Fallacy, in: The Sewanee Review, 54, 1946, pp. 468–488.

Wittgenstein, Ludwig: Philosophical Investigations. The German text, with an English trans. by G.E.M. Anscombe, P.M.S. Hacker / Joachim Schulte, Chichester / Malden 2009.

Žižek, Slavoj: On Belief, London / New York 2001.

Žižek, Slavoj: Afterword. Lenin's Choice, in: Vladimir Ilyich Lenin: Revolution at the Gates. A Selection of Writings from February to October 1917, ed. by Slavoj Žižek, London / New York 2002, pp. 165–336.

Žižek, Slavoj: Introduction. Between the Two Revolutions, in: Vladimir Ilyich Lenin: Revolution at the Gates. A Selection of Writings from February to October 1917, ed. by Slavoj Žižek, London / New York 2002, pp. 3–12.

Žižek, Slavoj: A Pervert's Guide to Family, in: Lacan.com, 2007. http://www.lacan.com/zizfamily.htm [last accessed 23 May 2022].

Žižek, Slavoj: From *Che vuoi?* to Fantasy. Lacan with *Eyes Wide Shut*, in: id.: How to Read Lacan, New York 2007, pp. 40–60.

Žižek, Slavoj: Event. A Philosophical Journey through a Concept, Brooklyn 2014.

Filmography

1776 (Peter H. Hunt, US 1972).

Babylon 5 (Joseph Michael Straczynski, US 1994–1998).
Battleship Potemkin (Sergei Eisenstein, SU 1925).
Bonnie and Clyde (Arthur Penn, US 1967).
Bound for Glory (Hal Ashby, US 1976).

Cleopatra (Joseph L. Mankiewicz, US / CH / GB 1963).

Der grosse König [The Great King] (Veit Harlan, DE 1942).
Drums Along the Mohawk (John Ford, US 1939).

Elysium (Neill Blomkamp, US 2013).
Enthusiasm: The Symphony of Donbas (Dziga Vertov, SU 1930).

Gone with the Wind (Victor Fleming, US 1939).

Heaven Can Wait (Warren Beatty / Buck Henry, US 1978).
Heaven's Gate (Michael Cimino, US 1980).

J'accuse! [I Accuse] (Abel Gance, FR 1919).
Joe Hill (Bo Widerberg, SE / US 1971).
John Adams (Tom Hooper, US 2008).
John Adams. Part I: Join or Die (Tom Hooper, US 2008).
John Adams. Part II: Independence (Tom Hooper, US 2008).
John Adams. Part III: Don't Tread on Me (Tom Hooper, US 2008).
John Adams. Part IV: Reunion (Tom Hooper, US 2008).
John Adams. Part V: Unite or Die (Tom Hooper, US 2008).
John Adams. Part VI: Unnecessary War (Tom Hooper, US 2008).
John Adams. Part VII: Peacefield (Tom Hooper, US 2008).

L'Anglaise et le duc [The Lady and the Duke] (Eric Rohmer, FR 2001).
La chute de la maison Usher [The Fall of the House of Usher] (Jean Epstein, FR 1928).
La coquille et le clergyman [The Seashell and the Clergyman] (Germaine Dulac, FR 1928).
La hora de los hornos: Notas y testimonios sobre el neocolonialismo, la violencia y la liberacion [The Hour of the Furnaces] (Octavio Getino / Fernando Solanas. AR 1968).
La mort de Robespierre (Georges Hatot, FR 1897).
La roue [The Wheel] (Abel Gance, FR 1923).
Land of the Blind (Robert Edwards, GB / US 2006).
Lawrence of Arabia (David Lean, GB / US 1962).
Liberty's Kids: Est. 1776 (Michael Maliani / Kevin O'Donnell / Andy Heyward, US 2002–2003).

MARIE ANTOINETTE (Sofia Coppola, US / FR / JP 2006).

NAPOLÉON VU PAR ABEL GANCE [NAPOLEON] (Abel Gance, FR 1927).
NICHOLAS AND ALEXANDRA (Franklin J. Schaffner, GB 1971).
NO QUARTO DA VANDA [IN VANDA'S ROOM] (Pedro Costa, PT 2000).

OCTOBER (Sergei Eisenstein, SU 1928).
OTTO; OR, UP WITH DEAD PEOPLE (Bruce LaBruce, DE / CA 2008).

RAGTIME (Miloš Forman, US 1981).
RED BELLS PART I: MEXICO ON FIRE (Sergei Bondarchuk, SU / MX / IT 1982).
RED BELLS PART II: I SAW THE BIRTH OF A NEW WORLD (Sergei Bondarchuk, SU / MX / IT 1983).
REDS (Warren Beatty, US 1981).
REED, MÉXICO INSURGENTE [REED: INSURGENT MEXICO] (Paul Leduc, MX 1973).
REVOLUTION (Hugh Hudson, GB / NO 1985).
RHYTHMUS 21 (Hans Richter, DE 1923).

SACCO E VANZETTI [SACCO AND VANZETTI] (Giuliano Montaldo, IT / FR 1971).
SHAMPOO (Hal Ashby, US 1975).
SLEEPY HOLLOW (Tim Burton, US / DE 1999).
SLEEPY HOLLOW (Alex Kurtzman / Roberto Orci, US 2013–2017).
STAR WARS: EPISODE IV – A NEW HOPE (George Lucas, US 1977).

THE BIRTH OF A NATION (D. W. Griffith, US 1915).
THE FORTUNE (Mike Nichols, US 1975).
THE GENERAL LINE (Sergei Eisenstein, SU 1929).
THE HOWARDS OF VIRGINIA (Frank Lloyd, US 1940).
THE PATRIOT (Roland Emmerich, US / DE 2000).
THE STING (George Roy Hill, US 1973).
THE TEN COMMANDMENTS (Cecil B. DeMille, US 1956).
TRIUMPH DES WILLENS [THE TRIUMPH OF THE WILL] (Leni Riefenstahl, DE 1935).
TURN: WASHINGTON'S SPIES (Craig Silverstein, US 2014–2017).

VENUS AVEUGLE [BLIND VENUS] (Abel Gance, FR 1941).
V FOR VENDETTA (James McTeigue, US / GB / DE 2005).

Name Index

Abel, Richard 75
Adams, Abigail 175–176, 180, 183–187
Adams, John 168, 171, 174–189, 191–195, 197
Adams, John Quincy 192
Adams, Nabby 180, 182–183, 185–186
Adorno, Theodor W. 18, 92
Alcibiades 57
Allen, Dede 128
Apollinaire, Guillaume 45
Arendt, Hannah 1–4, 7–9, 13–22, 24–37, 65, 77, 79–80, 82, 84, 91, 93–94, 104–110, 113, 115–116, 120, 132–133, 146, 151–152, 155–156, 161–162, 166–168, 170–171, 173–174, 176–178, 184–187, 189–191, 194, 200–203
Aristotle 49–50, 56–58, 62, 139, 194
Artaud, Antonin 118–119
Ashby, Hal 124, 202
Augustine 21, 44
Avedon, Richard 131

Badiou, Alain 110
Balázs, Béla 5, 41, 44–45, 52, 91, 96
Baron de Montesquieu, Charles de Secondat 107
Barrow, Clyde 128
Barthes, Roland 135, 137
Bazin, André 6, 39, 58, 74, 98, 120, 137, 197
Beatty, Warren 8, 66, 123–129, 134–135, 137, 141–142, 150
Beauharnais, Josephine de 84
Beckett, Samuel 191
Bedorf, Thomas 189, 191
Bellour, Raymond 71, 83
Benjamin, Walter 5–6, 17, 29, 40, 81, 145, 170–171, 177
Benveniste, Émile 134
Bergson, Henri 3, 51–56, 90
Bloch, Ernst 55–56, 119, 152
Blomkamp, Neill 56
Bonaparte, Napoleon 7–8, 67, 73–74, 84–85, 87–92, 99–105, 111–116, 201
Bondarchuk, Sergei 123

Branigan, Edward 112
Brownlow, Kevin 67, 73–74, 92, 114
Bryant, Louise 125, 131–133, 135–136, 139–144, 146–148, 157–166
Bühler, Karl 12
Bulst, Neithard 1, 19, 21–23
Burton, Richard 63
Burton, Tim 169

Canby, Vincent 129, 134
Carter, Jimmy 125
Cavell, Stanley 4, 9–10, 59, 120
Chaplin, Charlie 51
Chung, Jihae 15, 81–82, 92
Cimino, Michael 202
Cleopatra 63
Coppola, Carmine 73
Coppola, Sofia 187
Costa, Pedro 117
Couthon, Georges Auguste 73

Daney, Serge 117
Dang, Sarah-Mai 67
Danton, Georges Jacques 73, 99, 102–104
Deleuze, Gilles 3–4, 6–8, 10–11, 13–16, 51–56, 58, 65, 68–69, 72, 75–76, 79, 82–83, 85, 88, 90–91, 94–99, 104, 114, 116–121, 127, 132, 147–148, 152, 171, 182, 192, 194, 197, 200
Delluc, Louis 41
DeMille, Cecil B. 59, 195
Descartes, René 94–95
Desmoulins, Camille 22
Dickinson, John 178
Dillane, Stephen 177
Duc de la Rochefoucauld-Liancourt, François Alexandre Frédéric 28
Dulac, Germaine 118
Duncan, Isadora 137

Edwards, Robert 145
Eisenstein, Sergei 11, 16–17, 36, 94–96, 98–99, 104, 116–118, 120, 186, 203

Name Index

Emmerich, Roland 168
Engels, Friedrich 4, 20, 26, 29–30, 33, 96, 153–154
Epstein, Jean 2–4, 6, 15, 37, 39–52, 55, 58, 69, 74–76, 94, 97, 114, 116–117, 137–139, 154, 200

Fahle, Oliver 3, 41–42, 51, 85
Fanon, Frantz 203
Feige, Daniel Martin 172
Feuerbach, Ludwig 4, 20, 154
Fiedler, Konrad 12
Fisch, Jörg 1, 19, 21–23
Fleming, Victor 59
Fœssel, Michaël 76, 79, 93
Ford, John 168
Forman, Miloš 130
Förster, Lukas 66
Franklin, Benjamin 174–175, 176–178, 181, 192
Frederick II, Landgrave of Hesse-Kassel 169
Friberg, Arnold 195–197
Friedrich II 99
Fukuyama, Francis 199

Gance, Abel 7, 10, 15, 66–67, 72–76, 82–83, 92–94, 97, 99, 111, 114, 116–117, 201
George III 169, 189
Germann, Lukas 5
Getino, Octavio 203
Geulen, Eva 110
Giamatti, Paul 178
Gibson, Mel 168
Girshausen, Theo 50, 57
Goethe, Johann Wolfgang von 21–22, 104, 201
Goldman, Emma 130, 137
Grant, Cary 168
Griewank, Karl 19–20, 22–23
Griffith, D. W. 59, 168
Griffiths, Trevor 124–126, 133
Grindon, Leger 66, 123–126, 133–135, 137, 149–150
Grosser, Florian 31
Guattari, Félix 11, 13–14, 117, 119

Hall, Sheldon 66
Hamilton, Alexander 110
Hancock, John 180–181
Hansen, Miriam 81
Hardt, Michael 152
Harlan, Veit 99
Hatot, Georges 16
Haupts, Tobias 173
Hayakawa, Sessue 40
Hegel, Georg Wilhelm Friedrich 3–4, 30–31, 33, 134, 153, 172
Heidegger, Martin 95, 110
Heisenberg, Werner 48
Henry, Buck 125
Heraclitus 47
Herodotus 57
Heyward, Andy 169
Hilgers, Thomas 77
Hill, George Roy 130
Hitler, Adolf 92, 116–117
Hooper, Tom 9, 174–176, 189
Horkheimer, Max 92
Hudson, Hugh 168
Hunkemöller, Jürgen 129–130
Hunt, Peter H. 168

Jacobi, Friedrich Heinrich 21–22
James, Caryn 58
James, William 47
Jameson, Fredric 9–10, 30
Jay, Martin 199–202
Jefferson, Thomas 108, 155, 168, 174, 176–177, 181, 185, 192–193
Jesus Christus 113, 151
Johnson, Charles Leslie 129
Johnson, Mark 29–30, 97
Joplin, Scott 129

Kant, Immanuel 1, 7, 13–17, 28, 32–36, 76–83, 90–91, 93–94, 120, 133, 167, 186, 188, 200–201, 203
Kaplan, Nelly 67, 73
Kappelhoff, Hermann 11–13, 32–33, 59, 81, 86, 92–93, 95–98, 104, 134
Keaton, Diane 66, 123, 127, 129, 134, 140–142, 150, 159–160, 165
Kennedy, Robert 124

Name Index

Kepler, Johannes 53
Klee, Paul 177
Kleist, Heinrich von 130
Kluge, Friedrich 187–188
Koch, Gertrud 57, 81, 148
Koller, Wolfgang 15, 92
Konersmann, Ralf 145
Koselleck, Reinhart 1, 19–23, 29, 64
Kracauer, Siegfried 5–6, 39, 58, 81, 149–150
Kurtzman, Alex 169

L'Herbier, Marcel 97
LaBruce, Bruce 16
Lakoff, George 29–30, 97
Lean, David 59
Leduc, Paul 123
Lehmann, Hauke 10, 127–129, 144–145
Leibniz, Gottfried Wilhelm 83
Lenin, Vladimir Ilyich 27–28, 37, 146, 149–150, 153
Lippmann, Walter 137
Lloyd, Frank 168
Louis XVI 28
Lowry, Brian 66
Lucas, George 170
Lück, Michael 126
Lumière, Auguste 16
Lumière, Louis 16
Luther, Martin 23
Lyotard, Jean-François 79

Machiavelli, Niccolò 22
Maliani, Michael 168
Malick, Terence 187
Mankiewicz, Joseph L. 63
Marat, Jean Paul 73, 99, 102–104, 118
Marcuse, Herbert 25
Marinetti, Filippo Tommaso 39–40
Mark Antony 63
Marx, Karl 3–4, 20, 25–26, 29–30, 33, 56, 146, 152–154
May, Elaine 125
McCrisken, Trevor B. 169
McGovern, George 124
McKay, Craig 128
McTeigue, James 56

Meier, Christian 1, 21
Melville, Herman 13
Merleau-Ponty, Maurice 14, 64, 67, 71–72
Metz, Christian 70, 81, 134
Miller, Henry 133
Mohrmann, Judith 15, 79–80, 107
Montaldo, Giuliano 202
Morsch, Thomas 17, 81, 151
Muhle, Maria 190
Müller, Cornelia 97–98, 104

Ndalianis, Angela 173
Neale, Steve 66
Negri, Antonio 152
Nichols, Mike 125
Nicholson, Jack 127, 137, 159–160
Nixon, Richard 124

O'Donnell, Kevin 169
O'Neill, Eugene 137, 158–162
Orci, Roberto 169

Pacino, Al 168
Pappas, Peter 92
Pascal, Blaise 146
Pasolini, Pier Paolo 119
Péguy, Charles 171
Peirce, Charles Sanders 39
Penn, Arthur 123
Pepper, Andrew 169
Pétain, Philippe 93
Plato 47–48, 193
Plessner, Helmuth 12
Porter, Carolyn 150
Preußer, Heinz-Peter 104–105, 114
Proust, Marcel 95, 191–192
Pythagoras 48

Rancière, Jacques 17, 42, 74, 82, 193–195
Reagan, Ronald 123, 136
Rebhandl, Bert 173
Reed, John 66, 123–125, 131–133, 135–136, 139–144, 146–148, 150, 156–158, 161–166
Richter, Hans 40
Riefenstahl, Leni 92, 116–117

Robespierre, Maximilien de 16, 73, 99–101, 103–104, 107–109
Rohmer, Eric 202
Rosenbaum, Jonathan 131, 133
Rosenfeld, Sophia 155
Rosenstone, Robert A. 123–125, 134–135, 149
Rothemund, Kathrin 172–173, 191
Rothöhler, Simon 6
Roudenko, Vladimir 84–85
Rouget de Lisle, Claude Joseph 111
Rousseau, Jean-Jacques 47, 107
Rubens, Peter Paul 193
Rush, Benjamin 174–175

Saint-Just, Louis Antoine de 73, 107
Saussure, Ferdinand de 48
Schaffner, Franklin J. 61
Schlegel, Friedrich 23
Schlegel, Hans-Joachim 17
Schlesinger, Arthur Jr. 130
Schmitz, Norbert M. 145
Seiler, Cotten 18, 168–169
Seume, Johann Gottfried 169
Silverstein, Craig 169
Simmel, Georg 12
Sobchack, Vivian 6–7, 10–11, 14, 45, 58–72, 80, 82, 104, 128, 132, 144, 195
Solanas, Fernando 203

Sondheim, Stephen 136
Souriau, Étienne 58, 190
Speer, Albert 92
Stapleton, Maureen 137
Stern, Daniel 71
Straczynski, Joseph Michael 173

Taylor, Elizabeth 63
Tedjasukmana, Chris 3, 27, 52
Thomas Aquinas 22
Thomson, David 130, 133
Towne, Robert 125–126
Trotsky, Leon 149–150
Trumbull, John 192–195, 197

Vertov, Dziga 16, 145, 187
Voss, Christiane 57

Washington, George 174–175, 195, 197
Welles, Orson 119
White, Hayden 60–62
Williams, Linda 71, 151
Wittgenstein, Ludwig 59
Wundt, Wilhelm 12

Zinoviev, Grigory 152, 164
Žižek, Slavoj 146, 150–151, 154, 171

Film Index

1776 168

Babylon 5 173
Battleship Potemkin 17
Bonnie and Clyde 123, 125, 128
Bound for Glory 202

Cleopatra 63

Der grosse König 99
Drums Along the Mohawk 168

Elysium 56
Enthusiasm: The Symphony of Donbas 187

Gone with the Wind 59

Heaven Can Wait 125
Heaven's Gate 202

J'accuse! 202
Joe Hill 202
John Adams 9, 16, 18, 66, 121, 167–197, 201–202
John Adams. Part I: Join or Die 175, 195
John Adams. Part II: Independence 74–188
John Adams. Part III: Don't Tread on Me 189
John Adams. Part IV: Reunion 189
John Adams. Part V: Unite or Die 189
John Adams. Part VI: Unnecessary War 176, 189
John Adams. Part VII: Peacefield 189, 191

L'Anglaise et le duc 202
La chute de la maison Usher 51, 76
La coquille et le clergyman 118
La hora de los hornos 203
La mort de Robespierre 16
La roue 76, 202
Land of the Blind 145
Lawrence of Arabia 59

Liberty's Kids: Est. 1776 168

Marie Antoinette 187

Napoléon vu par Abel Gance 7–10, 14–15, 18, 66, 72–121, 127, 156, 174, 179, 197, 200–202
Nicholas and Alexandra 61
No quarto da Vanda 117

October 96
Otto; or, Up with Dead People 16

Ragtime 130
Red Bells Part I: Mexico on Fire 123
Red Bells Part II: I Saw the Birth of a New World 123
Reds 8–10, 18, 58, 66, 121, 123–166, 174, 186, 188, 201–202
Reed, México insurgente 123
Revolution 168–170
Rhythmus 21, 40

Sacco e Vanzetti 202
Shampoo 124–125
Sleepy Hollow 169
Sleepy Hollow 169
Star Wars: Episode IV – A New Hope 170

The Birth of a Nation 168
The Fortune 125
The General Line 99
The Howards of Virginia 168
The Patriot 168–169
The Sting 130
The Ten Commandments 195
Triumph des Willens 92, 116
TURN: Washington's Spies 169

Vénus aveugle 93
V for Vendetta 56, 146, 151

www.ingramcontent.com/pod-product-compliance
Lightning Source LLC
Chambersburg PA
CBHW050524170426
43201CB00013B/2068